VOICES OF THE FLEMISH WAFFEN-SS

About the Author

Having passed out from the Royal Military Academy Sandhurst, Jonathan Trigg served as an infantry officer in the Royal Anglian Regiment, completing tours in Northern Ireland and Bosnia, as well as in the Gulf. After working in the City, he now has his own business training the long-term unemployed to get them into work. His previous books include *Death on the Don: The Destruction of Germany's Allies on the Eastern Front*, *The Defeat of the Luftwaffe: The Eastern Front 1941–45* and *Hitler's Flemish Lions: The History of the 27th SS-Freiwilligen Grenadier Division Langemarck*.

Other Books by the Author

Hitler's Gauls – The History of the French Waffen-SS
Hitler's Flemish Lions – The History of the Flemish Waffen-SS
Hitler's Jihadis – The History of the Muslim Waffen-SS
Hitler's Vikings – The History of the Scandinavian Waffen-SS
Hastings 1066
Death on the Don – The Destruction of Germany's Allies on the Eastern Front 1941–44
The Defeat of the Luftwaffe – The Eastern Front 1941–45; Strategy for Disaster

VOICES OF THE FLEMISH WAFFEN-SS

THE FINAL TESTAMENT OF THE OOSTFRONTERS

JONATHAN TRIGG

AMBERLEY

Half-title page: The Flemish volunteer, Herman Van Gyseghem (front rank, third from right), on parade with his fellow SS-Vlaanderen members. (Courtesy Ronnyc De Paepe)

Title page: Waffen-SS officer candidates on parade at Bad Tölz. The Flemish Oostfronter, Oswald Van Ooteghem, is in the front rank sixth from the left. (Courtesy Oswald Van Ooteghem)

This edition published 2021

Amberley Publishing
The Hill, Stroud
Gloucestershire, GL5 4EP

www.amberley-books.com

Copyright © Jonathan Trigg, 2017, 2021

The right of Jonathan Trigg to be identified as the Author of this work has been asserted in accordance with the Copyrights, Designs and Patents Act 1988.

ISBN 978 1 3981 0327 6 (paperback)
ISBN 978 1 4456 6637 2 (ebook)

All rights reserved. No part of this book may be reprinted or reproduced or utilised in any form or by any electronic, mechanical or other means, now known or hereafter invented, including photocopying and recording, or in any information storage or retrieval system, without the permission in writing from the Publishers.

British Library Cataloguing in Publication Data. A catalogue record for this book is available from the British Library.

Typesetting and Origination by Amberley Publishing.
Printed in the UK.

CONTENTS

ACKNOWLEDGEMENTS

A book like this is never the exclusive work of one individual. It requires, and draws life from, a whole host of contributors and friends. I wish to thank a few by name if I may: my editor Shaun Barrington who initially almost challenged me to take on this task, my Belgian publishers who have been incredibly supportive, Michel Breiz and Chris Michel for their help in tracing veterans, Andy Bowie for his thoughtful and insightful comments on the text, Jimmy Macleod who as usual has proven himself a font of knowledge on the topic, and ever-willing to share his famous 'black book' of contacts and ex-Waffen-SS men, especially for sharing his correspondence with Jef Beutels and Toon Koreman's daughter. I would also like to thank Ronnyc de Paepe – formerly of the Belgian Navy – whose own work on the Oostfronters is both exhaustive and informative. Ronnyc very kindly let me see and read some of that work, and with his permission I have included some passages in the book.

Most of all I would like to thank the interviewees themselves; Oswald, Dries, Herman, Theo (and wife – congratulations again to both of you), Albert, Jan (and his son Philip),

Lucie and Madeleine. Without your patience, humour and hospitality this book would never have seen the light of day.

A special thanks must also go to Rudi 'Iggy Pop' Massart, my constant companion on my travels around Flanders and Germany – translator, driver, and fellow lover of 1980s pop music – it is no exaggeration to say that without Rudi this book would, and could, never have been written. Thank you Rudi.

Last, but not least I want to thank my wife Rachel and daughter Maddy who put up with me turning our relaxing holiday to Bruges into a 'working trip' with interviews and research, and for putting up with my near-obsessive approach, and for my son Jack for no other reason than I always mention him.

I would like to dedicate this book to Jan Munk and Els Van Gyseghem who will not see it in print, as to my sadness and regret they passed away before its publication.

A few comments on the text and how I have structured it. In such a gigantic cataclysm as the Second World War was, I thought it vital to try and place the events my interviewees talk about in a timeline of the war itself; what was going on in the conflict, how this might have shaped the veterans at that time – to give readers a sense of the wider war – so, for example, when the Flemish Legion were embroiled in the savage fighting on the Volkhov River in northern Russia in 1942, to indicate what was happening elsewhere along the thousand-mile frontline.

The interviews were carried out over a period of several months, and all of them were recorded on dictaphone, with most being filmed as well – all with the interviewees' permission, of course. I have attempted to ensure the translation from Flemish (the majority of the interviews were conducted in Flemish, Dutch, or a mix of the two with some pidgin German thrown in for good measure) is both accurate and achieves fluency. At all times I tried to keep the veterans on a chronological timeline so we would go from their early life, to the German invasion, to their enlistment, to training and first battlefield experience, and so on, but the interviews sometimes strayed from this as memories are not often linear, especially with people in their nineties or, indeed, with authors! The passing of time is important to remember: the veterans were describing and trying to recollect memories from over seventy years ago, and inevitably some facts, figures and dates might be a little jumbled or inaccurate. That's just life, and if any readers pick up errors I would apologise but also ask for some clemency, given the nature of the book. These are the recollections of the people who were there, and not a historian's almanac. Although, having said that, I was repeatedly struck by just how good the veterans' mental faculties and recall were.

Regarding terminology around the fighting in the East, I am aware that the Soviet Union was a country composed of literally hundreds of different peoples and ethnic groups, but the Oostfronters tended to use the term 'Russian' to cover them all, and so I have left it at that.

As to the views expressed in the interviews, they are those of the veterans themselves and not mine. I wanted them all to speak openly and so decided not to confront them with aggressive interrogation, but that doesn't mean I didn't provide a counter-view if I thought it necessary, or that I shied away from asking tough questions on the Holocaust and other Nazi atrocities. Suffice to say that I consider the Nazis to have been vile beyond description, and the Holocaust a crime that must never be forgotten, so I will leave the reader to think through their own views on what the veterans said. I always think part of a writer's job is to make the reader think, at least a little.

As most of the text is made up of interviews I have used a key to identify the veterans, unless it's obvious from the text, so Jan Munk is 'JM', Oswald Van Ooteghem is 'OVO' etc. The key is shown below.

Interviewees, place and DOB and final rank in the Waffen-SS or German Red Cross

Oswald Van Ooteghem (OVO): Born in Ghent, 14th August 1924. Rank – SS-Untersturmführer.

Herman Van Gyseghem (HVG): Born in Ghent, 6th May 1923. Rank – SS-Sturmmann.

Theo D'Oosterlinck (TD): Born in Bulskamp, 12th January 1924. Rank – SS-Oberjunker.

Lucie Lefever (LL): Born in Elverdinge, 7th September 1925. Rank – Schwester-helferin German Red Cross.

Dries Coolens (DC): Born in Ghent, 24th January 1923. Rank – SS-Oberscharführer.

Albert Olbrechts (AO): Born at 1 Sydenham Road, Croydon, south London, United Kingdom, 4th February 1915. Rank – SS-Sturmmann.

Jan Munk (JM): Born in Leiden, 6th June 1921. Rank – SS-Untersturmführer (substantive rank unconfirmed due to the end of the war).

PREFACE

Thousands of Flemish nationalist VNV members march down the Boulevard Anspach to commemorate the death in action of Reimond Tollenaere. (Courtesy Oswald Van Ooteghem)

Back in 2007, my book *Hitler's Flemish Lions* – a history of the Second World War's Flemish Waffen-SS units, the Flemish Legion, the Sturmbrigade and Divisions Langemarck – was published in the UK. In 2010 it was translated into

French, entitled *SS Flamands*, and published in Belgium for the French speakers in that country, the 3.6 million Walloons who predominate in the south. Then some four years later it made its way into Dutch and found its last incarnation as *Oostfronters* (East Fronters), this being the catch-all name used in Flanders to describe those Flemings who volunteered to go and fight on the Eastern Front during the Second World War. I was then asked by the Flemish publishers to fly to Brussels (Charleroi to be exact, infamously voted by the Dutch readers of the daily newspaper *De Volksrant* as the 'ugliest city in Europe') and do a series of interviews to help publicise the book. One interview involved me having lunch with a journalist from the Belgian edition of *Playboy* magazine! A second was held in the Army Museum in central Brussels for a television documentary exploring the Oostfronters phenomenon. The programme, *The Last Oostfronters* (http://www.chrismichel.nl/tv-reportages/de-laatste-oostfronters), subsequently aired on both the Belgian Flemish VRT and Dutch NTR channels, the mainstream free-to-air TV channels for both Flanders and Holland.

After a hair-raising journey back to the airport that evening, I sat on the plane whisking me homeward, and gathered my thoughts. What struck me most – apart from the hospitality of everyone I had met – was the reaction of all the interviewers to the subject at hand. The book considered the fact that after Belgium was invaded and occupied by the Nazis in 1940, several hundred young Flemish men volunteered to enlist in the Waffen-SS, and these hundreds then became thousands after the Germans invaded the Soviet Union in the summer of 1941. This was collaboration, pure and simple, and yet there was no hint of condemnation amongst the interviewers, no damning indictment of the volunteers, rather there was genuine interest, some surprise at the extent of it all, and for a few, if not a sneaking admiration, at least a measure of understanding and sympathy.

I was surprised at that reaction, which, in hindsight, was silly of me. After all, having researched and written a number of books about non-German volunteers in the Waffen-SS during the war, I had experienced at first-hand a whole gamut of views on the volunteers in their native lands. In France for example, the subject of collaboration and Waffen-SS recruitment is almost always met with denials and a blank refusal on the part of both officialdom and the majority of the populace to accept it ever happened. If pressed, the only usual concession to the truth given by a grudging Frenchman or woman is that if collaboration existed at all, it was something that only involved a small handful of degenerates who acted out of naked greed and self-interest and who can't even really be called French – tell that to the tens of thousands who filled the ranks of the *Milice francaise*, the LVF, or the SS-Charlemagne. At the other end of the scale, in the Baltic states of Estonia, Latvia and Lithuania, wartime collaboration with the Nazis is often wrapped up with the independence struggle against their giant Soviet neighbour and the horrors of Moscow's occupation in 1940–41. The controversial annual Waffen-SS veterans' marches through cities like the Latvian capital of Riga are viewed by some as occasions for national pride, just as they are seen by others as echoes of a past irrevocably blackened by violent anti-Semitism and association with the evils of Nazism. Scandinavia (I am generalising horribly here I know) and Holland are somewhere in the middle of that scale, if we can call it a scale; strongly anti-Nazi, libertarian democracies as they are, but also mindful of their part in the war and the motivations of their own Waffen-SS volunteers.

Flanders though is, perhaps, unique in this list – not a nation state in its own right, but a part of a thoroughly democratic, open society, very much at the heart of Europe and its EU institutions, with a tolerant and liberal population, prosperous and comfortable, but riven by its history, its Roman Catholicism, and its often turbulent relationship with Wallonia – the southern, French-speaking region to which it is yoked to form Belgium.

Nationalism, a desire for a country of their own, runs deep in the soil of Flanders fields and the cobblestones of its medieval cities and towns, it has seeped into the very fabric of the land and its people. The lion and the yellow and black of the Flemish flag are prisms through which so much of life, culture and politics are viewed by many – but by no means all – of the Flemish themselves, yesterday and today. This yearning for independence, to govern themselves and decide their own fate, translates into a generally ambivalent view among the Flemish themselves about the young men and women who went east to serve with the Wehrmacht in the war against Soviet Russia. For a minority, they are traitors who collaborated with an utterly detestable regime and were complicit in its crimes, while for another minority they were freedom fighters selflessly sacrificing their lives for Flanders: 'All for Flanders, Flanders for Christ' (*'Alles Voor Vlaanderen, Vlaanderen voor Kristus'*), while the majority view is somewhere between the two.

Overall this translates into what can be characterised as a genuine interest about the Oostfronters among a significant section of the population, and an atmosphere that allows the veterans themselves to speak openly about their experiences; this is manna from heaven for a historian.

This opinion was reinforced once I was back home in England as I began to receive a steady stream of correspondence through my publisher, mainly via email, from Flemings wanting to both congratulate me on the book (what scribbler doesn't like being told by a reader that they liked his book!), and politely make a correction or two to details in the text. Some went so far as to say that they knew one or more Oostfronters themselves and had always been fascinated by their story. As a lot of writers do, I kept up the correspondence, and over time it became clear that whilst the numbers of veterans still alive was decreasing fast as old age took its inevitable toll, there was an appetite among some of them to tell their stories before it was too late.

Then it struck me – here, perhaps, was one last chance to record at first-hand the memories of the Oostfronters themselves in their own words. As I researched the idea I realised three things; firstly, I would have to move quickly, time was very much against me with the youngest Oostfronters being in their early nineties. Secondly, the Oostfronters needed to be set in some sort of context, and there were others whose experiences I wanted to include to provide a fuller picture: a Dutch perspective from one of that country's Waffen-SS veterans who shared a language, a border and much more besides with his Flemish cousins; and women, whose role in the war had so often been side-lined or just omitted altogether. So I would interview an Oostfronter's wife, another's daughter, and an Iron Cross-winning Red Cross nurse. Lastly, and crucially for this book, what I realised above all else was that the majority of veterans I came across *wanted* to speak, they wanted to have their say, to leave a record. Perhaps nothing impressed this final point on me more than in my first face-to-face interview with a group of veterans when one admitted that apart from his lifetime partner no-one in his family – not his children, his grandchildren or his great-grandchildren, knew about his past. Rolling up his left sleeve, over a plate of sandwiches and some excellent coffee, to show me his faded, blue SS blood group tattoo, he shrugged at me and said, 'It's about time they knew. I'm not ashamed.'

Now, after many hours of exhausting, exhaustive but fascinating interviews, this book tries to capture their voices; so soon to be lost to the world.

I

BELGIUM: CREATION AND INVASION

In a letter to the then British Foreign Secretary, Lord Palmerston, the Austrian diplomat and arch-fixer Prince Klemens Wenzel von Metternich once memorably described pre-unification Italy as nothing more than 'a geographical expression.'[1] Almost a

A mass rally of Flemish nationalists before the outbreak of war. August Borms is among the crowd, as is Oswald Van Ooteghem's mother Gaby. (Courtesy Oswald Van Ooteghem)

century later, the same expression would be used by the author and academic, John Eppstein – 'Belgium is not a country, it's a geographical expression' – to describe the 30,528 square kilometres (11,787 square miles) of heavily populated land sandwiched between Catholic France to the south, Germany to the east, and Protestant Holland to the north.[2]

The reality is that Belgium, as a country, is split, with 60% of the present-day 11 million population being ethnically Flemish, and the other 40% Walloon. Non-Belgians may scratch their heads at the distinction between the two, but in Belgium itself it has been *the* defining division within the country since the provisional government of Charles Rogier (a Walloon) declared independence from the Netherlands on the 4th of October 1830, and the princeling Leopold Saxe-Coburg-Gotha (a German) accepted the constitution and the offered crown that came with it and became the first 'King of the Belgians' on 21st July 1831. The old continent of Europe then had itself a brand-new country, but it was one that began its life seemingly intent on sowing internal division rather than building nationwide unity.

The point of the lance that divided the Belgians from the get-go was fundamental – language. Perhaps understandably, the new state reacted against its former Dutch ties by declaring French, the native tongue of the country's Walloons, as the *only* official language. At a stroke the majority Flemings became second-class citizens as the administration, justice and higher education systems became linguistically alien. (There is an irony for those who wish to find it in the fact that the country's motto or rallying cry is today quoted in three languages: *Eendracht maacht makt, L'union fait la force, Enigkeit macht stark* – 'unity makes strength'.) This sense of French-speaking superiority was reinforced by the very founders of the state itself. Charles Rogier – twice the country's Prime Minister – explained his view of Flemish to one of his ministers soon after independence:

The first principles of a good administration are based upon the exclusive use of one language, and it is evident that the only language of the Belgians should be French. In order to achieve this result, it is necessary that all civil and military functions are entrusted to Walloons and Luxembourgers; this way, the Flemish, temporarily deprived of the advantages of these offices, will be constrained to learn French, and we will hence destroy bit by bit the Germanic element in Belgium.[3]

Rogier wasn't alone in seeing the Flemish and their language as in some way inferior and an obstacle to be overcome. The influential Walloon senator, Alexandre Gendebien, indulged in virulent racism by claiming that the Flemish were 'one of the more inferior races on the Earth, just like the negroes'.

Sentiments like these created a rift between Flemings and Walloons that has never totally healed – and the scab was violently ripped off by the tumult of the First World War. The slaughter of the trenches created resentment *within* all the combatant nations – not least between rulers and the ruled – as those who viewed themselves as excluded from power felt the blood price they were paying at the front entitled them to far more, both economically and politically. For the Flemish, across whose fields the battling armies flung their millions of shells and ground whole generations of their youth into the mud, this sense of injustice took firm root and led to calls for equality with their French-speaking countrymen.

This 'Flemish Movement' (Dutch: *Vlaamse Beweging*) was given a helping hand by the occupying Germans who developed a policy they called *Flamenpolitik* ('Flemish policy'), designed to help win over the Flemish to co-operation, and even collaboration, with the Germans. The Germans decreed that Dutch would henceforth be the official language in

Flanders and established a Dutch-speaking university, the Von Bissing University in Ghent. Inspired not by a sense of altruism but by a desire to divide and rule, Imperial Germany's *Flamenpolitik* failed to swing the population of Flanders decisively behind the invader but did manage to increase division within the country and poison the post-war atmosphere between the Flemish and the Walloons.

As the Continent desperately tried to recover from the war, continuing economic hardship and political dysfunction led to the birth and rise of fascist political parties and movements across western Europe in the 1920s and 1930s, many of them taking inspiration from Hitler and the Nazis, as well as Mussolini's Italy. None were voted into government by their electorates, although some rose from obscurity to become powerful organisations in their own right. Typifying the latter were Anton Mussert's *Nationaal-Socialistische Beweging* (NSB, National Socialist Movement) in the Netherlands, and Gustaaf 'Staf' De Clercq's *Vlaamsch Nationaal Verbond* (VNV, Flemish National League) in Flanders.

The spirit that motivated the NSB and its supporters has now, seemingly, disappeared, but the driving force for the VNV – the desire for more Flemish self-government, and even outright independence – is still alive and well.

With Europe wracked by political turbulence and instability, the Continent stampeded towards war, and at the beginning of September 1939 the tipping point was reached with Nazi Germany's invasion of neighbouring Poland. In a few short weeks the proud Polish Army and Airforce were annihilated, and the inhabitants of Warsaw had bombs rained on them by the Luftwaffe.

After the savagery and shock of the invasion of Poland, and the French and British declarations of war on Nazi Germany, all of western Europe waited for the hammer to fall and held their breath ... and they waited ... and they waited. Blitzkrieg became Sitzkrieg, and half a year passed without a shot being fired. British and French children, evacuated to the countryside to escape the expected air raids, went home. Reservists called up to the colours were missed, but life just went on. In the Third Reich, the Wehrmacht counted the cost of its subjugation of the Poles; 11,000 dead, 30,000 wounded, and another 3,400 missing, along with 300 panzers, 370 guns and 5,000 vehicles lost.[4] They made good their losses and prepared for their next order.

Then, at just after four in the morning of 9th April 1940, that next order came when German troops invaded tiny neighbouring Denmark. Six hours later it was all over and Copenhagen had capitulated. Attacked at the same time, Norway would hold out for no less than sixty-two days, but the real focus was on the West; France and the Low Countries. What would Nazi Germany do to try and avoid a repeat of its disastrous campaign in the First World War? A month later the world found out the answer to that conundrum. Following a brilliant plan laid out by a relatively unknown general of infantry, Erich von Manstein, the Wehrmacht launched a daring offensive across the River Meuse at Sedan, having somehow moved their panzers through the hitherto impassable Ardennes region. Having then broken the French line, the panzers raced for the sea, intent on cutting off the bulk of the British Expeditionary Force (the B.E.F.) and the cream of France's Army, along with their Belgian and Dutch allies who were fixed in place by a second, earlier, German offensive. Out-thought and out-manoeuvred, the Dutch surrendered after just four days, and within a fortnight the Belgians were teetering. The French – possessing what they considered to be the most powerful army in Europe at the time – scrambled to respond to events. The Prime Minister, Paul Reynaud, sacked his ultra-cautious and incompetent Commander-in-Chief, Maurice Gamelin, and replaced him with the equally ineffective Maxime Weygand. Weygand met Leopold III, the Belgian King, to try and shore up his fortitude, but came away from their meeting convinced the monarch had already consigned his country to defeat. Sure enough, just days later, Belgium surrendered. In Paris, Reynaud was said to be 'white with rage', while Britain's victorious Prime Minister of the Great War, David Lloyd George, said it would be hard to find 'a blacker and more squalid sample of perfidy and poltroonery than that perpetrated by the King of the Belgians'.[5]

With disaster staring them in the face, Britain did what it had to do for its own survival and launched Operation Dynamo – the miracle of Dunkirk – to salvage what it could from the unfolding debacle. Left to fight on more or less alone, the French did what they could too, but it was over within weeks. Hitler's Wehrmacht had accomplished in two months what their forbears had failed to achieve in four years: victory over France.

NOTES

1. Prince Metternich's letter to Lord Palmerston, dated 6th August 1847, was, of course, in French, as was all European diplomatic correspondence at the time. The wording the Austrian diplomat used was *'L'Italie est un nom geographique'*.

2. British Survey Handbooks series; *Belgium*, edited by John Eppstein, Cambridge University Press 1944.

3. Letter dated 1932 from Charles Rogier to the Minister of Justice, Jean-Joseph Raikem.

4 Evans, Richard J. *The Third Reich at War*, p7, Allen Lane.

5. Dank, Milton, *The French against the French*, p127, Cassell.

2

THE FIRST INTERVIEWS

Where to start? The answer was to start where the Oostfronters and the other interviewees themselves instinctively began their stories: with the invasion and occupation of their homelands. Everything they did up to that point was important, but it was necessarily a precursor. Their decision to join the Waffen-SS, to go and fight in the Soviet Union, the punishment they received in the aftermath – it was all a journey that began

Oswald Van Ooteghem at home in October 2016. (Author's collection)

at that one specific point. Without it everything would have been different, so that was it. We would begin with Adolf Hitler's decision to send his war machine to the west.

My own start point would be in the summer of 2016 as I drove from Bruges towards Ghent. Navigating the traffic of Flanders well-maintained highways, I mentally prepared to meet a group of men and women who had gone so far as to take up arms (or a nurse's uniform) to fight against the Soviet Union-as-was, in some of the bitterest battles ever seen in that most savage of all wars, in the uniform of the very country that had invaded their own; and not just any uniform, but that of the Waffen-SS. The Waffen, or Armed SS, is an organisation that evokes extreme emotion and deep controversy among most people who have come across its brief and bloody history. In a few short years it grew from being Hitler's personal, private bodyguard, into an army over half-a-million strong at its zenith that was an integral part of the German Armed Forces. Its ranks were mainly filled with native Germans, but also included hundreds of thousands of 'racial' Germans from outside the borders of the Third Reich, and non-Germans from more than twenty different countries and ethnic groups – such as the Flemish. From pretty amateurish beginnings, the Waffen-SS became a force that excelled in the art of war as its officers and men won justifiable renown for their military achievements. However, alongside the heroism of battles such as Kharkov and the Kilssura Pass, there was a darker side. The ruthlessness, fanaticism and disregard for human life that was part and parcel of the Waffen-SS fighting ethos also contributed to massacres such as Le Paradis, Oradour-Sur-Glane and Malmedy. It is these atrocities – and many others like them across the former Soviet Union in particular – that have primarily fashioned the image of the Waffen-SS since the end of the war, and helped make the pasts of the people I was going to interview so controversial.

The car pulled up in front of a smart, well-maintained house in a well-to-do cul-de-sac in an equally smart and solidly middle-class suburb of Ghent in Belgian Flanders. As is the custom in much of Continental Europe for white-collar professionals, on the wall next to the front door was a plaque with the owner's name, his job, in this case architect, and a list of his qualifications and accreditations. The doorbell rang and a well-dressed lady with a welcoming smile opened the door, shook my hand, introduced herself and led me through a narrow hallway into a large open-plan sitting room where I was clearly expected. As I entered the room, six elderly people, three men and three women, stood up and moved purposefully towards me to say hello: lots of handshakes, smiles and introductions, before everyone settled back down into their seats. I fussed around setting up my video camera on a tripod, adjusting the height and tilt to try and cover the whole room, putting my dictaphone on record and conspicuously setting it in the centre of the coffee table. I had just met some of the *Sneyssens* group; a name that meant nothing to me at the time, but a great deal to the people sitting in that room. I would soon learn that for them that name had meant fellowship, friendship, help and support, for sixty years and more – I was about to be given a crash course in it!

The lady who had welcomed me at the front door, Madeleine De Kie, poured deliciously chilled champagne into heavy, cut-crystal glasses, and told me to help myself to a large plate on the central coffee table covered in thick cubes of Turkish delight and other confectionaries. I declined and we all then toasted each other with raised glasses, before I launched into my prepared speech on the conduct of the interview we were about to start with my suggestions and requested permissions; so, did they mind me recording and filming them? All nods, good! I would be asking a series of questions and I was after straight answers – if they didn't know something or couldn't remember it then just tell me, there was nothing to be worried about. More nods. None of my questions were meant to catch them out or be confrontational, but they must understand that neither would I shy away from asking about very difficult topics – they needed to understand that too. To my relief on that one in particular they all fervently bobbed their heads up and down and voiced their assent. I picked up my pad and pen, leaned forward, and was about to ask my very first question when the owner of the house we were all sitting in looked straight at me and beat me to it.

OVO: First of all, we need to get the numbers right Herr Trigg. You said in your book, Oostfronters, *that there were around twenty thousand Flemish Waffen-SS volunteers during the war, well there were actually ten thousand of us Oostfronters, of whom around two thousand were killed at the front. There were lots of other Flemings in the Organisation Todt, the NSKK[1] and other parts of the Wehrmacht, but they weren't Oostfronters like us. These are the correct numbers.*

As it happened, I later interviewed another Oostfronter who vehemently disagreed with Van Ooteghem and his Sneyssens[2] friends, and thought the number of Flemish Waffen-SS was around the twenty thousand mark, but it was less the speaker's words and more the speaker himself that grabbed my attention that day.

Even sitting down as he was you could tell he was a big man. Tall and broad-shouldered, a full head of white hair, a mane almost, framing light blue eyes and a face that looked a lot younger than his ninety-two years. Indeed, the hearing aid tucked discreetly into his right ear was the only real sign of age. He was well-dressed in a comfortable way; chinos, pressed white shirt, tie and a powder blue jacket – it was summer – and the air in the room was warm, wafting gently in through the big windows from the tidy garden they looked out on. His voice was strong, used to being listened to, his hands gesturing to emphasise his points as he launched into his story. There was no mistaking it, this was Oswald Van Ooteghem, perhaps the most famous Oostfronter still alive. A framed photo of his father Herman, the former leader of the VNV paramilitary Grey Defence Brigade (*Grijze Werfbrigade*), stared down at us from one wall, facing an icon of the Madonna and infant Jesus on the other, a reminder that this was a devoutly Catholic household. Oswald Van Ooteghem, OVO for short, was born into a family of fierce Flemish nationalists in Ghent in August 1924. Still a teenager when Belgium was invaded and occupied by the Nazis, he volunteered for the German-sponsored Flemish Legion – the '*Legion Flandern*' – and in so doing became a soldier in the Waffen-SS; membership of which in itself the Nuremburg War Crimes tribunal declared a crime. He fought with the Legion on the Russian Front, was wounded several times, distinguished himself, and was promoted to officer rank. When the war finally ended, he took on a false German identity – Hans Richter – and lived in Germany to avoid the retribution being meted out to others just like him back in liberated Belgium. He found work as an architectural draughtsman, married a German girl and then in 1949 took the momentous decision to go home to Flanders and face the music. Arrested, he was held in the same prison as his father and a number of other Flemish nationalists and collaborators, before being convicted and sentenced to three years behind bars. By now the waves of bloody post-war revenge were subsiding, and OVO was granted early release just over a year later. Settling back into civilian life, he soon picked up his political activism again, and joined the Flemish *Volksunie* (People's Union), a party that from its establishment in 1954 until its collapse in 2002 was the main moderate voice of Flemish nationalism in Belgium, and as such was severely criticised by right-wing nationalist hardliners for being too accommodating. As a member of *Volksunie*, OVO sat on the East Flanders Provincial Council for almost a decade, spanning the late 1960s and early 1970s, becoming well-known in local politics. He made a name for himself in those years that enabled him to stand for elected office, and in 1974 he won a seat in the Belgian Senate representing the Ghent district of Eeklo, a rural area of around eighty thousand people according to the 2007 national census. OVO sat as a senator for thirteen years, combining his political role in the Belgian parliament with a seat on the Flemish Cultural Council. A diehard Flemish nationalist, just like his father before him, his overriding political philosophy throughout his career was the cause of Flemish independence. Now, almost thirty years after his time in elected politics had come to a close, Flanders, and its French-speaking neighbour Wallonia, are still united in the nation state of Belgium, but that is not for want of trying by Oswald Van Ooteghem.

Retired for many years, he is still well-known in the country, and is something of a legend in Flemish nationalist circles. He has never hidden his past; his membership of the Waffen-SS, his service as an Oostfronter, his conviction and imprisonment. Indeed, he is proud of it, and he wasn't alone in his actions either. The records are incomplete and occasionally contradictory, but research by the leading academic Kristof Carrein, into the SS's own *Fürsorgeamt der Waffen-SS und Flandern Wallonien*[3] archives, captured by the Soviets at the end of the war and only recently made available, would indicate that OVO was correct in his assertion that around ten thousand Flemings served in the Waffen-SS during the war. Bruno De Wever, a professor of Contemporary History at the University of Ghent, a leading authority in Belgium on the Oostfronters, and a man whose older brother Bart is a very senior Flemish nationalist politician today, agrees with that number, and explains that the lack of certainty is due to the fact that the number of volunteers fluctuated constantly during the war as men were injured, killed, or went missing, and new recruits went to fill the gaps. The picture is further complicated by the fact that many recruits successively served in different units. For example, a volunteer could have begun his service in the Flemish Legion, then been posted to its successor formation the SS-Sturmbrigade Langemarck, and then finally ended up in the SS-Division Langemarck, and be counted separately for all three. If the ten thousand figure is accurate – and let's assume it is – then this is still astonishing given the relative size of the Flemish wartime population, especially as it doesn't include the thousands of Flemings who, as OVO stated, joined other branches of the German Wehrmacht or paramilitary forces such as the Luftwaffe, the Kriegsmarine, the NSKK, and the Organisation Todt (the OT, military and infrastructure construction workers service).

Not that all ten thousand made it home, as OVO said. The Russian Front claimed a very high blood price from those who fought on it from both sides, and the Oostfronters paid their share in full; the Flemish Legion and Waffen-SS historian (and Oostfronter himself) Jan Vincx, agreed with OVO in his estimate that about one in five of the volunteers were killed and many more were wounded.

Back in OVO's sitting room, and to the right of the man himself, there was a petite, elderly lady, immaculately dressed and coiffured with designer spectacles that emphasised her piercing blue eyes and rather stern demeanour. She too was a Sneyssen, not an ex-soldier of course like OVO, but a former Red Cross nurse – Lucie Lefever. She had finished the war treating the wounded in the besieged city of Breslau (now Polish Wroclaw), and had a story to tell me of her service. As did Theo and Herman, the two other Oostfronters sitting quietly with their partners. Both men were in many ways mirror images of their host; smartly dressed, in their nineties, and startlingly alert for their age.

Sitting bolt upright was Theo – Theo D'Oosterlinck – the only one of the three men wearing glasses; gold-rimmed around his blue eyes, the same eye colour that all of them seemed to have in common, a feature associated with the Waffen-SS. Like Van Ooteghem, D'Oosterlinck had a hearing aid, and again like Van Ooteghem he had big hands and a strong grip. He was a quiet man, and most of the time during the interview he would be happy to defer to OVO, but when asked a question directly his voice would ring out, powerful and exact. He was dressed in a dark jacket, crisply ironed white shirt and dark tie, with a small distinct pin on his jacket lapel – a *berkenkruis,* or 'birch cross'. The 'birch cross' was the Oostfronters favoured way of marking their comrades' graves in Russia due to the ready availability of birch trees, and they had taken the name home with them to christen the monthly magazine they set up after the war to represent their views and keep each other informed. That pin was a sign, a symbol of who he was and what he had done in his youth. To most it would go unseen and unremarked, but not to anyone who knew 'the code'. To them it marked him out as an Oostfronter. The lady with him – shortly to become his second wife, albeit this was a secret from the rest at the time – was as well dressed as any other in the room. She sat calmly, listening to what was said, and occasionally glancing over at the other couple there, the Van Gyseghems.

Herman Van Gyseghem, clean shaven and grey-haired, was the only man not sporting a tie or jacket, instead he had an open-necked shirt tucked into brown trousers, above mirror polished shoes. Like D'Oosterlinck, he was quiet at first, his eyes seeming to stare somewhere into the distance, until he began to talk of the war, when it was as if he was back there, and the words just tumbled out. His elegant wife seemed quite frail. I later found out that just days before Van Gyseghem enlisted in the Waffen-SS in 1943, she had survived an American bombing raid on her home town of Mortsel near Antwerp; a raid that went badly wrong. Targeted to destroy the local Erla aircraft and motor works that was supplying the Luftwaffe, some eighty-two American Boeing B-17 Flying Fortresses dropped almost 250 tons of bombs in under ten minutes. Only a handful of bombs hit the intended target, but they were enough to start fires that more or less destroyed the factories. Tragically, much of the rest of the deadly payload landed on Mortsel itself, destroying and damaging nearly four thousand homes and killing 936 civilians, 209 of whom were children in four separate schools that took direct hits. A further 1,600 people were injured. Van Gyseghem's wife-to-be survived, but her mother and two sisters were killed. It was officially Belgium's worst loss of life in a single incident during the entire war. Following the mid-afternoon raid, Allied radio announced later that same day: 'The attack delivered excellent results...'

OVO was obviously held in high regard by everyone in the room, and both Van Gyseghem and D'Oosterlinck deferred to him, but out of respect and as a first among equals, rather than as any sign of submission. We were all guests in his house as well of course. They were all comfortable in each other's company and OVO in particular loved to talk of the lighter moments of their shared history with his comrades.

Herman Van Gyseghem (HVG): Once when I was at the front we had a weapons inspection, and the officer came around checking them all – our rifles, pistols and submachine-guns. He said mine was dirty and I got seven days' punishment – extra guard duties. I mean, seven days, when we were at the front! I couldn't believe it!

Van Ooteghem grinned and barked out, 'Well it was dirty wasn't it, so that's your own fault, boy!'

Van Gyseghem turned to me, shaking his head from side to side and smiled ruefully: 'Typical officer!'

Getting the numbers of Oostfronters right wasn't the only correction the veterans wanted to make to my previous book on the subject. It had been about them, their comrades, and the war they had fought. They presented me with a card listing mistakes I had made in the text, everything from the Flemish Waffen-SS officer '*Jack Delbaere*' actually being '*Jaak Delbaere*', to Hendrik Elias's wartime role in Ghent being as the 'Mayor' and not the 'Governor' as I had stated. Minor points in some ways, but important nonetheless. The pursuit of accuracy is never-ending.

Content that I would rectify my previous errors, OVO set off again, those big hands waving expansively in the air as he talked of history, geopolitics and Flanders' place in the world. He mentioned the failed experiment that had been the combined Dutch/Flemish/Walloon state back in the nineteenth century: the idea of '*Dietsland*' (the concept of the unification of Flanders and the Netherlands in one Dutch-speaking nation). He recalled that most famous of Flemish victories, Kortrijk, 1302, the Battle of the Golden Spurs and the humbling of the French, their Agincourt.[4] OVO talked of the fervour of anti-communist belief across Europe in the late 1930s and early 1940s, and kept on returning to that theme throughout the interviews: 'We had seen the big communist Russian bear attack little Finland, so why not Flanders?' He talked too of Flemish nationalism, the sense of grievance many Flemings had, and still have, against their Walloon, French-speaking neighbours, and he spoke of the VNV, the political party of his beloved father, and also of his idol and close family friend, the lawyer Dr Reimond Tollenaere.

After more than an hour of questions, answers and the ebb and flow of storytelling, we broke for a leg stretch and I used the time to wander around the room and the rest of the more-or-less open-plan ground floor to get more of a sense of the man who lived there.

The rooms were full, but uncluttered, oil paintings hung on most walls, mainly of ancestors, father, grandfather and so on, with photos of younger generations too, son and grandson. The furniture was substantial where it needed to be, thick, heavy wood and chest-high Chinese vases, delicate where it didn't. He was a reader; shelves groaned under the weight of lines of heavy volumes, an eclectic mix of works on art, politics and history, with pride of place given to books on Flemish nationalism by Elias and Tollenaere. OVO was clearly well-off without being ostentatiously wealthy, he valued comfort, his family, his religion and his politics, all integral parts of his make-up.

He invited us all to resume our seats and asked Ms De Kie to pour us some more drinks (he called her his 'guardian angel') with a twinkling eye and mischievous smile that made me wonder if he had been something of a lady's man in his youth. That image of the lady-killing nonagenarian was reinforced later during a subsequent break when he took me outside and showed me his car. No tiny little eco-car or Swedish safety-first box for OVO. His was a two-seat Mercedes convertible in bright yellow and black – the national colours of Flanders of course! He smiled at me, fingered the hole in his right ear lobe and said in his perfectly passable English, 'I like to feel the wind through my hair, and my ear!'

Before I knew it, the summer sun was fading into shadow and the session was drawing to a close. Very kindly, OVO had ordered in an afternoon tea of delicious open sandwiches and all manner of delicacies. There was more of his excellent coffee, all served by a smiling Madeleine de Kie, and as the Sneyssens interviewees tucked into the food, I reflected on what they had told me, and what they hadn't as yet.

Several things occurred to me straightway; to a man (and woman) they were proud of their service in the Waffen-SS and the German Red Cross, and they felt they had nothing to be ashamed of. Indeed, mid-way through my first bite, D'Oosterlinck rolled up his left shirt sleeve and showed me his SS blood group tattoo – 'O'. OVO did the same, but where his tattoo should have been was instead just a white scar about the size of a large coin, faded now, but matched by another on the other side of his arm. The latter was from a combat injury. For the former he had used a razor blade to cut off the blood group marking and claimed the two corresponding scars were from a through-and-through bullet wound. All this to throw any SS hunters off the scent. The second thing I noticed was a detail, but an important one: proud though they were of their service in the Waffen-SS, they hardly ever referred to it as such, or indeed the SS in general. They talked about the *Legion*, or the *Langemarck*, but not the *SS-Legion* or *SS-Langemarck*. Were they secretly ashamed, or was air-brushing out the Waffen-SS term a Pavlovian response, something they had learned over the years to avoid possible condemnation? To be sure, when I had brought up the subject of the Holocaust and Nazi atrocities they had all professed ignorance, and shock at what was done, and they were keen to point out the Soviets were also guilty of war crimes, which is undoubtedly true. It was a subject I wanted to return to the next time.

Another veteran who was proud of his service and saw no reason to hide it after the war, was the Dutch ex-SS Wiking Division soldier Jan Munk. Munk, or to give him his full name Johannes Nicolaas Munk, had been born in Leiden in June 1921 to a respectable middle-class family. He was tall, well over six feet, with the same big-boned body and prominent features that reminded me so much of Oswald Van Ooteghem. Now in his eighties, his mind was still sharp, his thin-rimmed glasses framing blue eyes and a large Roman nose. The hair, once dark and wavy, was now thin. He dressed smartly, a Wiking Division Association tie with a divisional insignia lapel pin worn proudly on his left breast. Munk, a young eighteen-year-old Dutch lad, was studying in The Hague while living in his aunt's house, when the invasion came.

I was called out of bed by the eldest of my aunt's three daughters, and from an attic window we watched German paratroopers jumping from their planes to occupy an airfield near the town. It was war. Panic set in among the Dutch soldiers guarding the airfield and they even started shooting at one another believing that they were shooting at the Germans. I decided that I had to go home, so I packed my clothes and personal items onto my push-bike, bought cigarettes with my last cash and set off for Leiden. I reached about halfway when I was stopped by the Dutch Army and advised to take cover in a ditch. There was some shooting along the road, but who was shooting at who I don't know.

Munk, a raw-boned young man standing over six feet tall, and sporting the round-rimmed glasses which he would wear his whole life, would go on to volunteer for the Waffen-SS and serve with them until the end of the war.

As the German Army, the *Heer,* marched triumphantly down the Champs Elysées in Paris, and Marshal Philippe Pétain established his Vichy regime, in Belgium the King decided against going into exile and instead 'retired' to his palace at Laeken where the Nazis placed him under house arrest.

Occupation in Flanders and Holland was to be a very different experience than in France. Dreadful though occupation was for all the defeated nations, Nazi treatment of Belgium and Holland differed from France in one crucial aspect: their prisoners of war. German camps were filled to bursting with the captive armies of the conquered countries; two million soldiers from France alone, a huge proportion of the nation's young men. Hitler chose to keep them behind the wire as a sort of insurance policy to guarantee French good behaviour, but this was not the case for the quarter of a million Dutch and half a million Belgian prisoners. In a master stroke of propaganda, the vast majority of the Dutch and Flemish Belgians were cursorily interviewed and then released to go back home. Official German policy was that all

Belgian NCOs, enlisted men and reservists who were made prisoners of war after the surrender were eligible for release. Any soldier in these categories who passed a linguistic test was theoretically entitled to an *Entlassungschein,* a Dismissal Pass, allowing him to return home. However, in practice this was extended preferentially to Flemish soldiers, while their Walloon comrades-in-arms frequently remained in POW camps until the end of the war. The policy was deliberately intended to exacerbate internal Belgian conflicts and foster support for the German occupiers in Flanders. Implementation of the policy was made easier by the fact that in 1938 the Belgian Army had been divided into separate Flemish and Walloon regiments. As a result, by February 1941, 105,833 out of 145,000 Flemish POWs had been repatriated.[5] This act engendered a wave of goodwill in Flanders towards the invaders that was further enhanced by German behaviour towards the rest of the civilian population and the institutions of the state. Some two million Belgians, a full 20% of the population, had previously fled south in front of the Wehrmacht's advance, fearful of a repeat of German mistreatment of civilians from back in the First World War. These refugees were now encouraged to go home and pick up their lives again.[6] The civil service, police and judiciary were all left in place, industrialists and farmers didn't suffer confiscations, and that barometer of Belgian life, the Roman Catholic Church, was likewise left alone. More than that, the Germans on the ground behaved impeccably towards the local populations, winning hearts and minds as the saying goes.

OVO: We were very heavily influenced by what happened after the Germans invaded and occupied Belgium. They'd captured tens of thousands of Flemish soldiers as the Belgian Army surrendered, and then instead of keeping them all locked up they just let them go home – just like that. They asked them a few questions and then it was 'thank you, you can go now.' This was very generous, and everyone in Flanders appreciated it. All those Flemish boys could go home. That had never happened before during war. Prisoners of war are usually kept to be used in the peace talks.

In Holland the situation was much the same, as the occupiers put on a show of respect to the local population.

JM: Upon my return home, most likely around 16th May 1940, I saw German troops in Leiden for the first time. We just stared, no-one turned their backs on them or behaved nastily. The nastiest rumour going around was that after occupying a town or village, the Germans would force their way into people's homes, drink their alcohol and then rape the women, young or old. The result in our area was that many people threw their alcohol into the water. I had a little boat and fished out a lovely Amstel beer barrel, it holds about ten gallons and today it decorates my dining room. This was the time when women did not wear trousers, and one day my sister Doortje was cycling past a young German private who looked at her legs. He whistled in admiration, but being very anti-Nazi she was not amused. A little further on she saw a German officer to whom she complained and who in turn reprimanded the young private. It has to be said that the behaviour of the German soldiers was extremely decent.

A seemingly benevolent occupation it might have been, but that is still a long way from one of the occupied putting on the uniform of the invader. So why did the Oostfronters do it?

OVO: We didn't do it for the pay that's for sure. From the start, we received one mark a day and then we got paid two Reichsmarks a day when we were at the front. A lot of us gave some or all of that money to charities such as the Red Cross anyway.[7]

Two primary motivations came up again and again; a fierce desire to fight communism – encouraged by elements of the Catholic Church – and a belief that fighting alongside the Germans would build up a debt that the Nazis would repay by granting Flanders and Holland independence in the new European order established after the war.

JM: I had just passed the final examinations for entry into the Dutch Army when the Germans overran Holland, and in my opinion the invasion was simply an act of war, just like the Danish and Norwegian occupations. I never had any strong political views except my anti-communist feelings. After the Wall Street Crash of 1929 there was a terrible economic crisis across Europe, and in Holland we had very high unemployment. There were riots in Amsterdam, and the Army and Navy were called in to help restore order. The Dutch government never got to grips with the situation, and just as elsewhere in Europe there was a fear of communism. On Sundays, Dutch Catholic and Evangelical congregations were warned by the clergy that this ideology would destroy Christianity and hundreds of years of European culture. We saw what was happening over in Germany; the people were cold, starving and unemployed, and then Hitler and his party changed all that dramatically. I remember the British press, such as England's Daily Express *newspaper, saying Hitler was 'the man who worked wonders'. Our own Dutch* Times *said that 'the fight against communism was a fight to the death.' I thought the Soviet invasion of Finland was foul and it just strengthened my anti-communism. I was surprised that no other country went to Finland's aid.*

HVG: The Catholic Church, and in particular the Jesuit schools and colleges, was very fanatical. They told us that you were either for Moscow or Rome, you couldn't be for both, and you had to choose.

They had a lot to do with motivating the young people of West Flanders in particular to do something for Flanders.

OVO: The big reason for volunteering was obviously the fight against Bolshevism, because Flanders was 90% Catholic. The Spanish Civil War had been fought and we'd seen the communists kill 6,000 to 7,000 clerics – priests, nuns, you name it. Moreover, the Russians had then attacked Finland. The newspapers here printed an image of the Russian bear attacking a little child called 'Finland' in its cradle … you remember things like that, it was very powerful at the time.

Interestingly, western European Catholicism wasn't universally of the same mind as the church in Flanders. An internal Nazi Party report of the time quoted a would-be Waffen-SS volunteer from Vienna who had turned to his local priest for guidance on enlisting and had then relayed that advice to his erstwhile recruitment officer: 'The priest told us that the SS was atheist and if we joined it we would go to hell.'[8]

What of Flemish nationalism and the so-called *Flamenpolitik*, was it the clarion call that led so many to join the Waffen-SS? Did Nazi Germany explicitly promise independence in return for the Oostfronters paying a blood price? Would both Flanders and Holland reap the benefits of a Nazi victory?

It was true that in October, Hitler had finally met Pétain and his premier, Pierre Laval, at the sleepy French town of Montoire in the Loire valley, and there, when he tried to get Vichy to fight alongside Germany against the British, he had said; 'Blood spilled in the common struggle will bind us together much more than treaties.'[9] Pétain though, had not taken the bait, seeing the Nazi leader's words as half-truths at best.

In Flanders, it was the VNV and its leader, Staf De Clercq, who would decide whether or not to tie the cause of Flemish nationalism to that of the Third Reich. One well-known historian said of the choice confronting De Clercq:

When Staf De Clercq in November 1940 decided on political collaboration without conditions he must have realized that he had to participate in the German war. De Clercq also had a dilemma, in that not collaborating militarily ran the risk of losing credibility with the militants in his own movement who may well have switched allegiance to his opponents.[10]

While the VNV was a party and a movement that in many ways was the antipathy of Nazism, staunchly pro-Catholic, fixated on independence rather than any idea of a 'common Europe', it was also one that at the same time was ripe for exploitation having as it did a clear sense of historic grievance against its French-speaking neighbours to the south.

OVO: There was always the Flemish-Walloon issue. France has always been the hereditary enemy of Flanders. For hundreds of years, the French have wanted to take Flanders – and they've tried – they wanted Brussels and its suburbs too and wanted to make Flanders French-speaking. This is a permanent movement, a permanent threat to the Flemings. We sought refuge with the Germans. The Belgian state was always a francophone state that tried to eradicate the Dutch and Dutch-speakers. All education was traditionally in French, then when the Germans came in the First World War they allowed us to be taught in Flemish, but as soon as the war ended it was back to French, even here in Ghent. So, the Flemish have always seen the Germans as friends. King Willem I founded the University of Ghent and Leuven. Previously we didn't have any higher education. In 1830, when the Dutch were chased off, the university 'Gallicised'. In 1914–18 the Germans then turned it the other way and 'Dutchified' universities. In 1918, the Belgians again Gallicised them after Germany lost the war, and it has taken years of struggle to finally get Dutch education for the Flemings. Even in Brussels, Dutch children in schools could only learn in French. The Germans promised implementation of bi-lingual language laws, which wasn't the case in Belgium at the time. Official signs here weren't in French and Dutch, sometimes only French. The Germans wanted to change that. So, the belief that the Germans would take Flamenpolitik *seriously became very strong. And the Germans said to us: 'if you want equal rights for Flanders after the war, in a new Europe, then you need to acquire this right at the front. You can have your own sovereign state, you can be taught in Flemish at school and university, but you must earn it!' Now we know better of course. As we've all seen in recent years, and I've often said myself; big, powerful countries have no friends, only interests. That is still the case.[11] We've all seen that happen in Iraq, Afghanistan, all over the Middle East. It's all about oil money and much less about ideology.*

When I asked the interviewees if they ascribed to this view, to a one they all chorused: 'At that time. Yes, we all believed it.'

However, Oswald Van Ooteghem remembered that not all of the VNV leadership were eager to collaborate with the Nazis.

OVO: In my area, there were certainly people who did not intend to collaborate, Hendrik Elias, who was a family friend and often in our home, was one such leader. He kept saying, 'no second activism'. During World War One some Flemings had, after all, co-operated actively with the Germans to try and achieve an independent Flanders, and it hadn't worked. Elias said the same thing would happen again and we couldn't trust the Germans.

However, the voices of men like Elias were drowned out amongst the rank and file of the VNV by its charismatic propaganda chief and the head of its uniformed paramilitary élite, the Black Brigade (*Zwarte Brigade*), Dr Reimond Tollenaere. The bespectacled Tollenaere had first studied law at Ghent University, becoming active in nationalist student politics there, before being appointed as head of VNV propaganda and winning a seat in the Belgian parliament in the party's breakthrough election of 1936, where it polled almost 14% of the total Flemish vote. To many young men of the time like Van Ooteghem, Tollenaere was simply magnetic.

OVO: Tollenaere was a personal and very close friend of my father. He lived in Oostakker, a suburb near here in Ghent. He was a lawyer and the head of propaganda for the VNV. He was a very good orator for the Flemish cause who spoke to lots of us both individually and collectively and inspired us to go and fight on the Russian Front. He was a family man too, with a wife and three young children, but still he went off to the front himself. Tollenaere didn't earn much money as a lawyer, mainly because he was always working so hard for the Flemish cause and the VNV, but then no-one really had much money in those days. In fact, you could say he worked himself to death for the VNV, but not as a lawyer. He was the youngest Belgian member of parliament too. At that time the train line between Ghent and Brussels was pretty poor, and he didn't have a car, so he often ended up spending the night at our house. Physically, as a man, he was about normal height, not too tall, about one metre seventy-five, he looked a bit like Theo here, the same glasses! People would do anything for him though, because he had charisma and personality. He radiated authority, and not just as the head of propaganda, it was he who said to us that by going to fight with the Germans 'we would earn for Flanders an equal place in a new Europe, so comrades, let's all get together.'

Tollenaere not only used his speeches and public meetings to expound his views, he also wrote extensively for the VNV's daily newspaper, *People and State* (*Volk en Staat*). Founded on 15th November 1936, it grew to a peak circulation of almost 50,000 copies a day and often carried lengthy pieces penned by the lawyer. In one such article in 1941 he wrote:

Flanders may soon have its own soldiers for the first time in centuries. Led by Flemish officers, contending under the lion flag, Flemish boys will sit in the steppes of Russia, testimony of the will to fight for our people. When we now prove in deed that we are willing to fight Bolshevism as the common European enemy, then later in building the new Europe we will have the right to speak. We have to demand an equal place for Flanders in a new Europe.

He also used it to give vent to the dark side of Flemish nationalism – a taint of anti-Semitism: 'The Jew does not belong to our people. Sentimentality should therefore not be taken into account.'

When the Wehrmacht launched its invasion of the West, Tollenaere, unsurprisingly – and a host of other prominent Flemish nationalists – considered by the government as potential fifth-columnists (although incredibly *not* Staf De Clercq) were arrested by the Belgian authorities and sent south under guard to France. In the chaos of the time many ended up dead, murdered by a firing squad of French gendarmes in Abbeville on 20th May. In total, twenty-two Flemish political detainees were killed that day. The evidence would seem to indicate that the police shot them not following some pre-planned order but rather out of panic as the German panzer advance headed straight towards them. By a stroke of luck Tollenaere was not among them, but there can be little doubt that the massacre affected him deeply, and spurred on his radicalism when he returned to Flanders after his own release.

OVO: We were very angry and horrified that some of our most well-known Flemish leaders were arrested by the Belgian government, taken to France and there they were shot in a park in Abbeville. Joris Van Severen [head of the extreme nationalist Verdinaso movement] was one of them. It was in May '40 when the Germans invaded and the Belgian security forces arrested the leaders of the VNV and many other right-wing organisations and deported them all to France. Many of them were killed on the road, others were mistreated. It was the Germans who liberated the survivors in France. For those people the Germans were liberators and not occupiers.

Tollenaere was not alone in being steered towards collaboration with the Germans by the Abbeville massacre. De Clercq too was moving in that direction, and on 20th April 1941 he made his first open – though fairly muted – appeal for VNV members to join the Waffen-SS. However, in a disturbing backdrop to De Clercq's call, the appeal coincided with the first screening in Antwerp of the infamous Nazi anti-Semitic propaganda film *Der Ewige Jude* (The Wandering Jew). After its public showing an extremist mob a couple of hundred strong – a few VNV members, but mainly rabid anti-Semites from the minority Flemish extremist *Volksverweering* (The People's Defence) movement – attacked two synagogues in the city and then set fire to the home of Marcus Rottenburg, the city's Chief Rabbi, in what became known as the Antwerp Pogrom. The local police and fire brigade arrived on the scene but were prevented from intervening by the Germans. There were between 65,000 and 75,000 Jews in Belgium at the time, the largest concentration being in Antwerp itself. The German military government had already tried to introduce anti-Jewish decrees forcing them to register and dismissing them from the civil service, the media and the legal sector, and while it seems that most civil authorities were pretty compliant to Nazi diktats on the Jews, the Belgian populace was less so. So, when the Nazis insisted that all Jews be identified by having to wear the Star of David on their clothes, large numbers of non-Jewish Belgians wore the emblem too in an act of mass civil disobedience in order to frustrate the discriminatory law, and the city of Brussels authorities officially refused to enforce the rule. In fact, as the Nazis' Final Solution began to accelerate from 1942 onwards, both the underground Belgian resistance and the local Catholic Church would endeavour to help their Jewish fellow citizens.[12]

Why was recruitment of Flemish and Dutch volunteers geared towards the Waffen-SS by the Germans, and not the mainstream German Army? The answer is complex, but can be boiled down to one major issue: power, and who wielded it in the Third Reich. Heinrich Himmler (the head of the SS – their *Reichsführer-SS*) was bent on expanding his own power by creating and growing an armed force that would be outside of the Army's control, and would serve Hitler, himself, and the Nazi Party as a whole, and be answerable only to them. This was the genesis of the SS's own armed wing – the *Waffen* or Armed SS. Understandably, the Army saw this as a direct threat and was determined to block it. Himmler found himself effectively shut out of the eligible manpower pool in Germany, so with the urging of his acolyte, the bullet-headed former physical training teacher Gottlob Berger, he turned his attention instead to the potential offered by what they both considered to be 'racially compatible' nations: Norway, Denmark, Holland and Flanders (not the Walloons whom they viewed as Gallic and non-Aryan). Berger, as head of the newly formed *SS-Erganzungsamt* within the SS Main Office, was charged with the task of establishing a new 'Germanic SS'. Germanics was the term used by the Waffen-SS to describe these populations that they considered to be fellow 'Aryans', such as the Scandinavians, the Dutch, the Swiss and the Flemish. Recruitment began pretty much straight after the Belgian and Dutch capitulations, with the first forty-five Flemish volunteers leaving to begin training in September that year. This was small-scale stuff though, and Berger soon upped the ante with the creation of the *SS-Standarte* (Regiment) *Westland* for both Dutch and Flemish volunteers. The response was positive, and within a few months recruitment was considered strong enough that a second formation was authorised – *SS-Freiwilligenstandarte Nordwest* – SS-Volunteer Regiment Northwest. By late spring 1941 somewhere between five and eight hundred Flemings were in the Westland and the Nordwest, amidst a total of about two thousand western European volunteers in all.

Then on the morning of 22nd June 1941 the world changed. Nazi Germany invaded its erstwhile ally, the Soviet Union.

At a stroke, volunteer recruitment for the Waffen-SS outside the Third Reich's borders was transformed from a niche appeal to diehard nationalists and non-German National Socialists, into a far broader 'crusade against Bolshevism'. The 'national legions' concept was now born, and a host of new formations sprang up; the *Legion Norwegen*, the *Freikorps Danmark*, the *Legion Niederlande*, and the *Legion Flandern* for Norwegians, Danes, Dutch and Flemish respectively, each of them acting as a repository for a new wave of recruitment. Now, by joining the SS-Legion Flandern a volunteer was not just collaborating with the Germans, but was joining the fight against the 'Red Menace'. Staf De Clercq now threw himself into the task and made his first major appeal to VNV supporters to enlist:

> The conspiracy of the old world of Judaism, of plutocracy and Bolshevism has now become clear. Even Soviet Russia has thrown off the mask and threatens European civilization; we must act to save Europe and save Christianity. All peoples must join together in the assault on Bolshevism. Flanders must also fight.

Expectations within the VNV sky rocketed. The Legion would be the beginnings of a new national army; Flemish officers would lead it, Flemish would be the language of command, and it would be subordinate to the political leadership of the VNV as the rightful government of Flanders. This was what they thought and hoped would happen.

Recruitment offices were set up across Holland and Flanders, with the one in Ghent being established in the famous *Vooruit* – a beautiful building that was the former home of arts and culture for the socialist labour movement built just before the First World War – and with Reimond

Tollenaere as the driving force behind the campaign, one of the first potential recruits through the door on 1st August was a sixteen-year-old Oswald Van Ooteghem. He had visited Germany with his father back in 1937, and had been hugely impressed by what he had seen as the nation underwent a resurgence under Hitler and his Nazi Party. With his father heavily involved in leading the VNV's Grey Defence Brigade, young Oswald had joined the VNV's youth wing, the *Nationaal-Socialistische Jeugd Verbond* (the NSJV, the National Socialist Youth Union), and was now queuing up with a thousand other young men to undergo the rigorous SS medical examination before being told whether he had been accepted or not.

OVO: Strictly speaking I was sixteen years old when I volunteered. Over one thousand volunteers reported to enlist, and only 405 were selected, the rest were turned away as not being up to standard. There were all sorts of people who volunteered; all sorts of different ideologies and reasons for volunteering. I left with the first group of the Flemish Legion. This was a very homogeneous political group because the VNV had called its members to join the Flemish Legion and so we did. At first, we weren't issued SS uniforms, we just had what we were wearing; VNV uniforms, Verdinaso, Rex, NSJV youth, Black Brigade, all sorts.

Standards were high, and the Waffen-SS was notoriously picky. Along with the usual Germany Army rules about height, medical fitness and lack of a prison record, the Waffen-SS had a sack-full of its own peculiarities, including Himmler's predilection to inspect photos of all potential officers, looking for 'Aryan' characteristics. It also had a near-obsession with dentition; over ten per cent of otherwise suitable volunteers were rejected at the time for poor teeth.[13]

So, with fewer than half of the volunteers being considered suitable, the profile of the accepted 405 new recruits was somewhat surprising, with idealistic teenagers like Van Ooteghem being the exception and not the rule. Firstly, Van Ooteghem's extreme youth was exceptional. The average age of that first cohort was actually 26 years and 6 months. Statistically they would be the oldest cohort of Flemish volunteers recruited during the war. The average age of all the ten thousand Oostfronters combined, would be between twenty-two and twenty-three years at enlistment. The majority of the volunteers were unmarried, and almost a third were members of the VNV, although remarkably some twenty per cent had no party affiliations at all. As a student, Van Ooteghem was in a minority, and no occupation predominated with the men coming from all walks of life, although miners were pretty common.[14]

Theo D'Oosterlinck (TD): Without my parents knowing, I signed up to join the Flemish Legion. I was just eighteen years old. When I enlisted I was still in school. I was born on 12th January 1924 in Bulskamp, a small town near Veurne, but when I was six we moved to Ghent where my father had got a job as a customs official in the port. I was technically-minded so I signed up in 1940 – when I was sixteen or seventeen, I can't remember exactly – for a preparatory course to train as a technical engineer, but after a while I quit the course because I had decided I wanted to volunteer for the Legion and go fight on the Russian Front. My family weren't hugely political, but my father was in the VNV. I only told them I was going about five days before I was due to leave on the train to take us to training. My mother especially was not very happy about it, but my father had fought in the 1914–18 war so he couldn't really say anything against it. Anyway, there were a lot of arguments at first, and during those five days we were always fighting at home. Then

I just had to leave. But at least they knew, there were quite a few who left without their parents knowing anything at all.

OVO: One of my comrades told his parents: 'I'm just going out to buy a pack of cigarettes', and the next thing he was on the train to the Eastern Front.

Lucie Lefever (LL): Lots of us told a few lies so we could enlist. At that time you had to be twenty-one years old or have the permission of your parents to sign up, so quite a few people said their parents had agreed when they hadn't. I was eighteen years old when I volunteered and both my parents gave their permission for me to join.

HVG: There were lots of young people who wanted to volunteer, but as we used to say at the time some of them only volunteered with a 'little finger in the air' and not an outstretched arm! They didn't really want to do it. With me it was different. I wanted to join right from the start. Flemish politics has always been bipolar: you're either a moderate or a fanatic. The way we used to think was like this, 'This is the goal we have in mind. That takes precedence over everything. It is all or nothing.' During the occupation there was no room for moderation. You chose to fight the Bolsheviks or you chose the Resistance.

OVO: That's right, you were either for going to the war, or not. In the middle was a big grey mass, we called them 'wait-and-sees'.

HVG: I came from a pretty fanatical family. My sister had already left Flanders to join the German Red Cross, and when I learned that the Germans were going to set up a European army I knew I had to volunteer. So as a young Fleming it was natural that you put on a uniform and went to fight against Bolshevism, and when I volunteered in 1943 (I was twenty years old at the time) my mother was very proud of the fact that I was going to fight against Bolshevism. My mother was always trying to help the Germans.

LL: My father was always a strong VNV'er, very Flemish-minded. Mother was less so, but even so she was OK with it all. She didn't forbid me from volunteering and so I asked her if I could go join the German Red Cross. She said yes. I had no nursing experience but she knew I would be looked after. The conditions of service were very good: there was strict oversight of the girls, no going out with men or to bars during your work, and we were protected. Red Cross Sisters who didn't behave, who went off with soldiers or other men, or just went out drinking and so on, well they were sent home. As for me and the other girls we were sent to Germany to learn about nursing.

Further north in Holland it was much the same for Jan Munk and his fellow Dutch volunteers. Munk, like Van Ooteghem, had also visited Nazi Germany before the war and been impressed by what he'd seen.

JM: You have to realise that in Holland during the war, the mentality was that you were either pro-Allies or pro-Nazi – you couldn't stand in the middle, that was unthinkable. My family weren't politically active. Father was a medical doctor and wasn't a member of any party. The great majority of Dutch people were strongly anti-Nazi, certainly my parents were, my younger brother joined the resistance as did my elder sister's husband. I remember back in 1935/36 we went to Germany by car to a restaurant that was famous for cooking a special trout dish. In the town when we arrived there were flags flying, it was a beautiful summer's day and we saw groups of Hitler Youth boys and girls marching and singing, they all looked so happy. I thought it was wonderful until my father said to his friend: 'Look at all those Nazi children. Isn't it terrible, they will grow up to no good.' My family had always *been anti-Nazi but not anti-German, and I think that it was at that moment when my father made that comment about those youngsters, whose happy marching and singing I thought was so marvellous, that I became pro-Nazi. My mother's sister was married to a doctor, and they were both very pro-Nazi - Marietje and Louis Del Baere from The Hague – they were both very active members of the Dutch NSB, and I used to talk with them a lot, but they never influenced me, it was always my choice. I was always at loggerheads with my anti-Nazi father because of it all.*

Oswald Van Ooteghem had no such issues with his father of course, but his mother was an altogether different kettle of fish. She was not pleased with her teenage son abandoning his education and running off to go soldiering.

OVO: My father was proud of me volunteering of course, but it was difficult for my mother, but then you'd expect a mother to be worried about her son. As it was I could look for inspiration to Reimond Tollenaere who had volunteered as well and so was leaving his wife and three children. He wasn't just the chief of propaganda for the VNV, he set an example to us all in his uniform. Men like Jef Van De Wiele[15] only joined later. As for Tollenaere, he went to Russia and sadly died a few months later in Koptsy near Novgorod.

Still just sixteen years old, five days after his medical examination and acceptance into the Flemish Legion, Oswald reported at Brussels North station and climbed on board a train bedecked with flowers and victory slogans written in chalk and whitewash on the sides of the carriages. The platform was packed with people, not just volunteers and their families saying emotional goodbyes, but crowds of young girls and well-wishers singing and cheering and waving the recruits on their way.

OVO: I left on the 6th of August 1941 with the first contingent. I became seventeen on the 14th of August. My mother was pretty upset when I left, as you might expect, but we were a militant family and my father was the leader of the Grey Brigade of the VNV and he understood. For us this was about history. Remember that back in 1302 there was a great battle at Kortrijk against the French – the Battle of the Golden Spurs – and now it was like that time again, there was an atmosphere of heroism, it was a time for Flanders, to sacrifice everything for Flanders if we had to, to fight and die for Flanders!

The train pulled out slowly from the station and, with its 400+ Flemish volunteers, headed east. Its destination was the Polish village of Pustkow near the former Polish Army cavalry training camp of Debica. Here, deep in rural south-eastern Poland, the SS would build a huge military training base they would christen *SS-Heidelager*. This would be where the Flemings and the Dutch would have their first taste of German military discipline.

Jan Munk's experience was not dissimilar to Van Ooteghem's, although he chose not to join the Dutch Legion, but instead opted for the SS-Wiking Division. Intended by Himmler and Berger to be mostly manned by western European volunteers, the Wiking would always be mainly German, but throughout its existence it would always have hundreds, if not thousands, of Dutch, Flemish, Norwegian and Danish volunteers in its ranks, not to mention Swiss, Finns and even some Swedes.

JM: In my final year at school I was asked 'If you are so pro-German why don't you join them?' I felt that a Dutch unit could not show the same strength and discipline as the Germans, so I decided to join the Waffen-SS direct. On the 28th of May 1942 I went to the recruiting office in The Hague with two friends who then failed the selection board. I was on a train from the main railway station the next day with approximately one hundred other volunteers, of whom thirty-five had volunteered for the Waffen-SS Wiking, and the rest were for the Legion Niederlande or the NSKK as ambulance or truck drivers. A couple of days later we arrived at Sennheim in Alsace.

NOTES

1. The National Socialist Motor Corps, German: *Nationalsozialistisches Kraftfahrkorps, NSKK,* a paramilitary organisation of the Nazi Party that officially existed from May 1931 to 1945. The group was a successor to the older National Socialist Automobile Corps (NSAK), which had existed since April 1930. The NSKK served as a training organisation, mainly instructing members in the operation and maintenance of motorcycles, cars and trucks. The NSKK was further used to transport Nazi Party officials. With the outbreak of World War Two the NSKK was used to provide drivers for various branches of the German Armed Forces. Members drove ambulances, supply trucks and so on. Non-Germans, including Flemings, were also recruited into its ranks, among the Flemish volunteers were the 2nd Company of the NSKK's 4th Regiment who disappeared to a man during the fighting at Stalingrad after ferrying supplies from the airfield at Rossosh into the stricken city. Over 4,000 Flemings volunteered for the NSKK, compared to over 30,000 in the Organisation Todt (4-5,000 alone in its guard service) and only some 500 who enlisted in the Kriegsmarine.

2. The Sneyssens group, named after Cornelis Sneyssens, a well-known medieval Flemish hero immortalised

by the Flemish nationalist poet Albrecht Rodenbach. Sneyssens won fame as the bearer of the flag of Ghent at the Battle of Bazel on 16th June 1452. The battle was fought between an army under Philip III, Duke of Burgundy, and the rebel city of Ghent. The battle was part of the Ghent Revolt against Burgundian rule. After some early embarrassing defeats (such as the 1452 Battle of Nevele), Philip III had mustered some 30,000 men and led them into Flanders to crush the uprising once and for all. The Flemish leader, Wouter Leenknecht, had gathered an army of some 13,000 men in the village of Bazel to oppose the Burgundians. Marching to nearby Rupelmonde, Philip finally lured the Flemish out of their defensive positions after two days of manoeuvring. Meeting them on open ground, the Burgundians defeated the rebels, with two thousand of them killed or captured, and the rest fleeing towards Ghent. During the panic, one of the rebels managed to kill Corneille of Burgundy, Philip's favourite bastard son. In revenge, Philip had all his prisoners killed and laid the entire area to waste. Sneyssen had his hand holding the Ghent standard cut off, but refused to let the flag fall and held it with his other hand.

3. The *Fürsorgeamt* was the welfare office for Waffen-SS volunteers from across Flanders and Walloonia, which provided volunteers and their families with financial and other assistance during the war.

4. Pierik, Perry, *From Leningrad to Berlin – Dutch Volunteers in the Waffen-SS 1941–45* p58, Aspekt. Pierik characterised Kortrijk as the victory of Flemish '*kerels*', literally 'blokes' i.e. normal citizens from Ghent and Bruges, against the detested 'southerners' as the French-speakers were collectively called.

5. '*Ceux de XIIIB: Recueil de Textes extraits du Mensuel de L'Amicale des Anciens Prisonniers de Guerre du Stalag XIIIB*'. *Centre Liégois d'Histoire et d'Archaeologie Militaire.* Retrieved 1 September 2013.

6. Evans, Richard J. *The Third Reich at War*, p382–384, Allen Lane.

7. Dank, Milton, *The French against the French*, p192, Cassell. Volunteers for the French LVF were paid at the same level as German Army soldiers, but using the set exchange rate between the French franc and the German Reichsmark. This meant French volunteers received twenty francs a day plus an additional twenty francs for every day in combat, plus a family stipend of 1,200 francs a month.

8. Evans, Richard J. *The Third Reich at War*, p505, Allen Lane.

9. Dank, Milton, *The French against the French*, p39, Cassell.

10. Weaver – De Vos 24/12/1993.

11. This echoes the famous comments made by Henry John Temple, 3rd Viscount Palmerston and British Foreign Secretary; 'We have no eternal allies, and we have no perpetual enemies. Our interests are eternal and perpetual, and those interests it is our duty to follow.' Speech to the House of Commons on 1st March 1848).

12. Evans, Richard J. *The Third Reich at War*, p387, Allen Lane.

13. Dank, Milton, *The French against the French*, p192, Cassell. Two-thirds of volunteers for the French LVF were rejected on medical grounds; bad teeth, poor eyesight and varicose veins being the biggest issues.

14. From Willy Massin's work; *Limburgers in het Vlaams Legionen en de Waffen-SS* (Diest: W. Massin, 1994),

containing a social analysis in his study on the Limburg volunteers in the Flemish Legion and the Waffen-SS based on the personal records of 530 volunteers who enlisted 1941-1944. The mining areas of Limburg – the easternmost province of Flanders – provided the largest number of volunteers (over 65%), most of which came from the city of Genk. Seventy per cent of the Limburg volunteers were unmarried. Mining was a very large industry in Limburg, while the number of college students was significantly lower than in the other provinces. Based on transport lists (and statistics) the age of the volunteers remained substantially constant throughout the course of the war.

15. Thirty-eight-year-old Fredegardus Jacobus Josephus (Jef) van de Wiele was the founder and leader of the *Deutsch-Vlämische Arbeitsgemeinschaft*, the German-Flemish Labour Group, better known as DeVlag. DeVlag wanted an 'Anschluss' with the Third Reich and for Flanders to formally become a part of a Greater German Empire.

3

TRAINING: MUD AND DISILLUSIONMENT

Recruits for the 1st Company Legion Flandern in training; Oswald Van Ooteghem is standing second from left, Albert Olbrechts is standing on the far right. (Courtesy Oswald Van Ooteghem)

Comprehensive and realistic training, conducted by well-qualified and experienced instructors, was the very bedrock of German military excellence in the Second World War. That system of training was designed for one goal, and one goal alone; to produce troops of the very highest quality able to fight and win across any expected battlefield. While understanding their national legions would undergo specifically 'German' training, the VNV and NSB leaderships back in Flanders and Holland respectively had extracted key concessions from the Nazis regarding the unique 'non-German' ethnicity of the new recruits. These concessions included the appointment of a Roman Catholic chaplain for the Flemish, the creation of their own medical corps, the use of the Dutch language wherever possible, the participation of Staf De Clercq and Anton Mussert in the appointment of senior Legion officers, with direct liaison between the Legions and the political leadership of the VNV and NSB and, crucially, the appointment of Flemish and Dutch NCOs and officers to lead the troops. As it turned out pretty much all of these promises were discarded by the Germans even before the first drafts of volunteers drew their kit. The military authorities decided that German would be the language of both training and command, that no Catholic chaplains would be brought on board – the SS always had an antipathy towards organised Christianity – and that there would be no encouragement to any political oversight of the Legions from back home. However, the biggest blow to the hopes of the volunteers was dealt in the selection and appointment of the NCOs and officers of the two Legions. Deeming the majority of ranking Dutch and Belgian recruits as not up to standard, it was decided that Germans would fill the majority of command posts right from the start. This would mean that fewer than half the officers in the Legion Niederlande would be Dutch, and that the one Flemish NCO in the Flandern would stand out like a sore thumb amongst his seventy-seven German counterparts.[1] As far as the SS training authorities were concerned, the men climbing down from the train carriages in Poland were going to be trained like every other volunteer, like it or not, and the watchword of that training was 'tough'.

During my first interview with the Sneyssens group, when I asked my initial question on that training and what it was like, all three men looked at each other, smiled with a sort of grim remembrance and then, remarkably, all made the same hand gesture: they put their right arms out in front of them, clenched their fists and turned them to the right as if they were tightening a screw. D'Oosterlinck then said: 'It was tough. Simple as that.'

OVO: Our training camp was in Debica, Poland. It was hard and unforgiving. From early in the morning until late in the evening we were shouted at and given orders. It was very physical. The food wasn't very good; greasy, which led to a lot of upset stomachs amongst us. Then we were transferred to Arys in East Prussia [now Polish Orzysz] on 7th September. Then our company was deployed. The reserves stayed in Graz in Austria at first, and then were sent east to join us. That's when Theo joined the Legion.

TD: Yes, I was actually trained near Graz in Austria at a place called Litzendorf. There was no light training at all. We Flemish were dealt with very strictly. The German trainers talked, shouted and used swear words at us all the time. Discipline was everything, so when they said 'lie down' you did it, whether there was mud or water or whatever on the ground just do it. Our barracks had to be very tidy. The lockers had to be clean, with everything in them clean, ironed and in good order all organised. If not, then it was pulled out and thrown on the floor and you had to start all over again.

Enlisting in 1943, Van Gyseghem was sent to the alternative training centre for European SS volunteers at Sennheim in Alsace, but it seemed little had changed since the Heidelager days back in 1941.

HVG: A small anecdote if I may. In the barracks, in our bunk rooms, we all had a locker where we kept all of our uniform, equipment and belongings. These lockers had to be perfect, with everything clean and in its proper place. If the duty officer of the day came around and inspected it and it wasn't in order, he would pull it all out and throw it over the floor. You then had to pick it all up, clean it up, and put it back properly, and he would come and re-inspect it to make sure it was right this time.

Jan Munk, like Herman Van Gyseghem, was also trained in Sennheim, where his experiences were much the same as those of his Flemish brethren.

JM: The training concentrated on discipline. We were taught to march, to sing, to look after ourselves and to realise that an order had to be obeyed. We were never asked to do anything unreasonable like jumping out of a window without knowing how high up it was, but they excelled in teaching us to take cover. Once we had to exercise in a field which had been flooded, frozen over and then partially thawed. There were pools of icy water everywhere and at first everyone tried to keep dry by supporting themselves on their toes and hands, but after a while as we grew tired this became elbows and knees, and eventually when we realised how futile it was we threw ourselves down properly. We even enjoyed ourselves by trying to topple the NCOs by aiming for them as we dived for cover. Later, after our first contact with the enemy, you realised just how good our training had been. Everything was in German, the majority of foreign volunteers were Dutch or Flemish, but we had French-speaking Belgians, some Frenchmen, Danes and Norwegians too – four companies in all in the barracks. Our day started at 5.30am with breakfast in our own room, which then had to be cleaned. This was followed by roll-call, then the daily activities of square-bashing, weapons drill, marching and lessons in all aspects of army life, so we learnt to recognise all types of tanks, both ours and those of the enemy, and what we had to do if one approached us. Cleaning was also something special! If they told you that your room, rifle or uniform had to be clean, they meant clean! Saturday mornings was always our major cleaning session, including doing the corridors and stairs on our hands and knees.

The Swedish Waffen-SS volunteer, Tage Lindborg, echoed much of what Jan Munk said about Sennheim and its diverse mix of nationalities: 'There are so few Swedes. It's mostly Norwegians, Danes, Dutch, Flemish Belgians and Swiss. Yes, here there are all damn nations.'[2]

Being subject to strict military discipline and undergoing hard, physical training is one thing but the Flemish in particular (and the Dutch to a lesser extent) were physically and verbally abused to such an extent that the entire national legion concept was endangered.

OVO: Mentally it was tough. As the Flemish Legion, we were promised a Flemish command, with our own officers and our own spiritual and medical support, but this soon proved to be an illusion. As Flemings we were welcome, but only under German command as part of the Waffen-SS, and without a separate framework. A number of volunteers didn't want that, so they left and went back home. I decided to bite my tongue and stay. I didn't want to dishonour my family. So, I made my oath of allegiance to the supreme commander of the German Army in late October, on the 25th, and that was that. Two weeks later we were loaded onto a train and went east, to Tilsit, Riga and then Pleskau [in Russian, Pskov].

TD: We were trained using the German language, no Flemish was used. The officers were all German, and as far as they were concerned the language of training was German.

JM: We did not admire our instructors – all Germans by the way – but we certainly respected them, and some we liked. Only once did we have a Rottenführer who for some reason did not like the Flemish and treated them badly. At Christmas 1942 we found him lying on the floor, dead drunk, so we got hold of his heels and dragged him down the stone staircase to the cellar. In the cellar we threw him in one of the long water troughs and turned the cold tap on. We then beat him with our belts. Other instructors saw us doing this but turned a blind eye, and after that the Flemish recruits didn't have another problem with him.

The man put in charge of training those first batches of volunteers was Otto Reich, a forty-nine-year-old East Prussian Oberführer who had started his SS career as one of Sepp Dietrich's original 120 volunteers for the SS-Leibstandarte back in the 1930s. He had fought in World War One and then gone on to serve in the freebooting, right-wing Freikorps before Dietrich came calling. An uncompromising disciplinarian, Reich was at best indifferent to his charges, as was the first nominated commander of the Legion Flandern, Michael Lippert.[3] Lippert, like Reich, was a Nazi fanatic, and under their dual leadership, treatment of the recruits was so bad that one Dutch volunteer even committed suicide and news spread fast back home about the poor treatment being meted out.[4]

Mussert's response was to send his right-hand man, the Brussels-born Cornelis Van Geelkerken[5]– to go and see for himself what the conditions were like, and to talk directly to the volunteers. The tall and serious Dutchman was incensed by what he found, and after he reported back to Mussert, the NSB leader appealed angrily to both Berger and Himmler to rectify the situation or face losing NSB support for recruitment.

As for the Flemish, De Clercq's response to the reported abuse was to write a five-page confidential letter to both Heinrich Himmler and the German Military Board. In it, he didn't pull his punches:

These considerations and decisions are absolutely of a highly confidential nature. Neither our people nor Germany have anything to gain by the disclosure of the problems and abuses, dissatisfaction, indignation and hostility … a feeling of suspicion and unrest among the surviving legionnaires and the German-friendly Flemish population would be developed …. Indignation … would be so huge … the relationship between the Germans and the new Flanders would be significantly harmed."

De Clercq went on to criticise what he saw as bad faith by the Germans in preventing direct contact between, and oversight of, the Legion by the VNV leadership, and the disparaging language often used by the German training staff to the recruits about the VNV itself, and him in particular.

Was the Waffen-SS being sloppy in its training, or were Berlin's orders being disregarded locally by the staff? As Jan Munk pointed out, there is some evidence for the former, but not of the latter. In reality, the root of the problem lay in the wildly differing aims of the Waffen-SS and the VNV and NSB. Mussert and De Clercq wanted control over the Dutch and Flemish Legions respectively to support the political aims of their parties. Specifically De Clercq wanted the Legion to help spearhead Flanders' case for independence but the Waffen-SS didn't really want Flemish nationalists, rather they wanted young Flemings they could train to be part of the new Nazi élite they intended to establish across Europe once they had won the war. As De Wever put it:

The intentions of the SS authorities were the same in Flanders, the Netherlands, Denmark and Norway: they wanted to form an élite that would strengthen the Greater Germany ideal. The intention was to mould leaders for the future, firmly convinced, we would say indoctrinated, with the idea that Flanders was only one of many clear and future jewels in the crown of the Greater German Reich.

So, the intentions of the Waffen-SS were opposed to those of the VNV. Berlin wanted the volunteers to become proper 'German' SS men, 'even if it was at the expense of the original commitment motives of many Flemish nationalist and / or Catholic-inspired volunteers.'[6]

By the time Jan Munk enlisted the following year, this central conundrum was still at the very heart of the Waffen-SS training machine. Passing out of Sennheim on 6th July 1942, the young Dutchman was sent by train to Lendorf barracks near Klagenfurt in Austria for further infantry training. En route he contracted bronchitis and was sent to hospital for treatment, and then a convalescent home amidst the Austrian lakes. Upon returning to Lendorf he was put on six weeks of light duties, which he detested as he was set to work in the kitchens and officers mess at first, before being put on better duties in the armoury. He resumed full training on 6th September.

JM: I'd already missed two groups of Dutch recruits who had come and gone while I was sick. I was then based in Klagenfurt with the 1st Ersatz Company, Block Room 85, there were four of us Dutch, two Danes, a Fleming, one Norwegian and a Swede – we nearly always spoke German, it just made things easier. Our immediate superior was a Rottenführer, four rooms made up a platoon with an Unterscharführer in charge, and four platoons made up a company under the command of a Hauptsturmführer or an Untersturmführer. I was rather good with the MG34 machine-gun so I received special training as an MG No.1. I was scheduled to join the SS-Wiking Division, one of the most interesting divisions within the Waffen-SS, with Estonian, Finnish, Flemish, Walloon, Dutch, Danes, Norwegians and Swiss volunteers, as well as 'volksdeutsche' [ethnic Germans from outside the borders of the pre-War Third Reich] from Hungary, Rumania, Poland, Yugoslavia and even the Soviet Union! They all made the very brave decision to fight for the German Army as individuals.

This was far more what the SS authorities wanted rather than recalcitrant Flemish nationalists, but Munk was clear that for most of the volunteers their own countries came first – and that went for him too. In late July 1944, he was slated to go to the famous Waffen-SS *Junkerschule* (Officer School) at Bad Tölz, tucked away in rural Bavaria, and attend the 4-month 18th Wartime Shortened Officers Course. This was the fifth course for non-Germans and would end up being the last before the war ended. He was promoted to *Standartenjunker* after passing the first part of the course, before he and his classmates reacted to an outburst by an arrogant German officer instructor.

JM:There was a heated argument between one of our instructors and one of the Danish Standartenjunker over whether Germany should annex other European countries – the German officer said yes they should, and our Danish comrade said no they shouldn't. I was always against Holland being annexed by Germany, and we all agreed with our Danish comrade. Feelings were running very high, and we felt a gesture was needed. So, the next day we all paraded in our uniforms as usual, except that now all the volunteers were wearing their countries' national badge on their lower left-hand sleeve, which we never did, only ever wearing our divisional or regimental cuff-title. No-one said anything but a few days later the German instructor was posted to the front.

Back in 1941, the Legion Flandern had moved from Debica to Arys in East Prussia to continue its training, and then onwards to Riga in Latvia, and finally the front. The Reichsführer-SS Command War Diaries contained a single entry dated 6th November that would be momentous for Oswald Van Ooteghem and his fellow volunteers.

6 November 1914: On the orders of RF-SS the Legion Flandern was attached to 2nd SS Infantry Brigade and was to begin its march from Arys, East Prussia to Tossno [in Russia near Leningrad] at 0700hrs on 10 November.

It had barely been three months since the train had rolled out of the Brussels North station. Were they ready or were they rushed, and if so why were they rushed? The Dutch author and historian, Perry Pierik, was clear in his view: 'The Flemish legionnaires weren't trained exceptionally well, and as a consequence suffered very high casualties.'[7]

It is true that the Flemings were the first national legion to be sent to the front. The Frenchmen in the German

Army-backed *Légion des volontaires français contre le bolchévisme (LVF)* arrived in Debica in southern Poland for their training from September 1941 onwards, and weren't committed to the Operation Typhoon battles of Army Group Centre until the beginning of December. As for the Dutchmen of the Legion Niederlande and the Norwegians of the Legion Norwegen, they would only enter combat in February 1942, while the Danes of the Freikorps Danmark would arrive even later, in May that year. There were specific reasons for some of these delays, but it's difficult not to suspect that at least a measure of the thinking behind the decision to send the Flemish forward so early was the German belief, held at the highest levels of command, that the war in the East was more or less won, and so whilst it didn't much matter in the military scheme of things, it would be advantageous politically to have some non-German European volunteers taste action at the front before it was all over.

Hitler himself had already said as much back in July to Joseph Goebbels, (Hitler's Minister of Propaganda and Gauleiter of Berlin) who had recorded in his diary: 'The war in the East was in the main already won.'

Hitler's comment echoed the view of the Chief of Staff of the German High Command, General Franz Halder, who wrote in his diary in the same month: 'So it's really not saying too much if I claim that the campaign against Russia has been won in fourteen days.'[8]

Having said that, a secret report compiled in the spring of 1942 by the SS's own security service, the *Sicherheitsdienst* (SD) detailed a commonly held belief among the German public itself that the Waffen-SS were poorly trained in comparison to the Army, and that as a consequence its men were often 'recklessly sacrificed'.[9] No matter what the reasoning was, the Flemish were going to war.

NOTES

1. Rikmenspoel, Marc J., *Waffen-SS Encyclopedia*, p136, Aberjona Press.
2. Larsson, Lars T. *Hitler's Swedes – A History of the Swedish Volunteers in the Waffen-SS*, Helion.
3. Lippert would end the war commanding Dutch Waffen-SS troops in the hastily-formed 34th Landstorm Nederland Division, before being tried and convicted after the war for his part in the murder of the SA leader Ernst Röhm in Stadelheim prison during the infamous Night of the Long Knives in 1934.
4. Pierik, Perry, *From Leningrad to Berlin – Dutch Volunteers in the Waffen-SS 1941–45*, p58, Aspekt.
5. After the war Van Geelkerken was sentenced to life imprisonment, but released early in 1959. He died aged 75 on 29th March 1976 in Ede in the Netherlands.
6. De Wever – 24/12/ 1993.
7. Pierik, Perry, *From Leningrad to Berlin – Dutch Volunteers in the Waffen-SS 1941–45*, Aspekt.
8. Evans, Richard J., *The Third Reich at War*, p188, Allen Lane.
9. Ibid, p505. Over 900,000 men served in the Waffen-SS during the course of the war, with 34% of that number listed as fatalities.

4

TO THE FRONT!

No-man's land for the Legion Flandern on the Leningrad front. (Courtesy Oswald Van Ooteghem)

What Oswald Van Ooteghem, Theo D'Oosterlinck and their comrades would find in Russia was a war that Hitler and Berlin may have thought would be over very shortly, but was in fact only just beginning, and would go on to claim the lives of well over thirty million people in an orgy of violence and blood-letting the like of which the world had never before seen.

The Flemish Legion were bound for the Wehrmacht's Army Group North and its assault on Soviet Russia's second city and the very cradle of the Russian Revolution – Leningrad. There were no true backwaters on the Russian Front, but this was about the closest there came to being one. The smallest and least mobile of the three German Army Groups launched into the Soviet Union back in June, Army Group North's commander, *Ritter* Wilhelm von Leeb, was an artilleryman by background and renowned in the German military as perhaps its greatest exponent of defensive warfare. His seminal work on the subject included the line: 'the aim of the defensive is to hold, that of the offensive to win, it is easier to hold than to win.'

This was not an officer with a deep affinity for armoured warfare and the new concept of blitzkrieg, rather he was a general beloved of detail and thorough planning, whose performance in leading a diversion against the French Maginot Line back in 1940 had earned him a much-coveted Field Marshal's baton. A devout Catholic with little time personally for the Nazis, von Leeb was a tall, taciturn man, his shaved head topping a thin face almost perpetually set in a scowl. His fellow Feldmarschall, Sigmund Wilhelm List, commented on his lack of sense of humour: 'If von Leeb ever tried to smile, it would crack his face.'[1]

Given his own temperament, lack of military resources, and the difficulty of the terrain, criss-crossed as it was by innumerable rivers, lakes and streams, and thickly covered by semi-trackless forests stretching for hundreds of miles, it was perhaps not a huge surprise that von Leeb had been unable to reach and capture Leningrad in a lightning campaign over the summer and early autumn. Although he was not helped at all by the attitude of his Finnish allies; happy to advance and liberate their former territory ceded to the Soviet Union following their defeat in the Winter War, they refused to continue their offensive beyond that and threaten the whole of northern Russia. Neither could he look for support or succour to his ultimate boss in the Reich Chancellery, who made his views about the city crystal clear to his field marshal in late September:

> I have decided to erase the city of Petersburg [originally St Petersburg as it is today, then Petrograd, then Leningrad] from the face of the earth. I have no interest in the further existence of this large city after the defeat of Soviet Russia.[2]

In practical terms this meant von Leeb was not given the troops or equipment necessary to capture the city, only to surround it and begin a siege which Hitler thought would starve this immense city of three million people into submission. In scenes reminiscent of the Western Front in the First World War, the Germans dug miles of trenches around the city, and artillery and aircraft were used to continually bomb and shell it, wreaking death and destruction on its inhabitants and defenders. An estimated one million civilians would die from hunger and bombardment in that first dreadful winter, and food became so scarce that people were forced into eating cats, dogs, rats from the sewers and even boiling down their wallpaper to eat the glue. No fewer than 886 Leningraders were arrested by the city authorities for cannibalism.[3]

Behind the snaking trench lines of von Leeb's besiegers was a vast hinterland of forest and swamp ideally suited for the thousands of partisans and resistance fighters who now made it their home. These men and women were a mixed force; many were Red Army personnel stranded behind German lines after their summer advance, while many others were ordinary villagers and townsfolk determined to protect their Motherland against the invader. Controlled, and often supplied, by Moscow they were a powerful threat to the rear areas of their enemy – a German Army that had a deep-seated historic antipathy towards 'irregulars' and whose invariable response to them was the use of massive and often indiscriminate force. Back in September 1939 as the Wehrmacht thrust into Poland, the then-commander of Army Group North, Fedor von Bock, issued the following order to his troops on how armed resistance was to be dealt with: 'If there is shooting from a village behind the front and it proves impossible to identify the house from which the shots came then the whole village is to be burned to the ground.'

His men took him at his word, and within two months a total of 531 Polish towns and villages had been destroyed and 16,376 Poles executed for continuing to resist the invaders.[4] The same would happen in the Soviet Union but on an altogether larger scale.

Unable to dedicate enough regular Army troops to try and subdue the partisans, Berlin fashioned two ad hoc Waffen-SS formations to try and help do the job, the 1st and 2nd SS Infantry Brigades. The 1st was sent to support Army Group Centre, while the 2nd went north.

These units, each around 6-8,000 men strong at any given time, were to fight an often extremely brutal war where atrocities and massacres were almost commonplace. In the West we often think of 'resistance' as a pretty small-scale affair – small groups of plucky freedom fighters armed with a few rifles and submachine-guns blowing up the odd train or truck. This was most definitely not the case in Russia as the RF-SS War Diaries of the time make plain:

> 4 November 1941: 1st SS Infantry Brigade report; In a brisk battle with a partisan group near Vogeoff, 94 partisans were killed and a small arsenal of weaponry was captured as follows: 21 x 8.5cm artillery pieces, six cases containing 2,000 flares, 44 x hand-grenades plus rifle and artillery ammunition. The field pieces had to be destroyed as they could not be easily transported out of the area.

Twenty-one pieces of artillery is nothing less than full-scale warfare, and capturing them was clearly a notable success for the SS infantrymen, but the dark side of their operations was never far away. Another excerpt from almost a week later reads:

> 10 November: 1st SS Infantry Brigade report; Guard posts at the POW camp south of Skurovka were assailed by automatic weapons fire from the outside and by pistol fire from the inside. A search for the culprits was unsuccessful, but the camp commandant decided that 25 prisoners should be shot as an example to hopefully prevent future sabotage.

This was the type of formation and the campaign they were waging that the Flemish would be pitched into. The RF-SS

Command War Diaries had a number of entries for the Flandern over its first few weeks in theatre:

15 November: The arrival of the SS-Legion Flandern with 25 officers, 2 officer candidates, 79 NCOs and 1010 men with 140 vehicles was reported at its billet in Tarrassovo.

20 November: Legion Flandern was put to work fighting partisans and accounted for two [its first reported action, with another operation on the 25th that didn't result in any casualties to either side].

27 November: Flandern and other brigade troops strafed by Soviet aircraft, no casualties. [First aircraft attack for the Flemings.]

3 December: Search commandos sent out by Flandern and the Brigade motorcycle platoon returned to quarters after 5 days of operating in the field against the terrorists [the term routinely used by the Germans helping them justify atrocities]. Many strongpoints and isolated villages they operated out of were destroyed.

Then came a fight that left the first Flemish dead of the campaign.

4 December: at 1115hrs Red Army soldiers launched a raid into the Escort Battalion RF-SS security zone 9 km west of Olomno; a company of the Escort Battalion along with a part of the Legion Flandern counterattacked. In the course of fierce fighting the enemy was routed but six Flemish SS men were killed and three more were wounded. The Escort Battalion lost one killed and three wounded.

This was how Oswald Van Ooteghem saw it.

OVO: By that time the Flemish Legion had gotten some new volunteers and was over a thousand strong, and we'd had more training in Latvia and Russia. The atmosphere was pretty good. The Germans had advanced rapidly almost to Leningrad – now St Petersburg of course – and we were told the Flemish Legion would be used primarily as an occupying army. Yet soon we suffered our first casualties. During an ambush near Tossno by partisans – armed resistance fighters operating in civilian clothes behind the front lines – a few of our boys were surprised and killed at a village called Olomno. I was ordered to stay in the village and wait for reinforcements which were coming to pick up a broken-down field kitchen wagon. It was cold and I decided to warm up in the house of a farmer along with a comrade. Once back outside, we found that the rest of our patrol had already gone. We had to find our own way back to camp in the dark and the cold, following right behind each other. It was pretty scary I can tell you.

Theo D'Oosterlinck also experienced that first winter at the front, and then the spring and summer of 1942.

TD: We left for training from the station at Antwerp, there were about 150-200 of us, all volunteers. In Graz, where we did our training, we were told we were going to be an 'ersatz' company – a replacement company – to replace fallen comrades at the front from the first contingent back in the summer. In the Flemish newspapers, like Volk en Staat and de Gentenaar, we used to see obituaries appearing regularly of boys who had been killed on the Eastern Front. We used to talk about it among ourselves. We had four months of training, and then it was on the train north to the front, to Leningrad, to the siege lines around Leningrad that is. When we got there we were spread out in little groups along the line to plug the gaps. I was assigned to the 2nd Company, and my commander was Helmut Breymann, he was Austrian. He was a father figure to us, a very good man and a fine officer. He left and went to the Dutch later on, and I heard he was killed at Narva in 1944.[5] One of the platoon chiefs was Martenson [SS-Untersturmführer Sven Martenson]. I saw him again at the Lüneburgerheide [German Army training area and formation point for the SS-Sturmbrigade Langemarck], twice actually. Anyway, when it was winter in the siege lines we stayed in our trenches. They had been dug by the SS-Polizei Division when they were stationed there, and were still full of snow. We cleared them by shovelling it out and building walls of snow so we could walk around and be safe. Supplies could be brought up to us in the line under the cover of the snow, it was good. Then as it got warmer the ground became very marshy, very wet. The weather was good, and we were sent to a 'sappe', a forward combat post in front of our main trenches. We could see the skyline of Leningrad from there.

With Van Ooteghem and his comrades in the far north of the Soviet Union, Jan Munk went to the far south by train through the rolling steppes of Ukraine.

JM: Our pay was one Reichsmark and six cigarettes a day, and from this meagre amount we had to buy writing paper, razor blades and just about everything else, including the boot polish we all needed. This only changed on 29th March 1943 when we were marched to Klagenfurt station with a band playing and there we were met by women and girls with flowers and useful gifts like razors, soap, pencils and paper. We were put into goods wagons with big sliding doors on the side — eleven men plus a sergeant in each wagon — and then off we went. We were told then that our former pay of one Reichsmark was being increased to two Reichsmarks plus we kept our six cigarettes allowance. Not only

*that but the food got better, and there was more of it, we were
even sometimes given tins of meat from Denmark and chocolate
from Holland, which made me smile. Then we would just open
the doors and sit on the floor with our legs dangling outside as
we watched the countryside pass by for kilometre after kilometre.
We were all impressed by the enormous vastness of the Russian
countryside that the Germans had managed to occupy.*

For the Flemish it was the cold and snow of northern
Russia, but for Jan Munk as a newly-trained member of the
SS-Wiking Division it was the baking sun and endless blue
skies of southern Ukraine.

JM: *I joined the 1st Company, the Westland Regiment, in the Slavjansk
area in late March '43 [eastern Ukraine]. They had just returned
from the front to lick their wounds and absorb the replacements
like me. We were quartered in a tiny Russian village, just a row of
houses on each side of an unsurfaced road with a water well in the
centre and their earth-latrines behind the houses. We were very well
treated by the Russians, and we shared our food with the Russian
family, who in turn gave us lovely fried eggs, fried potatoes and
gherkins from their vegetable plot at the side of the house. We slept
on the floor without straw or bedding, just digging a small hollow in
the hard earth floor for our hip and wrapping our jack-boots in a
pullover as a pillow. I always slept well … My first fight was not really
a combat. We had joined our unit but we newcomers were still very
green. We were told to march in a long line until we came to a deep
crater in the flat ground. We were told a small group of partisans
had taken cover in there after being parachuted in behind our lines.
A Flemish soldier was stupid enough to go to the edge and was
promptly killed. His friend, furious, did the same, firing his rifle down
at the Russians, but he was also shot. We just lobbed hand-grenades
in until it was all quiet. There were eight of the Russians I think, and*

when we went down into the crater we found a large metal case full of Russian money and weapons. The money was useless to us so we used it as toilet paper, or to roll cigarettes.

Legion Flandern went into winter quarters a week or so before Christmas 1941 around the small town of Talsen and its neighbouring villages, and there they celebrated their first festive season in Russia. However, the Christmas and New Year hangovers were barely gone before an almighty disaster began to enfold the *Ostheer* [the Germany Army in the East].

I am sitting with my comrades in a dug-out, in the half-dark. You have no idea how lousy and crazy we all look, and how this life has become a torment for me. It can't be described in words any more. I've only got one thought left: when will I get out of this hell?[6]

This shocking admission from a soldier's letter to his wife back home, wasn't written by some poor Soviet conscript shivering in front of blitzkrieg, but by a German soldier shivering in front of a Soviet onslaught. In a desperate gamble to end the conflict before the turn of the year, the Ostheer had launched Operation Typhoon to capture Moscow and finish off the Russian bear. It had failed. Mere miles from the Kremlin, with Wehrmacht soldiers seizing Moscow tram tickets for souvenirs, the offensive had run out of fuel, out of ammunition, out of men and out of time. 'General Winter' and Georgy Zhukov had waded in on Moscow's behalf and the 5,000 horses that every German infantry division still relied on in this mechanised age to pull its artillery, supplies and heavy equipment, were dying in their traces just as Napoleon's had done more than a century before.[7]

Beginning on 6th December, the Red Army had launched a massive counter-offensive on the Moscow front that sent Army Group Centre reeling backwards, and almost caused its complete destruction. Tens of thousands of Germans were killed, and masses of equipment were lost as worn out German units were crushed in the snow. It was the first major Soviet victory of the war, and it signalled the end of Hitler's dream to conquer the Soviet Union in a lightning campaign.

NOTES

1. Mitcham Jr, Samuel W., *Hitler's Field Marshals*, p125, Guild.
2. Evans, Richard J., *The Third Reich at War*, p202, Allen Lane.
3. Glantz, David M., *The Battle for Leningrad 1941–1944*, BCA, & Jones, Michael, *Leningrad – State of Siege*, John Murray.
4. Evans, Richard J., *The Third Reich at War*, p20, Allen Lane.
5. Born in Austro-Hungarian Trieste on 9th February 1911, Helmut Breymann joined the Austrian SS Regiment Der Führer before going on to briefly serve in the Nordwest. After serving with the Flandern he was promoted to become commander of the 2nd Battalion of the Dutch Waffen-SS 48th General Seyffardt Regiment. He was killed alongside most of his men during the fighting at Narva in July 1944, although he was officially designated as Missing in Action and only finally declared dead by the District Court of Vienna on 13th October 1949.
6. Evans, Richard J., *The Third Reich at War*, p208. Letter from German Army soldier, Alois Scheuer, to his wife.
7. Ibid, p3.

5

THE LEGION AT THE VOLKHOV AND LADOGA

A rifle marks the makeshift grave of a Red Army soldier on the Volkhov front. A German Mark III panzer lies destroyed in the background. (Courtesy Oswald Van Ooteghem)

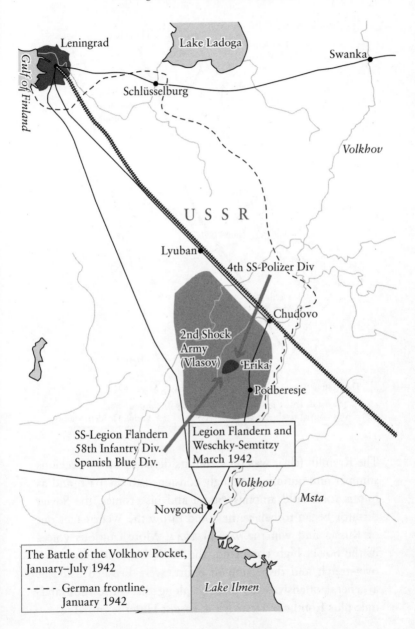

Leningrad

Gulf of Finland

Lake Ladoga

Swanka

Schlüsselburg

Volkhov

U S S R

Lyuban

4th SS-Polizer Div

Chudovo

2nd Shock
Army
(Vlasov)

'Erika'

Podberesje

SS-Legion Flandern
58th Infantry Div.
Spanish Blue Div.

Legion Flandern and
Weschky-Semtitzy
March 1942

Volkhov

Msta

Novgorod

The Battle of the Volkhov Pocket,
January–July 1942

– – – – German frontline,
January 1942

Lake Ilmen

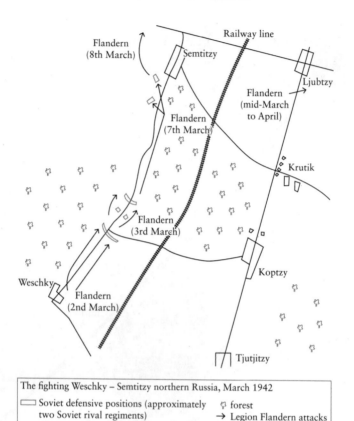

Flandern
(8th March)

Semtitzy

Railway line

Ljubtzy

Flandern
(mid-March
to April)

Flandern
(7th March)

Krutik

Flandern
(3rd March)

Koptzy

Weschky

Flandern
(2nd March)

Tjutjitzy

The fighting Weschky – Semtitzy northern Russia, March 1942

Soviet defensive positions (approximately
two Soviet rival regiments)

forest

→ Legion Flandern attacks

The Kremlin felt it was on a roll, its disasters of the previous summer and autumn seemingly consigned to the past, and as hubris took hold amongst Stalin and his cronies, the Soviet dictator began to believe he could throw the Wehrmacht out of Russia and win the war in 1942. More cautious voices in the Soviet high command, the STAVKA, who warned of overstretch and dispersion of effort, were brushed aside as a general offensive was ordered along the entire thousand-mile-plus frontline: 'Destroy the Fascist Hitlerites now!'

On the northern front, the Soviets began their assault against the Ostheer on 7th January, their infantry, cavalry and tank troops washing round German strongpoints and creating two pockets – '*kessels*'– with over 100,000 Germans trapped within; General Count Walter von Brockdorff-Ahlefeldt's II Corps at Demyansk, and the far smaller Kholm Pocket of Lieutenant-General Theodor Scherer's 281st Security Division. Calamity stared Army Group North in the face, and every man who could carry a rifle was called to the front. In Talsen the Flemish Legion got their orders, climbed aboard their trucks and headed east to the line near the Volkhov River.

Wilhelm von Leeb struggled to maintain his Army Group's position and asked permission to withdraw his troops back west behind the Lovat River to re-establish a coherent front line. Hitler refused, believing the best way to win was for the soldiers to stand and fight where they were. Utterly disillusioned by what he saw as undue interference and amateurism from Berlin, von Leeb resigned on 16th January and was succeeded by the commander of his own Eighteenth Army, Colonel-General Georg von Küchler. Küchler, the conqueror of both Holland and Paris back in 1940, was an artilleryman like his predecessor, but faced with the same problems as the man he replaced, he chose a radically different solution. Realising that Hitler wouldn't allow a retreat, he surmised that the key to German success lay in holding the main road and rail junctions until the spring thaw left the Red Army spearheads stuck in the mud as their supplies ran out. He could then counter-attack to snuff out those same beleaguered spearheads. But until that happened he ordered his men to hold their ground. It would be the hugest dogfight.

The German Eighteenth Army, to which the Legion Flandern belonged, improvised by combining disparate formations into ready-to-go *kampfgruppen* (literally 'battle groups'), those masterpieces of lashed-together units that were so often the saviours of the Ostheer. Flandern itself was grouped into *Kampfgruppe Debes* alongside the Reichsführer-SS Begleit Battalion (RF-SS Escort Battalion) and the SS Anti-Aircraft Detachment 'East'. Ordered to help contain the Red Army breakthrough and prepare the ground for a counter-attack, the Flandern was involved in extremely heavy fighting around the villages of Koptsy, Weschky and Semtitzy (the Oostfronters lumped the latter two together and christened it the battle of Weschky-Semtitzy), tiny specks on the map that would loom large in the memories of the veterans down through the years.

OVO: In the spring of 1942 we were deployed in the battle for the Volkhov, near Novgorod, about two hundred kilometres south of Leningrad. We had to fight the Russians of course, but there was also another enemy: the freezing cold. The temperature would drop at night to minus thirty, or even forty degrees centigrade. We didn't have proper winter coats, no fur hats and no warm boots, and trying to advance in the snow and ice was almost impossible. Frostbite was a real problem. Toes, fingers and parts of men's ears froze and fell off. Whoever fell asleep in the snow, they never woke up. Then we were hit by a hammer blow – Reimond Tollenaere had been killed. The only senior VNV leader who had gone to the front with us was dead. I met him a few days before his death and it was freezing cold, around 40° below zero, and he said to me 'Oswald, have courage, it's tough but we will get through it.' What can I tell you, he was my mentor. We heard that he had been killed by friendly fire from Spanish artillery. The Russians were only a few hundred metres away and the gunners got their zeroing wrong. The Spanish were from their Blue Division ([the Spaniards earned their nickname from the colour of the shirts they wore on arrival in Russia] who fought against the Russians. Tollenaere was just thirty years old and left behind a wife and three children.

I went to Podberesje, a godforsaken village, where Tollenaere had been put into a temporary grave, and saw his grave marker. I felt sick. In the village itself I saw another terrible sight: against the church wall were the mutilated bodies of many dead German soldiers. Ears, hands and genitals had been cut off. Some of them were completely naked and had been doused with water by the Russians and left to freeze to death. I didn't have time to think much about it though as it was getting dark and I needed to find some place warm to sleep to get through the bitterly cold night. I actually spent the night in the church itself, and stuffed a load of newly-arrived Feldpost [Germany Army field post system] letters inside my clothes. They helped keep me a bit warm at least.

The losses were huge. The Spanish troops from the Blue Division were completely demoralised. One day in February – the 18th I think – we were ordered to help rescue the remains of a company from the Blue Division who had been cut off near the village of Bolsjamosje. We advanced and came under fire from a Russian anti-tank gun, and we all took cover. I found what I thought was an empty bunker and went down into it as fast as I could. I couldn't believe it when I saw it was full of Spanish soldiers who were sitting there making little wooden crosses. They didn't even look up at me but just carried on what they were doing. They had made a load of crosses for their fallen comrades and they were now making their own, carving their own names in the birch wood. They were sure they were going to die.

Then on another occasion I had to stand guard against possible Russian attack, and my sentry position was behind a wall of bodies of Russian soldiers – all frozen solid. Our boys had built it for protection. There was an arm, a frozen arm, that stuck out of the wall. That image was with me for years. I couldn't get it out of my mind. It haunted me.

Almost grudgingly, the Germans themselves were now acknowledging the fighting qualities of the Legion, as witnessed in the Wehrmacht's daily bulletin from the 10th of February: 'In the successful defence of heavy mass attacks by the enemy, the Württemberg 25th Motorized Infantry Division and the SS-Legion "Flandern" distinguished themselves especially ...'

For Van Ooteghem those eighteen or so months in northern Russia left a tide of memories. An idealistic sixteen-year-old teenager had left his home and family and found himself in a world of snow, mud, forests and death. No matter what he had done since, that time clung to him like a second skin, and it was almost inevitable he would return, and so he did in the early summer of 2008.

Then in his eighties, he went back and saw it all again in his mind's eye. He took a flight to St Petersburg and, along with a driver, headed out into the countryside in a four-by-four, away from the city and the airport and out into the forests, fields and swamps of his wartime service.

Away from the metalled highways and modern infrastructure of Russia's second city, Van Ooteghem was soon swallowed up in a landscape that hadn't changed much at all in the decades since he was last there. The roads were little more than tracks, pot-holed and badly maintained, and lining them all were the endless ranks of fast-growing birch trees heading off to the horizon. Signs of human existence were few and far between; the odd single-storey wooden house or cabin, a veranda and clap-board cladding, the odd curious dog or pecking chicken. After miles of more of the same Van Ooteghem arrived at the first destination on his list, the village of Tossno, site of the Legion's first battles back in late 1941.

It isn't much to look at; a clutch of houses edging a couple of streets, with an old rundown Soviet-era community centre the only sign of the Revolution that began a few miles away. Van Ooteghem wasn't in Tossno to see how much – or how little – it had changed since 1941, he was there to meet a German, Uwe Lemke. Lemke is a Regional Director for the *Volksbund Deutsche Kriegsgräberfürsorge* (the German people's War Graves Commission)[1] with responsibility for northwest Russia and the estimated 300,000 German and allied soldiers thought to lie unidentified across this vast area of several thousand square kilometres. 'It is an immense task, but we don't just dig indiscriminately. We cast around until we are sure that we will find something. I've been here fifteen years and in that time we have found some 100,000 corpses. Maybe I can perhaps keep working here until I retire.'

Lemke uses old photos taken by soldiers at the time, and makes sure he speaks to local farmers and villagers – in this region people don't tend to move around much, and in all likelihood the old were there during the war and can remember what happened. Once he has enough evidence to instigate a dig he clears it with the Russian authorities – far easier now that soviet communism itself has been buried – and then it's down to him and his small gang of workmen.

According to Lemke's information there is a good chance that soldiers from Army Group North's 12th Infantry Division are lying in the swampy ground just a few hundred metres from the centre of the village, and maybe some Flemish too – that's why Van Ooteghem is there. The German holds up an old photo: 'Look, this must have been where the church was, and there was a small cemetery with wooden crosses. We are not just looking for bones, we want to put a name to the dead, and hopefully bring some peace to their family.'

Lemke sets his men to it, aware that prying eyes may be watching. Grave-robbers abound out here, and they work in teams to grab anything they can sell on eBay or a host of militaria websites. As Lemke says: 'We have a history of souvenir hunters; badges, gold teeth and rings, coins ... We cannot protect everything, and often we work in open spaces. It is unfortunate but unavoidable. Therefore, we work first on the places that are most vulnerable to looting.'

Digging away, one of Lemke's locally-hired workers – Yevgenny Demidov – makes a find. Bones: a tibia, ribs, and then the skull. Then the piece they really wanted, his ID tag. This was Corporal Erich Probst, a Mecklenburger like the majority of his comrades in the division with the snorting bull insignia. He was reported missing in action on 12th September 1941. He was killed three weeks after his thirty-first birthday. All that is left of him is placed in a blue plastic bag. Demidov has been doing this for some time: 'What were these guys doing here? So far from home. I always wonder. It's sometimes the little things that make it special; rings, medals, sometimes old photographs and handwritten letters from loved ones, the most unusual thing we have ever found was a skull with one glass eye in it, which I had never seen. No, they were not enemies. They were just young men with dreams and expectations. They were defending their country. The rest is politics.'

Erich Probst ended up being one of sixty dead soldiers found in the Tossno dig, and they were all taken to the German military cemetery at Sologubowka, where the victims of the Leningrad fighting are usually buried, while those from the Volkhov battles are mainly laid to rest to the south of Novgorod. Supported by the Russian government, the two sites are huge – in Sologubowka alone there is room for 80,000 graves – although there are no individual graves, only a few symbolic headstones and stone tables where the names of the victims are engraved. Hardly any are Flemish. Of the 100,000 men found by Lemke and his team by 2008, only fifty have been Flemings, and none were found at the Tossno dig.

Frustrated, Van Ooteghem moved on to the second village on his list, Podberesje. The four-by-four bounces along the half-roads and then there it is – the church he sheltered in overnight and where he stuffed Feldpost letters into his jacket to keep warm – it is still there. The car stops and he wanders around but there's nothing to see, and no dig taking place here, so it's off again. The drive becomes increasingly difficult and Van Ooteghem remembers something a comrade told him about this region. 'Once, a comrade told me he that was out on a patrol and came across a group of local Russian villagers who were very surprised to see 'German' soldiers. They didn't even know there was a war going on. I dismissed his story at the time as a soldiers' bluff, but now I begin to understand. Out here, entire villages can't be reached.'

Next it was Bolsjamosje, where Van Ooteghem found the Spaniards making their own grave crosses, and just as with Podberesje there is little except a sense of anti-climax. The village was almost deserted, only one house still occupied by an old lady who is too stubborn and too Russian to move. She was a little girl during the war and remembers the Spanish and the Germans, and how the partisans came afterwards and punished the village for not resisting the invaders as hard as the guerrillas thought they should.

In the back of the four-by-four Van Ooteghem had two wreaths, both decked out in the national colours of Flanders, with one dedicated to who else but his mentor, and the man who – alongside his father – was the biggest influence on his young life, Reimond Tollenaere.

'There is no politics behind this. This has nothing to do with ideology. This is a personal tribute to a father who had more courage than anyone ever. A rebel, a passionate orator who always lived for his convictions, and a man who left his family behind for Flanders. I saw his son recently and told him I would lay a wreath for him. He was very happy about that. "He who is without sin let him cast the first stone." Well I have many sins. I will not throw stones.'

Among the trackless forests that Van Ooteghem was navigating well over half-a-century later, Georg von Küchler's strategy was paying off by early March 1942, and he launched an attack on the Volkhov to seal off the biggest penetration of his lines, and try and trap two whole Soviet armies in a massive pocket of his own. As their part in the plan, the Legion was tasked with pushing the Soviets away from a major road between the villages of Weschky and Semtitzy. The fighting would be fierce. Semtitzy in particular would be a site of horror, with both sides pouring men into the fight as the village swapped hands over and over.

OVO: In March we had some real success when after a couple of night attacks in the snow we took Semtitzy from the Russians. Then I had a lucky escape. We had driven the Russians back and then gone on to break through their positions. There was a Russian soldier on skis who must've been coming back to the village itself from a patrol, when all of a sudden he sees a soldier in German uniform lying in the middle of his old position. He unslung his rifle off his back and put it in his shoulder all ready to shoot me. Luckily one of my friends, who was heading off to get us some more ammunition, saw the Russian and took aim at him. The Russian hesitated – only for a moment – as our uniforms must have confused him. The Russians were all dressed in white, whereas we were only wearing white jackets, so he probably wanted to make sure he wasn't going to shoot one of his own side. Anyway, my friend aimed right at him, a shot rang out and he hit the Russian in the throat. The body fell right next to me. I was alive because one of my comrades had been quicker than the Russian and had shot him dead first. He saved my life. I frisked the Russian and found a couple of pictures in his pocket. I kept one for luck and it became my talisman, I kept it with me wherever I went. After the war my wife got a bit bored of it to say the least, as I hung the photo above our bed as a kind of lucky charm, and I used to speak to it, to him, to that Russian, every night. It was a tiny photo though and I lost it some years ago when we moved house.

I was an infantryman in the 1st Company at the time² and then later on I became a Kriegsberichter — a war reporter. I was wounded in that fighting, I got a piece of shrapnel, a splinter in my left foot, and I got frostbite too, in both of my feet. It was during that fighting that we lost another good comrade, Kamiel De Wilde from Stekene. We were out on a patrol when the Russians let us fall into an ambush. They let us walk undisturbed on a trail surrounded by big snow-drifts. When we were close enough to them they started to shoot at us. They used mortars and rifle grenades as well, and a grenade landed between De Wilde and me. That's when I took the splinter in my foot. De Wilde was hit far worse than me, he took one in the chest. As he lay there he said to me: 'Tell my mother that her son died for Flanders.' Some of Kamiel's family came to see me after the war to hear the story of how he died, but his mother didn't come.

We were ordered to carry out an attack on a line of Russian bunkers. Twenty-five Russian bunkers we took. We were even mentioned in the 'Wehrmachtbericht' [the daily bulletin from the Wehrmacht that sometimes singled out units and individuals for special mention]. The bulletin said: 'Among other actions the Legion Flandern managed to take twenty-five enemy pillboxes in heavy close combat.'³ As for me I had the wound in my left foot. That was my first proper injury at the front, and as I was recovering it was suggested to me that I could do some reporting and take some photos. I still had to fight as well of course. That's when I first became a war reporter, whilst I was still serving in the Flemish Legion at the front.

On 12th March the Legion was pulled out of the line and sent into corps reserve. Arriving back in relative safety the roll was called out. Only 101 survivors answered it. Van Ooteghem was not one of them as he had been evacuated to the rear for medical treatment, his first sojourn with the doctors but not his last. Arriving back in Germany in the middle of March, he was visited by his parents, before being discharged and sent to a convalescence company in Graz where he received notification of his award of the Wound Badge in Black.

OVO: You start to reflect about what happened years later, actually the older you get the more you think about it. How crazy was I? Shooting at people I didn't know, and you're not even mad at. It was almost like being on a shooting range – like in a fairground – where you're just trying to hit the target. The Russians had white camouflage uniforms, so we held our rifle sights up towards the trees as they were brown in colour. When the tree all of a sudden went white in colour we knew we had to shoot. We knew that a Russian was walking by the tree. When the tree became brown again after we'd fired a shot we knew we had hit him. It was madness, horrible, just horrible.

The fighting at Weschky-Semtitzy was typical in many ways of the endless list of small-scale engagements which formed such a large part of the whole Russo-German War, and was in itself a big step in the development of the Flandern as a fighting force, and for the men in it. Its own (German)

Operations Officer noted the following points in his report on the Legion's conduct during the battle: [4]

1. *Poor reconnaissance of enemy field positions and strength. The attack was not conducted with air and artillery support.*
2. *Too few German officers and NCOs have been in the companies. As soon as the company commander is killed or wounded ... the attack stalls. As soon as a new leader arrives, the attack resumes. The troops are good but lack leadership.*
3. *Insufficient liaison between regimental headquarters and the Legion.*
4. *Unsatisfactory evacuation of the wounded.*
5. *Unsuccessful coordination with Spanish units in flank.*
6. *Artillery fired on registration points, rather than by direct observation from the front lines.*

Critical though this report is, there can be no doubt that Oswald Van Ooteghem and his comrades helped secure a significant Ostheer victory as the Volkhov Pocket collapsed along with the Soviet units within it, and the self-same report did indeed praise the Legion for its excellent coordination with neighbouring German units, and for handling ammunition, supplies and general logistics well.

However, the outcome of the battle wasn't an unqualified victory for the Ostheer. The days of herds of bewildered Red Army soldiers meekly tramping into German captivity were ending as news of the barbarity of Nazi mistreatment of Soviet POWs had gotten through to the Red Army, as testified to by one Red Army member: '... they say there's no shelter, no water, that people are dying from hunger and disease.'[5] So they now preferred to fight to the end rather than surrender. Only 32,000 Soviets were captured in the battle, in terms of the fighting in the East, a drop in the Red ocean.

By early May, both Kholm and Demyansk had been relieved, although German casualties had been horrific. In Kholm almost half the five thousand-odd defenders had been killed. And as a sign of his appreciation, Hitler promoted Küchler to Field Marshal. For the Flemish, and the Dutch of the Legion Niederlande who had played their full part too, it was time for medals to be handed out. Eighteen Niederlande members received the Iron Cross 1st Class, and 158 the 2nd Class award. Sixty-two Flemings received the 2nd Class, and nine the 1st Class, including the first ever to a Flemish soldier, Jules Geurts. The other eight went to German members of the Flandern.[6] The Flandern then received some well-earned rest, spending Kortrijk Day on 11th July parading in front of their new temporary commander, the Austrian Josef Fitzhum. The break didn't last long.

By now the tide of the whole war was beginning to turn against the Third Reich. In far-off North Africa, the 'Desert Fox' Erwin Rommel was defeated by Bernard Montgomery and his Eighth Army at El Alamein in October, and the Americans landed in French North Africa to complete their victory. In southern Russia, the seemingly unstoppable advance of Friedrich Paulus's Sixth Army was held at Stalingrad, and in the north a fresh Red Army offensive in late October to relieve Leningrad was only just beaten off by a depleted Army Group North.

Oswald Van Ooteghem had recovered from his foot injury and frostbite, had taken leave for most of June, had spent time in Berlin preparing for his new role as a war correspondent, been promoted to SS-Sturmmann, and was back in the line; but not for long.

OVO: In late November '42 I took part in a counter-attack against the Russians and was wounded again. This time I got shot in the right arm, in the upper arm. The Russians were using explosive bullets. The bullets made a circular motion so that when they hit you they caused really serious injuries. Luckily, I was wearing lots of layers of clothes at the time, including a thick jacket. The bullet exploded in the jacket and that saved me from a very bad wound. I had to walk through the night back to the field hospital a few kilometres behind the lines to see a doctor. I was walking and had to keep pressure on my arm at the same time to try and slow the bleeding. After a while I was stumbling, and then somehow managed to reach the doctor where I passed out from blood loss. I came to a few days later and since then I've never been able to remember the details of that night. Some of the hair from my woollen vest got stuck in the wound and it got infected. The wound was infected for a long time. After that I went back to being a war reporter, as I told you before, in the SS-Standarte 'Kurt Eggers'.[7] I was posted back to Berlin in January 1943, and was given some leave. When I was a war reporter our senior commander in Berlin was Gunther D'Alquen.[8] When we were at the front we were quite independent, it was like being a little 'freebooter', we could easily move from one unit to another, writing reports, taking photos and so on.

D'Oosterlinck remembered that time too.

TD: The ground was dreadful, it was all very swampy and full of insects. The Russians were quite far away from us really, and it was usually fairly quiet in the line. We shot at them occasionally to show them that we were still there. We used one heavy machine-gun with tracer rounds and we used flares too. We were never attacked by partisans. It was decided that we needed to connect up two hills we were defending – you know, by digging trenches between them so we could go from one hill to the next under cover from artillery and snipers. The digging was done by Hiwis [Hilfswillige, ex-Soviet prisoners who had volunteered to help the Germans]. They came to work at night. They were prisoners of war but wanted to help the Germans. They were given food for the work, and were looked after. For them it was about survival. They did not fight with us though.

I went on leave after that, it was one of the best trips ever. I went to Estonia and eastern Germany and we saw everything become greener and greener as we went west. It was so nice to see. Then we went home. We could tell our stories everywhere we went and we could drink, meet, drink some more. After three weeks we had to return to Leningrad, but I didn't make it back. While we were on the way I was told that I had to go to Debica instead, so off I went.

Back in Flanders, big changes were afoot as the war dragged on. Food, or rather the lack of it, was beginning to be a serious issue that came to dominate people's thoughts and conversations. The official daily ration across Belgium was 1,300 calories a day, the same as in France, but three hundred calories less than in Norway for some reason.[9] There's nothing like hunger to fuel people's anger, and the VNV was not immune to the growing popular unrest with German rule. When De Clercq himself unexpectedly died of a heart attack on the morning of 22nd October in Ghent, he was succeeded by that close friend of the Van Ooteghem family, Hendrik Elias. Elias was no fan of collaboration with the Nazis, rightly believing that they would not grant the Flemish their independence, and under his leadership official VNV support for further Waffen-SS recruitment turned decidedly lukewarm.

At the front, the legionnaires also had a tough life to say the least, but they were shielded from some of the material deprivations of the war that affected their countrymen and women back home. Members of the armed forces had priority on food, so the meat ration for a soldier was over three times higher than for a German civilian, while the bread ration was twice as much. Troops even got real coffee when it was available, and not the *ersatz* substitute made from acorns that the civilians had to put up with. They could usually get hold of tobacco and alcohol.

JM: Our rations would nearly always arrive on time when we were at the front. The field kitchen staff would buy cattle, potatoes, vegetables, etc. whatever they could get hold of really, and the meals were almost always tasty, and there was lots of it. If the food-carriers couldn't get through because of enemy fire – artillery or snipers – then you just had to wait, that happened a few times, but we always got the food in the end. I was never really hungry at the front, even later in the war.

NOTES

1. The War Graves Commission is dedicated to finding and identifying German war dead. Established after the First World War, it is mainly funded by public donations, but receives a small amount of financial support, roughly 10% of its expenditure, from the German Federal government.

2. The 1st Company was led by SS-Obersturmführer Peter Nussbaum who was killed in action by a rifle grenade in the fighting at Weschky-Semtitzy on 2nd March 1942. The same fighting also left the 4th Company's Kamiel De Wilde dead and Jan Delbaere wounded.

3. The actual Wehrmachtbericht of 14th March 1942 said: 'In various attacks on the central and northern front, the enemy's attacks were unsuccessful: the enemy was

thrown out of his positions and the SS-Legion Flandern took twenty-five hostile bunkers.'

4. Legion Flandern: Kriegestagebuch, T354/653/235-39.

5. Evans, Richard J., *The Third Reich at War*, p182, Allen Lane. Diary of Soviet Army commissar Nikolai Moskvin.

6. Pierik, Perry, *From Leningrad to Berlin – Dutch Volunteers in the Waffen-SS 1941–45*, Aspekt. XXXVIII Army Corps awards to 2nd SS Infantry Brigade.

7. In January 1940, the SS decided to organise its own propaganda unit. Initially a company of three platoons, one covered the Leibstandarte SS-Adolf Hitler, one the Totenkopf and one the SS-VT – this latter formation eventually became Das Reich. The unit's headquarters was in Berlin where its articles were censored by the Armed Forces High Command, the OKW – Oberkommando der Wehrmacht. As the Waffen-SS expanded so did the propaganda unit with new platoons raised to cover new divisions as they were formed. In August 1941, the unit was formally recognised as a battalion. It continued to grow and even had its own radio station, so that by November 1943 it was upgraded to the status of an independent regiment, and hence the SS-Standarte 'Kurt Eggers' was born. The honour title 'Kurt Eggers' was the name of the former editor of the SS weekly paper, *Das schwarze Korps,* The Black Guard, who was killed serving with the Wiking Division in August 1943 near Belgorod.

8. The editor of the SS weekly newspaper The Black Guard, and commander of the SS-Standarte 'Kurt Eggers' was SS-Standartenführer Gunther D'Alquen. D'Alquen was a professional journalist who headed up the regiment until the end of the war. The Black Guard

itself was published on Wednesdays and distributed free of charge, and every SS member was encouraged to read it. It was anti-Semitic and anti-communist. The first edition appeared on 6th March 1935, with 70,000 copies printed. In November of the same year, the number reached 200,000 and by 1944 750,000. The newspaper saw some very limited distribution outside Germany.

9. Dank, Milton, *The French against the French*, p341, Cassell.

6

KRASNY BOR – HELL IN THE SNOW AND THE END OF THE LEGION

The Red Army's victory at Stalingrad is usually regarded as the turning point of the war in the East, although amongst so many titanic battles fought in the Russo-German conflict

Flemish volunteer and war correspondent Harry De Booy – on right – best friend of Oswald Van Ooteghem, killed in action at Krasny Bor. (Courtesy Oswald Van Ooteghem)

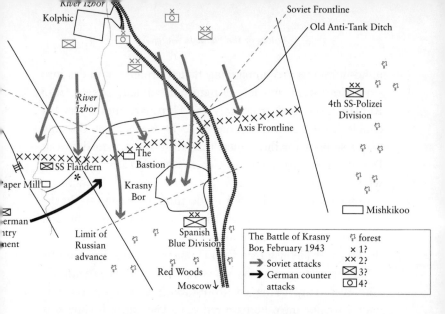

The Battle of Krasny Bor, February 1943
→ Soviet attacks
→ German counter attacks

🌲 forest
× 1?
×× 2?
⊠ 3?
▣ 4?

Map labels: River Izhor, Kolphic, Soviet Frontline, Old Anti-Tank Ditch, River Izhor, 4th SS-Polizei Division, Axis Frontline, SS Flandern, The Bastion, Krasny Bor, Paper Mill, German Infantry ment, Limit of Russian advance, Spanish Blue Division, Mishkikoo, Red Woods, Moscow ↓

it is sometimes hard to pinpoint one defining battle in that see-saw struggle. The Sixth Army's commander Friedrich Paulus had broken with Prussian military tradition in not committing suicide as Hitler felt his last-minute elevation to Field Marshal demanded, and instead had stumbled into captivity and surrendered his forces. Germany had then not only lost its first entire field army since the disaster at Jena back in 1806, but also its largest and most powerful formation on the Russian Front. When the fighting in Stalingrad finally stopped and the columns of shivering, lice-ridden, and half-starving captives shuffled off to their almost-certain death, a full ten per cent of the entire Ostheer was wiped off the order of battle: three panzer divisions, three motorised infantry divisions, one Jäger division, one anti-aircraft division and no fewer than thirteen infantry divisions, plus another twenty or so additional regiments and battalions of artillery and support troops, not to mention elements of two other German armies, the Fourth Panzer and Second. The scale of loss in men and equipment was mind-numbing. Accompanying their German comrades into extinction went no fewer than two allied armies from Rumania, one each from Italy and Hungary,[1] and a very big chunk of the Luftwaffe in the East.[2] In comparison, the only major setback for the Soviets that season was their defeat at Rzhev, where Army Group Centre's Ninth Army bled them white.

In the north, the STAVKA made another attempt to lift the siege of Leningrad, now well into its second year. The first stage of that relief battle in January 1943 saw the death of the first ever Flemish Iron Cross winner, Jules Geurts, shot by a Red Army sniper, as the Soviets pounded away relentlessly and eventually managed to establish a slender six-mile wide corridor into the battered city. The entire lifeline was still under the noses of the German guns, but Army Group North's grip had been fatally weakened as supplies flowed into the city. Determined to lift the siege completely, the Red Army tried again in early February, launching a big offensive on the 10th. Known by the Germans as the Third Ladoga Battle (and the Soviets as the Second), Vladimir Sviridov's forty-thousand-strong 55th Army formed the western arm of a Red Army pincer designed to encircle a large part of Georg Lindemann's Eighteenth Army and free Leningrad once and for all. Sviridov's first major objective was a small town lying on the main Moscow-Leningrad railway line and highway called Krasny Bor.

Today, Krasny Bor is just another suburb of St Petersburg, some twelve miles or so from the centre of the city. It is a peaceful, run-of-the-mill sort of place, with unremarkable streets and quiet shop fronts, all built since the end of the war, as the old town of brick-built buildings has long since been swallowed up by the surrounding forests and swamps. The motorway – the M10 – and the railway, are still there as they were in 1943, although the big intercity trains don't stop at the small local Popovka station. The new town's five thousand or so inhabitants mainly commute, or work in the local pipe-making factory that is the area's biggest employer. Every day, the townspeople walk by three monuments, all dedicated to the dead. One commemorates those who fell during Russia's Civil War, whilst the other two are for the thousands killed in and around their town in February 1943.

The battle fought at Krasny Bor that February wasn't decisive like Kursk or Stalingrad, neither was it massive like the great encirclement battles of Kiev or Uman in 1941, it was just one of hundreds of medium-size actions fought throughout the four years of the Russo-German war; relatively unremarkable to the rest of the world, but burned forever into the memory of the men who fought it.

If Krasny Bor is remembered for anything at all in the wider annals of the war it is chiefly for the bloody involvement of Emilio Esteban-Infantes's Spanish 250th Infantry Division. Worn down to a fighting strength of just 5,900 by the eve of the Soviet offensive, the Spaniards would lose a total of 3,645 men killed or wounded, and another 300 missing presumed dead or taken prisoner, during the battle, a truly staggering seventy per cent casualty rate. So terrible were the casualties in fact, that the Red Army offensive's first day was nicknamed 'Black Wednesday' in Franco's Spain. By comparison, the involvement of a few hundred Flemings was relatively minor, but try telling that to a surviving Oostfronter! For them, and for all the Oostfronters, Krasny Bor would pass into folklore as one of the toughest battles the men from Flanders would ever fight.

The battle began with a ground-crushing artillery bombardment that decimated the Spanish ranks, but as the

Soviet 55th Army then launched its attack, the line held – the Spaniards having a well-earned reputation as being tough fighters, and even though they were initially pushed back they did not break, and this allowed the German command to rush reinforcements up, including the Flandern, who were thrown into the battle as soon as they arrived. Oswald Van Ooteghem is now one of the very few veterans of Krasny Bor still alive.

OVO: Anyway, I'd been wounded in my arm – shot as I told you – and after I had recovered I went home for some leave, and then went to Berlin to learn a bit more about being a war reporter. A while later I went back towards the front and had a wonderful experience when I managed to go and visit the old imperial palace at Tsarskoye Selo, about twenty kilometres south of Leningrad. It was sumptuous. It is in the town of Pushkin now. I interviewed the resident architect and even got photographed at the palace gates. The pictures look like holiday snaps!

When our visit was over I was then sent with my friend and fellow war reporter Harry De Booy to Krasny Bor, where there was a big battle going on, as the Russians were trying to break the long siege of Leningrad using lots of their infamous T-34 tanks.

I first met Harry in Graz where both of us were recovering from our wounds and we were put in a replacement company together. I received word there that I had been awarded the Wound Badge in Silver and the Iron Cross 2nd Class. That's also where Harry and I were both told we would be going back to the front as Kriegsberichter. Harry was multilingual and the playboy of the Legion: he had been a steward on the Hamburg-America Line and had learned languages there.[3] He was selected as a radio reporter – a broadcaster – and I was selected to take photos and write articles for the press.

We got to Krasny Bor in February 1943, and it was really dangerous I can tell you. The Germans were doing everything they could to hold their positions, including counter-attacking with their new Tiger tanks [Major Richard Marker's 1st Company of Heavy Panzer Battalion 502, which was credited by the end of the battle with no fewer than 163 Soviet tank kills]. The road from Leningrad to Moscow became a road of death at Krasny Bor. If you looked to the right of the road you could see fresh troops, new panzers and loads of ammunition, all heading to the front, and then when you looked to the left you saw our soldiers piling up the dead and wounded. The scenes were horrific. The noise was overwhelming. Tanks were coming from all sides, and I saw men killed when they put their heads up above the top of their trenches and then failed to bring them down quickly enough when a tank rolled over their trench – the tracks just took their heads clean off. It was pure hell, everyone was up to their hips in melt water and blood. Every day we were shelled; artillery, mortars, grenade launchers, and even naval guns from Kronstadt [the Soviet Baltic Fleet naval base]. They bombarded us for hours. The Russians wanted at all costs to break the encirclement of Leningrad. Finally the Russians were able to make a breach in the front. The Spaniards were caught off guard and lost thousands of men there. To bridge this gap, the Flemish Legion and the Latvian Legion were deployed. We succeeded. When we arrived at the front, the panzer battle was still going on. With all the heavy bombing going on Harry and I took refuge in an underground Luftwaffe bunker. It was full of soldiers already; some were alive, some were dead and some were wounded. There was a Luftwaffe officer present. He saw our cuff-title [a black ribbon worn around the left cuff with writing in silver thread that identified them as war reporters] and that we were Kriegsberichter. The officer was angry with us because he feared that we had drawn the attention and fire of the enemy. He spoke to us and used the word 'halbsoldaten' – 'half-soldiers'. At the time we war reporters were sometimes called half-soldiers by the boys in the line, because they thought we didn't fight as fully as they did, but Harry didn't like being called a half-soldier, he felt insulted. He was a holder of the Iron Cross 2nd Class that he had received very early on for his achievements at the front. He was a good soldier and always threw himself into the fighting. He said he would show this officer that he was not a halbsoldat. There were anti-tank mines in the bunker, and he grabbed hold of one to go and crack a tank. I went outside as well. We rushed from one shell crater to another. We were shot at. A shell never fell again in exactly the same place, that's what we thought … not a precise science we knew but it was all we had. What exactly happened next is hard to describe, but unfortunately at some point a tank shell exploded near to both of us and we were both hit by the shrapnel. I wasn't wounded all that badly, but Harry had been hit in the chest, near his heart. We were in a crater that was full of mud and filthy water and I held him as he kept on saying my name: 'Oswald, Oswald, Oswald …' He died in my arms calling my name. A good friend was dead. I've remembered that picture my whole life. I was deeply affected by Harry's death. He was a flamboyant guy in the prime of his life, and was a real lady killer with his jet-black hair – he was the Don Juan of the Legion. A few hours before his death he told me that he was in deep trouble because he had got married to a girl in Antwerp, and had had to marry another girl in Hamburg, but really wanted to marry a third girl he'd met in Berlin! We were sitting together on the train to Riga where we disembarked to go to Krasny Bor, and I'd joked with him that the only answer was to get himself killed in action. Harry was born in Amsterdam, but was Flemish, he didn't have any family as far as I knew so I didn't have anyone to visit after the war to tell them how he died and that I was with him at the end.

Getting wounded at Krasny Bor by the same shell that killed Harry was the third time I was injured at the front. I got shrapnel in my left thigh, elbow and cheek. I was stumbling around and then luckily I got a ride back to the field hospital from a Swedish war correspondent.[4]

The Russians were stopped from breaking through the lines, but they were taking ground bit by bit. The losses were dramatic. The Flemish Legion ceased to exist, and what's left of it was later added to the SS-Sturmbrigade Langemarck.

Oswald was different when he spoke of Harry De Booy. It wasn't a hugely discernible difference, no fake sentimentality – hand-wringing, eyes misting over with long glances up to the ceiling – rather it was the small things; a tightening around the eyes, a slackening off of the expansive hand gestures with which he punctuated his answers to my questions. This isn't the first time he has spoken of Harry's death, not by a long chalk, but it's still there, the loss, the grief of it. He was stuck in a shell-hole, peppered with shrapnel, in the middle of a bitter battle, and it had all shrunk down to Harry – his friend – his chest covered in blood and lying dead in his arms. War at its rawest, at its most human.

For the Flandern, its losses were indeed as dramatic as Van Ooteghem said. Apart from Harry De Booy, Krasny Bor cost the Legion over four hundred men killed or wounded, with only forty-five left alive and uninjured at battle's end. Soviet losses were just as horrific, with their infantry divisions reporting casualty rates of anywhere between fifty and seventy per cent. Krasny Bor's memorials to the dead are well-deserved.

OVO: I ended up spending three months in the hospital after Krasny Bor. After my recovery I had to report to my chief in Berlin in my role as a war reporter. I'd originally been selected because I used to write pieces for youth magazines and journals back in Flanders before the war and the SS authorities had seen them and liked them and thought I could carry on writing in the Legion. There were quite a few of us Germanic war reporters as we were called, and at one point in August 1943 we went on a tour of Belgium and northern France – I never really knew why we did it, no-one ever told me and I never asked. After all it was a chance to go home and see Flanders. There were lots of different nationalities on the tour; Germans of course, Flemish, Danish, Dutch. We visited the Westwall [Nazi Germany's much-trumpeted Siegfried defensive line built between Germany and France], Langemarck and the memorial there [the site of a 1914 battle where thousands of young German volunteers were killed. The site is very symbolic for Germans, somewhat akin to the Somme and Verdun from the British and French respectively]. And of course, we went to Brussels. It was a very good trip.

After Krasny Bor, Van Ooteghem's war service would quieten down for well over a year, before he was flung back into the teeth of the conflict in the spring of 1945, and by then he would be fighting within the borders of Germany itself. In the meantime, he spent a short time in the Ukraine covering the 1st Panzer Army, before being posted back to Berlin once more.

He did however, return to Krasny Bor, the last stop on his 2008 memorial trip to honour his old comrades. Present-day Krasny Bor is a mile or so away from the site of the original town and this makes finding the battlefield difficult. In the end, it is only a series of water-filled depressions in the ground that give it away; these were once trenches and bunkers, mortar and shell craters, now they are part-covered by straggly scrub and stunted trees, the undergrowth piling up in and around them. Grand it is not. This is no Waterloo or Bosworth Field, with hundred-foot commemorative pillars, flag-bearing standards and visitor centres with gift-shops – this looks the sort of place fly-tippers would use to dump their rubbish, or joy riders to burn their stolen cars. It looks abandoned and unloved. It is depressing, and yet it is the face of much of war; grubby, half-forgotten and unremarkable except for the events that happened there in a past that is rapidly disappearing. Van Ooteghem wandered around, trying to fit the terrain into the jigsaw of his memories of that savage battle. 'This is where Harry died, and the older I get the more I think about it. When I was young I was shooting at people I didn't know, and now I look back and realise it was madness. I should have rejected it all, and I'm sorry I did not, but I did what I thought was right. I once read a book entitled "No-one goes free", and it said that in death, everybody is equal, and that someone isn't a "good" or "bad" war victim, they're just a victim, after all who hasn't done wrong in their life? I thought I was fighting the good fight. I'm old now and will soon be gone, but I still believe that whoever does something out of conviction should not feel guilty.'

At Krasny Bor Van Ooteghem met up again with Uwe Lemke and his team of Russian diggers from the War Graves Commission. Down and down they went into the soft, wet earth, black water seeping into the holes and trenches they dug almost as quickly as they could empty them. Van Ooteghem's comrades were found there, thirty-two of them. The Oostfronter had another wreath for them, much the same as his one for Reimond Tollenaere, with a black and yellow ribbon, but this one had a different inscription: 'Digging in the East – Greetings from Flanders'. (For a full list of the Flemings found on the 2008 Krasny Bor dig, see Appendix A).

NOTES

1. See Trigg, Jonathan, *Death on the Don – The Destruction of Germany's Allies on the Eastern Front 1941–44*, The History Press.

2. See Trigg, Jonathan, *The Defeat of the Luftwaffe – The Eastern Front 1941-45*, Amberley.

3. The transatlantic *Hamburg-Amerikanische Packetfahrt-Actien-Gesellschaft* or HAPAG for short, now part of the global holiday company Hapag-Lloyd.

4. Larsson, Lars T., *Hitler's Swedes – A History of the Swedish Volunteers in the Waffen-SS*, p225, Helion. Oswald Van Ooteghem's fellow war reporter and saviour was the twenty-seven-year-old Swede, SS-Untersturmführer Carl Svensson. Svensson was reporting on the fighting at Krasny Bor at the time when he saw Van Ooteghem, picked up the wounded man and took him to the nearest field hospital. Van Ooteghem passed out in the truck and never knew the identity of the correspondent until told in 2011 by Lars T. Larsson during the course of research for his book.

Above: Flemish nationalism has always been both a mass movement and a family one; a VNV rally for young Flemish women and girls. (Courtesy OVO)

Below left: Oswald Van Ooteghem's father – Herman – was an ardent Flemish nationalist who headed the VNV's paramilitary Grey Brigade before the war. Convicted of collaboration he died in St Gillis prison in Brussels on 15th May 1962. (Courtesy OVO)

Below right: Oswald Van Ooteghem's mother – Gaby Van Ooteghem-Guenther – who, along with her husband, was prominent in Flemish nationalist circles and very influential in her son Oswald's life. (Courtesy OVO)

Above: Herman Van Ooteghem (front rank, fourth from right) on parade in Brussels with his Grey Brigade, being inspected by the VNV's leader – Staf De Clercq. The man to De Clercq's right and just behind him is the senior VNV leader, Joris Van Steenlandt. (Courtesy OVO)

Below left: The Flemish Rexist, Albert Olbrechts, in 1940 in his Belgian Army uniform. (Courtesy Albert Olbrechts)

Below right: Albert Olbrechts in his Waffen-SS uniform with his first wife Liddy Proost in 1943. (Courtesy Albert Olbrechts)

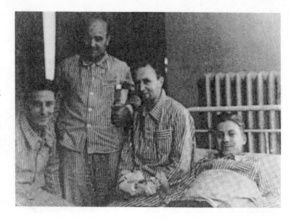

Albert Olbrechts (lying in bed) in hospital in Riga, Latvia. He spent several weeks there recovering from illness after his service on the Leningrad front with the Legion Flandern. (Courtesy Albert Olbrechts)

Albert Olbrechts (far left) and other Waffen-SS volunteers meet the Walloon Rexist leader Leon Degrelle (third from left in the suit) at the Dréve de Lorraine. (Courtesy Albert Olbrechts)

Above left: Albert Olbrechts (left) at the European Veterans Athletics Championships in Zittau, Germany, in August 2012. Olbrechts competed in the 100m race and was the only competitor in the 95-99 years age group. His time of 34.04 secs was beaten by the French runner on the right, Romain-Henri Maynard (the only entrant in the 90-94 years age group), who won gold with a time of 20.89 secs. (Courtesy Albert Olbrechts)

Above right: Albert Olbrechts, aged 101 years old, at home in Karlsruhe, Germany. (Author's collection)

Above left: The Dutch Waffen-SS volunteer and member of the Wiking Division, Jan Munk. (Author's collection)

Above right: Jan Munk and his beloved English wife Mauveen. Munk sports his favourite SS-Wiking tie. (Author's collection)

Below: A teenage Oswald Van Ooteghem (front right) parades with other young Flemish nationalists. (Courtesy OVO)

Oswald Van Ooteghem (front rank, second from left) as a VNV drummer-boy. His future Legion Flandern and Sneyssens comrade, Oswald Cromme Lynck, is two to his left with glasses. (Courtesy OVO)

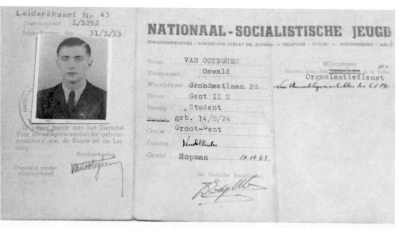

Oswald Van Ooteghem's ID card, identifying him as a leader in the Flemish National Socialist Youth – the youth section of the VNV. (Courtesy OVO)

Above: Oswald Van Ooteghem's *Soldbuch* (his Waffen-SS ID card). Every member of the Wehrmacht was issued a Soldbuch, it detailed their rank, service record, awards etc. (Courtesy OVO)

Below left: Oswald Van Ooteghem in his Waffen-SS uniform with field-cap. (Courtesy OVO)

Below right: Some of the first wave of recruits for the Legion Flandern; Oswald Van Ooteghem is second from the right, and Dries Coolens is second from the left. Centre in field-grey uniform is Roose, and Bert Vertriest is on the far right in glasses. (Courtesy OVO)

Training at Debica in occupied Poland for Legion Flandern volunteers. From left to right: Bert Vertriest, Oswald Van Ooteghem, John Brysinck and Dries Coolens. (Courtesy Dries Coolens)

The decorated Flemish Oostfronter, Dries Coolens, and his late wife. (Courtesy Dries Coolens)

Left: Flemish Waffen-SS volunteers crewing a mortar on the Russian Front. Dries Coolens would spend his entire wartime service in the mortar units of the Legion Flandern and the Langemarck – both brigade and division. (Author's collection)

Below: Dries Coolens in his nineties at home in his retirement flat in Metzingen, Germany. Coolens's flat is full of memorabilia from his Waffen-SS service, including the *berkenkruis* (birch cross) symbol above the wardrobe behind him. The Legion Flandern illustration he is holding is by the celebrated Flemish artist, Frans Van Immerseel. (Author's collection)

Dries Coolens's *Pro Justitia* ('For Justice') – the legal document used by the post-war Belgian government setting out the crimes an individual was convicted of, and the punishments meted out. Like most Oostfronters, Coolens was accused of 'taking up arms against the Belgian State'. (Author's collection)

Dries Coolens holds a presentation case that includes his Flemish lion badge, his cuff titles for both the Flandern and Langemarck, and his various decorations for bravery and service, including; the Iron Cross 1st and 2nd Class, the Close Combat Clasp, the Infantry Assault Badge, Tank Destruction Badge and Wound Badge. (Author's collection)

Above left: The SS-Vlaanderen volunteer, Herman Van Gyseghem, before his acceptance into the Waffen-SS in 1943. Van Gyseghem is one of a tiny handful of veterans still alive who served in the Langemarck's armoured unit. (Courtesy Ronnyc De Paepe)

Above right: Herman Van Gyseghem's best friend, Christiaan Dispa. Dispa was accepted for the Flandern when Van Gyseghem was turned down due to his poor eyesight. Dispa is wearing his Infantry Assault Badge, his Wound Badge in Silver (2nd Class for 3-4 wounds) and his 'Frozen Meat Award' – earned by men who had served in Russia over the dreadful winter of 1941/42. (Courtesy Ronnyc De Paepe)

Christiaan Dispa's grave at Krasnoje Selo on the Leningrad front. The forest of crosses were all made from the abundant local birch trees – hence why the 'birch cross' became a symbol for the Flemish volunteers. When Dispa was killed Herman Van Gyseghem was distraught. His loss was never forgotten. (Courtesy Ronnyc De Paepe)

Above: Herman Van Gyseghem's sister, Frieda (nurse on the right), met her German fiancée, SS-Hauptscharführer Marten Brandau (far right holding her arm) when he was recovering from wounds in Krakow hospital. They became engaged but he was killed in action in Russia in October 1944 shortly before their wedding. (Courtesy Ronnyc De Paepe)

Below left: Herman Van Gyseghem at home in Ghent in 2016. (Author's collection)

Below right: A few weeks after this picture was taken Herman Van Gyseghem's wife, Els, sadly passed away and Herman moved into a retirement home. (Author's collection)

A Flemish-crewed Sturmgeschütz from the Langemarck. The figure on the left is Herman Van Gyseghem's friend and commander, August 'Gus' Heyerick. The NCO on the right holding the cigarette is another Fleming, SS-Rottenführer Ponet. (Courtesy Ronnyc De Paepe)

A platoon of Flemish Sturmgeschütze. The Langemarck was one of a very few non-German units to be allocated armour. (Courtesy Ronnyc De Paepe)

Oswald Van Ooteghem's instructor and one of the very first Flemish volunteers for the SS-Nordwest Regiment, Marcel De Kie. (Courtesy Madeleine De Kie)

Oswald Van Ooteghem with his 'guardian angel' Madeleine De Kie. (Author's collection)

Wounded Flemish Oostfronters in hospital in Russia. Oswald Van Ooteghem stands at the back with the crutch. The soldier in the middle with the glasses is Dries Coolens. (Courtesy OVO)

Memorabilia of Oswald Van Ooteghem's Waffen-SS service, including his ID documents, Wound Badge, Infantry Assault Badge, Iron Cross ribbons, rank tab and Flemish lion insignia. (Author's collection)

Above left: Reimond Tollenaere (on left) was the head of propaganda for the VNV and one of the first officers in the Legion Flandern. His brother Leo is on the right, and their mother is sitting. (Courtesy James Mcleod)

Above right: Reimond Tollenaere's death at the front to friendly fire sent shock waves through Flemish nationalist circles. His funeral in Brussels was a huge event. Here, his wife and one of his three children are flanked by Italian and Spanish military dignitaries. (Courtesy OVO)

Below: Thousands of uniformed VNV men parade in Brussels's Grote Markt (Grand Place) for Reimond Tollenaere's funeral. (Courtesy OVO)

Tollenaere's funeral procession marches down the Boulevard Anspach. The Black Brigade members dip their flags and give an eyes left in tribute to the wounded Legion Flandern men marshalled on the steps of the Brussels Stock Exchange. (Courtesy OVO)

Convalescing Oostfronters at Reimond Tollenaere's funeral. (Courtesy OVO)

Conrad Schellong, German commander of the Legion Flandern. (Courtesy OVO)

Slutzk on the Leningrad front. Conrad Schellong's headquarters bunker is in the cellars of the factory on the right. (Courtesy OVO)

Above: Some Oostfronters take a break from the Leningrad front to visit the Catherine Palace at Pushkin. From left to right; Oswald Van Ooteghem, Harry De Booy, Renaat Vaes, Albert Olbrechts. (Courtesy OVO)

Left: Oswald Van Ooteghem (on left) and his friend Harry De Booy (second from left) take a cart round Tsarskoye Selo. (Courtesy OVO)

Right: Fifty years later Oswald Van Ooteghem went back to Tsarskoye Selo on pilgrimage. (Courtesy OVO)

Below: A battery of German multi-barrelled *Nebelwerfer* rocket launchers bombard the Soviets at Krasny Bor. (Courtesy OVO)

Above: Tigers of Major Richard Marker's 1st Company, Heavy Panzer Battalion 502, rumble into battle at Krasny Bor. (Courtesy OVO)

Left: A commemoration service at the Langemarck battle site in West Flanders. From left to right: the influential Flemish priest Cyriel Verschaeve, unknown German officer in peaked cap, Tony Van Dyck (head of the *Germaansche SS in Vlaanderen*), Raf Van Hulse (Flemish war correspondent platoon leader), Schindelmaier, Miel Goossenaerts (in black in the shadows), the Devlag leader Jef van de Wiele (in black with peaked cap), and Paul Suys (head of Rex Vlaanderen). Conrad Schellong is in front. (Courtesy OVO)

The Walloon Rexist leader, Leon Degrelle (centre) with Oswald Van Ooteghem (behind Degrelle over his right shoulder) and other Army and SS men. (Courtesy OVO)

Brussels Grote Markt in 1943. Oswald Van Ooteghem (centre) sees the sights as part of his tour away from the front. Raf Van Hulse is behind him over his right shoulder and Miel Goossenaerts is over his left shoulder. (Courtesy OVO)

Oswald Van Ooteghem regales a young lady with stories from the front. The sea-mew emblem on her left cuff identifies her as either an NCO or officer in the VNV's female youth branch, the DMS (*Dietsche Meisjes Scharen*). (Courtesy OVO)

Another young woman is enthralled by Oswald Van Ooteghem – this time in Hanstedt, Germany in 1945. (Courtesy OVO)

Oswald Van Ooteghem spent most of 1944 in training; first in Graz, then at the Waffen-SS Officer School at Bad Tölz, and then lastly at Beneschau. In this photo he is training with a flamethrower. (Courtesy OVO)

Moving with the flamethrower on an exercise. (Courtesy OVO)

Oswald Van Ooteghem (centre) digs a trench with comrades – some things in the infantry never change! (Courtesy OVO)

Oswald Van Ooteghem (second rank on the left) and fellow officer candidates drill at Bad Tölz. (Courtesy OVO)

Right: Oswald Van
Ooteghem's locker at
Bad Tölz, filled with
all his possessions.
The Waffen-SS prided
itself on the fact that
all members left their
lockers unlocked
as a demonstration
of trust in their
comrades. (Courtesy
OVO)

Below: Oswald
Van Ooteghem
(second from left
wearing the helmet)
training on an
MG34 machine-gun.
(Courtesy OVO)

Left: It wasn't all hard work though, there were days when Van Ooteghem could relax. (Courtesy OVO)

Below: Oswald Van Ooteghem (right) and fellow Fleming Fons Goeman (left) do some sun-bathing in the summer of 1944. Bad Tölz academy is in the background. (Courtesy OVO)

Bad Tölz encouraged fitness through sport, and the academy offered more than twenty different disciplines, including skiing in the Bavarian mountains. (Courtesy OVO)

Back in Russia it was a different story. A Flemish anti-tank cannon crew shell the Soviets in the buildings opposite. (Courtesy OVO)

Another Flemish anti-tank unit engages the Red Army. The figure on the right with the field cap is the Flemish artist, Frans Van Immerseel. (Courtesy OVO)

The Flemish Red Cross volunteer Lucie Lefever (front rank, third from the right) in Bruges on the 28th August 1943. (Courtesy OVO)

Some of the Sneyssens veterans group in the summer of 2016 in Van Ooteghem's house, in Ghent; from left to right: Theo D'Oosterlinck (sitting), Oswald Van Ooteghem (standing), Lucie Lefever (sitting) and Herman Van Gyseghem (standing). (Author's collection)

Theo D'Oosterlinck and his new wife in their flat in Ghent the day before their honeymoon cruise on the Rhine. (Author's collection)

The Oostfronter and only survivor of his company from the fighting at Jampol – Theo D'Oosterlinck. (Author's collection)

Adolf Hitler and SS-Obersturmbannführer Richard Schulze – the Adjutant of the Reich's Foreign Minister, Joachim von Ribbentrop. (Courtesy OVO)

Above left: After the war Schulze (on the right) changed his name to 'Schulze-Kossens', worked as a salesman, wrote several books and kept in touch with many of his former Waffen-SS comrades. He is at a reunion with Oswald Van Ooteghem (on the left) and ex-SS-Obersturmführer Jef Francois (centre with glasses), who succeeded Joris Van Severen to lead Verdinaso after the former's execution by the French police in 1940. (Courtesy OVO)

Above right: Oswald Van Ooteghem giving another speech after the war during his time as a leading Flemish nationalist politician. (Courtesy OVO)

Oswald Van Ooteghem gives a speech back home in Flanders during the war. (Courtesy OVO)

In November 2013 Oswald Van Ooteghem was still giving speeches! (Author's collection)

7

6TH SS-STURMBRIGADE LANGEMARCK, THE WIKING AND THE UKRAINE

The spring of 1943 wrought dramatic changes for the fortunes of the Third Reich, the Ostheer, and the Flemish Oostfronters and their families back home in Flanders. The calamity at Stalingrad had been bad enough, but worse was

Flemish volunteers in the Sturmbrigade Langemarck. Dries Coolens, fourth from the left, stands with his best friend on his right – Karel Goeman. Coolens would be the only one from the photo to survive the fighting in the Ukraine. (Courtesy James Macleod)

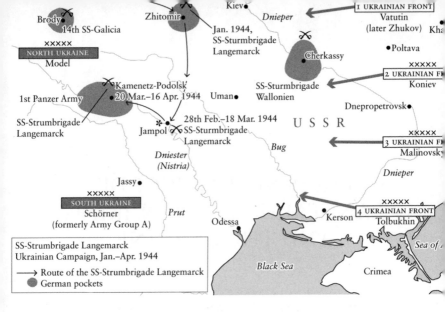

SS-Strumbrigade Langemarck
Ukrainian Campaign, Jan.–Apr. 1944

→ Route of the SS-Strumbrigade Langemarck
⬤ German pockets

to come for Berlin in May, as the frail North African front collapsed in Tunis and a third of a million more German and Italian soldiers went into Allied captivity – although those men had an infinitely greater chance of survival than their captured Sixth Army comrades, of whom only one in eighteen would ever make it home alive.

As for the Flemish Legion, the end of March saw the survivors pulled out of the frontline to rest, before they were sent west, back to their old stomping ground at Debica in Poland to lick their wounds and reform. As the legionnaires took up their bed-spaces in the barrack rooms, and unpacked their kit into the empty lockers, events were unfolding in Berlin and across Flanders that would radically alter their future.

The first question the Flemish would have to face now was how to find the reinforcements they needed to fill the gaps in the ranks. This wasn't a problem for the Flemish alone, the enormous losses in the East in 1942 had presented Nazi Germany with a manpower crisis. The Reich's population, large as it was, was simply not big enough both to fill the ranks of the Ostheer and man the factories, mines and farms back home to produce the equipment, resources and food needed to win the war. Berlin's solution, in broad terms, was to step up recruitment for the Wehrmacht and the Waffen-SS, while backfilling the gaps this created in the civilian labour force with masses more non-German foreign workers, getting them to the Third Reich by force if necessary.

The Nazis had recruited abroad for workers from across Western Europe pretty much as soon as their conquest campaign of 1940 was over. At first it was strictly voluntary, with the Germans portraying working in Germany as some sort of nirvana, complete with favourable rates of pay, excellent living and working conditions and additional benefits such as paid holidays and subsidised housing. In Belgium, the Germans trod extra carefully at first, aware that the legacy of the deportations they had carried out in the First World War were still fixed in the popular imagination. What they did do was institute a wage freeze locally which was designed to make Germany more financially attractive as a work destination, but initially at least they did little more than that. That situation changed dramatically in late March 1942 when Fritz Sauckel, the *Gauleiter* (chief Nazi Party official responsible for all administration of a region/ area) of Thuringia, was made General Plenipotentiary for Labour Deployment. This rather grandiose title was in reality a cloak for his real role – minister for forced and slave labour. Sauckel's first major success in the West was to agree a scheme called *la releve* with Pierre Laval and his Vichy government. Under the terms of the programme brokered by Pétain's chief minister, for every three skilled French workers who volunteered to go and work in Germany, one French

POW would be sent home. Just over 80,000 Frenchmen who had languished in German cages since 1940 were released under la releve, with 240,000 workers going the other way to take the total of French labourers in Nazi Germany to 666,000 by the end of 1943.¹ Even this was no way near enough – compulsion was needed. In France, this translated into the detested *Service du Travail Obligatoire* (STO – Compulsory Work Service) brought in by Vichy in October that year, that soon trapped every man between the ages of 21 and 30, before later press-ganging boys of sixteen and grandfathers of sixty.

As for Belgium, some 180,000 of its citizens voluntarily signed up to go to Germany, before compulsory service almost doubled that number. One Flemish volunteer worker was Jef Beutels.

In September or October 1940 I went to Kassel in Germany as a voluntary engine worker in the Henschel factory [Henschel made both aircraft for the Luftwaffe, and panzers including the Tiger for the Army]. I was only sixteen and so I had to do a special course with other youngsters, which helped a lot with the German language especially. In the beginning of '41 we Flemish boys working at Henschel formed ourselves into an NSJV group. We then got better food, and more of it, and better accommodation and treatment all round. We were protected by the factory police as well, as we lived near their homes.

In February or March 1942 Dr Jef Van De Wiele and his staff came to Kassel. The Flemish workers helped DeVlag organise meetings with Van De Wiele and he then talked to us about the SS-Vlaanderen and we were all recruited. As we then made up a pretty big group of SS men, one of Van De Wiele's staff stayed with us – a man named Van Dam from Antwerp. He got us our uniforms and gave us our basic training. More Flemish lads joined us and soon I was made a group leader for the Henschel boys, and Frans Clinckaert from Aalst did the same for the Junker boys [the nearby Junkers aircraft factory]. Clinckaert later died in Russia.

On Sundays we had training or singing lessons – the rest of the week we worked in the factories. As our uniforms were black, lots of the German civilians thought we were officers and saluted us – it was very military! When we marched through the centre of Kassel on Sundays we always attracted a lot of attention we Henschel and Junkers lads.

The local police used us as helpers for the bombing raids as well and we were always on stand-by. When Kassel was bombed by the Allies we saved many lives, and had to risk our own many times. We were awarded the War Service Cross 1st Class in recognition of what we'd done. By now we had grown to sixty members and went to meetings of thousands of other SS men in Hamburg, Göttingen and Braunschweig.

In June 1942, Clinckaert and myself were sent to Sennheim for a six-week military training course, and when we returned to Kassel we were both promoted to Unterscharführer. We then had to take charge of training the other boys, but we were still supervised by Van Dam.

In August 1943, our entire group – without any exceptions – volunteered for the Waffen-SS to go and fight in Russia. Many of our comrades died or went missing out there. I saw six or seven of them back in internment and that was probably all that was left of our Kassel group.[2]

By no means were all foreign workers as happy about the situation as was Beutels, and resentment in the West to this labour conscription was significant and ultimately fed the Resistance with recruits and support. However, by comparison, the countries of the occupied East fared infinitely worse than their western counterparts. Poland for example, was effectively 'looted' of much of its working-age population. Already by the autumn of 1941 there were one million Poles working in Germany, of whom only 15% were volunteers[3] and across the border in Belarus, the Ukraine and western Russia, whole villages were razed and their populations shipped west at gunpoint. Even this was better than the treatment meted out to the Jews. The SS authorities at Auschwitz hired out their Jewish inmates for three Reichsmarks a day to the giant chemicals combine I. G. Farben's synthetic rubber plant at Monowitz. There they were worked to death.[4]

The Reich did not benefit as much as it thought it might from this sea of press-ganged humanity. Conscripted foreign worker and slave labour productivity was notoriously low. In Germany's coalmines, POWs only dug out half as much coal per shift as Flemish miners did in their native Limburg pits.[5] Foreign workers from the West were also entitled to go on leave, and once home many of them simply disappeared and never went back. In just one factory, I. G. Farben's plant in Ludwigshafen, sixty-eight per cent of western workers given home leave in the summer of 1943 absconded.[6]

With Sauckel doing his utmost to man German factories, mines and farms, it was time to try and plug the yawning gaps in the Ostheer, and the Waffen-SS would play its part, in particular by trying to hoover up recruits amongst ethnic Germans living outside the borders of the Reich, the so-called *volksdeutsche*, and by redoubling efforts to attract more non-German volunteers such as the Flemish – but not as replacements for the old national legions.

Berlin felt that the legions had had their day, and what was needed now were new, larger formations that would act as operational 'running mates' for the premier Waffen-SS panzer formations, and would be more 'politically reliable' into the bargain. So were born the *SS-Sturmbrigaden*, the SS-Assault Brigades.

Degrelle and his Walloons, now co-opted into the Waffen-SS as honorary Aryans, became the 5th SS-Freiwillige (Volunteer) Sturmbrigade *Wallonien*, tied to support the Wiking Division, while the Dutch became the 4th SS-Freiwillige Panzergrenadier Brigade *Nederland* attached to the new Nordland Division. As for the Flemish, their Legion was dissolved at the stroke of a pen and overnight became the 6th SS-Freiwillige Sturmbrigade *Langemarck* allied to the élite Das Reich Division. The French, not quite as revered in SS circles as some of their more teutonic brethren, formed their own sturmbrigade, the 8th, and were attached to the Horst Wessel Division, down the Waffen-SS's martial pecking order.

In Flanders, at VNV headquarters, the news that the Flemish Legion was no more was greeted with dismay. The Party had not been consulted by the Germans on the decision, and rightly felt slighted. Hendrik Elias now began to fundamentally rethink the VNV's position on collaboration with the Germans. He was supported in this reassessment by other influential nationalist voices such as that of the well-known Catholic priest, Father Jules Callewaert, who wrote to him in early April 1943 stating that the VNV's policy of backing Germany to win the war at all costs was wrong because the Nazis had not given Flanders any cast-iron guarantees about the future. 'The slogan "Hitler knows everything and will solve everything" can only be spoken and believed by naive squibs ...'

Elias was also heavily influenced by the political street-fight he was in with Jef Van De Wiele and his DeVlag movement. Allied with the SS-Vlaanderen,[7] they struggled for supremacy with the VNV on the streets of Flanders, a dogfight between Elias's Flemish nationalists and Van De

Wiele's 'Flemish-Germans' – a battle DeVlag was winning despite the fact that their viewpoint was only shared by one per cent of their fellow Flemings. Not that this bothered DeVlag: 'We are the élite, we will say what is best for our people.'

Needless to say, this was anathema to Elias and the VNV's cherished ambition for an independent Flanders. However, the VNV was irrevocably losing political ground to DeVlag, and confrontations between the two were becoming more frequent, particularly as the Germans began to shift their support away from the former and towards the latter.

The dissolution of the Flemish Legion, 'supposedly for military reasons, in reality, for political reasons', had been a thunderbolt for Elias, and news from the war only served to focus his mind further. In the West, the Anglo-Americans followed up their success in North Africa by invading Sicily in early July, and clearly were very soon going to be in mainland Italy. As for the East, Hitler's gigantic offensive gamble at Kursk had failed, and the subsequent Red Army counter-offensives had pushed the Ostheer back hundreds of miles as the Germans lost another 170,000 men and almost 800 panzers. True, Soviet losses at 1.6 million men and 6,000 tanks were far, far higher[8] but Moscow could replace them, Berlin couldn't.

Elias made his decision. On 14th August 1943, he formally announced the suspension of all cooperation between the VNV and the SS, and the withdrawal of active VNV support for Waffen-SS recruitment. Elias was no fool though, and knew just how dangerous the game was that he was playing, so to soften the blow he made it clear the VNV would still work for a German victory, and would not stop its support for recruitment, but rather switch it to the Organisation Todt and the *Kriegsmarine,* the Third Reich's navy.

Elias's announcement inevitably damaged recruitment for the new Sturmbrigade Langemarck. DeVlag in particular tried to step up to the plate, but it didn't have the VNV's street muscle and popular support, and its relative failure was no surprise to the Flemish historian, Frank Seberechts: 'DeVlag lacked the substructure of the Flemish movement and the Flemish nationalists. It was only held together by a National Socialist cement, and so seemed to be bigger and better than it really was.'

Lacking the clout of the VNV, DeVlag found an ally in its recruitment drive in the form of the influential Catholic priest from Alveringem, Cyriel Verschaeve. Verschaeve, a learned writer and celebrated thinker, was a bespectacled and grey-haired sexagenarian with the air of an absent-minded professor, and was seen by many Flemings as perhaps the most powerful spiritual leader of the Flemish people, and his endorsement was a powerful boon to the SS recruiters. Hundreds more young Flemings now signed up back home, and they were joined by some 1,500 volunteers from amongst the Flemish foreign workers in the Reich as the Nazi Armaments Minister Albert Speer finally allowed Berger and his acolytes to go fishing in that particular pool.

As the Flemish were convulsed with political in-fighting and the birth of the Langemarck, Jan Munk was with the Westland Regiment near Isjum on the River Donetz in early July 1943 as the Red Army weathered the storm at Kursk.

JM: At the start of July '43 we had a period of time where we would climb into our Opel Blitz trucks and drive from A to B, then back again, several times. Each time we were told to look like other units; so sometimes we painted on different divisional signs, took off our camouflage uniforms, put them back on, changed our weapons, and so on. It must have driven the partisans spying on us bananas! Our driver was Flemish and he was incredible, always somehow getting us through the thick mud and keeping the truck going so we didn't have to get out and push.

Then one day, we were on a ridge overlooking a valley in which was a small village surrounded by fields of sunflowers. Me and a German soldier, Roeder, were told to follow a hedgerow and recce the village. Everything looked fine and we couldn't see anyone. We reported back and then sat and waited for about an hour. I think our officers didn't believe the village was empty despite what we had reported. Then, from out of the sky Stukas arrived and attacked the place, and we advanced. The village was actually full of Russians, and they suddenly emerged from the barns and the haystacks. We attacked and took the village. As a medic, I treated my first wounded, one of our machine-gunners who had been shot in the helmet. The bullet had made an almost complete circle of it before it was deflected off. It had made a nasty mess of his scalp though. I bandaged him and went to the next one. He was a Rumanian volksdeutsche who was crying for his mother. He had been shot in the right thigh, and when I cut his trousers away I saw the blood just pumping out. I told him I was getting some help but he died a few minutes later of course. I then saw the effect the Stukas had had on the Russian T-34 tanks, the buildings and the enemy soldiers – lots of dead. These dead soldiers, both our men and the enemy, made a big impression on me. I asked myself why one man had been hit and not another, and a bit of my 'it won't happen to me' feeling disappeared.

We carried on marching and approached two woods with a field in between. We were told to expect Russian fire and as we got half-way across we came under murderous rifle and machine-gun fire, which was concentrated on the officers, NCOs and machine-gunners. We re-grouped, waited a while and attacked again. This attack failed too. We had a third go but had to turn back. As we fell back I hid behind a lone tree. Then I heard an officer shout, 'Munk – over here.' I was more afraid of being thought a coward *than I was of being hit so I grabbed my machine-gun and ran zig-zag back to our line. We suffered about seventy-five per cent casualties in those three attacks.*

The next morning we advanced again and this time the Russians were in full retreat. We reached the top of a hill and could see the Donetz – or at least a tributary of the river – and we could also see the Russians wading up to their waists to try and cross it and escape. There were masses of them in the water and on the far sandy bank, all of them trying to reach the nearby woods. The losses of the previous day had frightened me and intensified my emotions so much that for years I wasn't able to talk about what happened next to anyone except my wife. My number 2 was with me, carrying two full ammunition boxes, and all I had to do was lie down behind my beautiful MG34, aim and shoot. I could see where my bullets were hitting so I could correct my aim as necessary as I kept on firing and firing. For the very first time I really enjoyed killing those bastards. I hadn't felt like that before. It had always been a case of hitting him before he hit you, but this was different. That day I killed so many of them, and I enjoyed it.

… We were learning all the time. The old hands taught us, from the experiences they had learned the hard way, how to survive, and most of us took notice. Later on, when we were the old hands, and received new replacements, we tried to teach them too. There is no doubt at all though, that whenever we fought the majority of casualties were always the new recruits.

Munk and the Westland were given no let up as the Red Army tried to capitalise on its victory further north at Kursk, and soon they were struggling to hold the Donetz line. By this time more and more of the new recruits arriving with the division were volksdeutsche from the Balkans and Southeast Europe, primarily Rumania, and Munk was allotted one of them as his Number 2.

JM: On the 17th we retook positions left by retreating Army units. Those trenches and bunkers were lovely and were full of food, socks and underwear and tobacco. Just as I was helping myself I was told to report to my company headquarters – I was furious – but this order probably saved my life as the bunkers were overwhelmed a short time later by a Russian tank attack and all my comrades were killed.

At that time my Number 2 was the son of a Rumanian farmer, whose German could only be described as 'not too bad'. His willingness however was second to none, as was his strength – what a Samson! Whereas every other gunner would carry the regulation two boxes of ammo, he would carry four, grinning the whole time and keeping up the pace. Russian infantry were crossing in front of our trench and I opened fire. The machine-gun jammed – there was a shortage of brass so bullet cases were made of steel and they jammed in the barrel sometimes – and as I was trying to fix it I felt a blow to my right shoulder as if someone had hit me with a sledgehammer. I had been hit but it didn't hurt. Then I heard a noise to my right, and I turned to look at my Number 2 as he was about to lift a box of ammo, just as he was hit through his left temple. He didn't know anything about it and fell dead.

Wounded, and with his number 2 dead, Munk fell back from his trench as the Russians got closer. As he ran he found his commander lying on the ground.

I was told he was dead. A bullet had entered his skull near his left eye and exited from his left ear-lobe. It looked bad, but then he moved! I put his arm around my neck and carried on down the trench. I was joined by another Dutchman who had been hit in the thigh. After a while I lifted my commander into a fireman's hold on my shoulders. This hurt my wounded shoulder a lot. My comrade was behind us, keeping the Russians at bay with his rifle, who seemed just as scared as we were.

Munk managed to get his badly injured commander to safety and was then treated in a field hospital before being sent home on leave.

As Jan Munk recovered from his injury, two young Flemings were enlisting to take their place in the ranks of the Oostfronters – one as a soldier, and the other as a nurse in the German Red Cross – the *Deutsche Rote Kreutz* (DRK).

The latter was a young girl from West Flanders, Lucie Lefever. Lucie is now a sprightly lady with immaculately coiffured hair and a firm but gentle handshake. Short in height, her blue eyes are still very keen as they fixed on me across the table in Oswald Van Ooteghem's living room. She is clearly well-liked and respected by her fellow Sneyssens, particularly Van Ooteghem, who smiles whenever he talks to her.

LL: I was born on 7th September 1925 in West Flanders in a little village, and I volunteered in August '43. I was sent, with a number of other Flemish girls, to Bad Salzungen in Thuringia. There we were trained for three months in all nursing skills. At that point I contracted diphtheria – you know, croup – and I dropped out of my group for a period of three months and was quarantined. By the time I was well again my group of volunteers from back home had finished their training and were gone, so I had to join up with a course of German girls. Then at Easter 1944 I was sent to the infirmary in Breslau in eastern Germany to begin my work. I was there until the end of the war.

Lefever wasn't the only DRK connection to the Sneyssens. Sitting across from her was Herman Van Gyseghem whose elder sister Frieda had left her studies at the Language School in Ghent to enlist in the DRK on 5th February 1943. Just twenty-one, Frieda was sent to Spa, near Malmédy on the border, for her training. After passing out from Spa she was posted to the Koberzyn hospital near Cracow in Poland.[9] As for Herman himself, he was a student at Ghent High School in 1940 when the Nazis invaded. A talented linguist like his sister, he was studying German and was also learning the violin at the nearby Academy of Music. Fired up by the Nazi call to arms, Van Gyseghem was just seventeen years old when he went with his best friend, Christiaan Dispa, to the *Werbestelle Flandern* recruiting office in the same Vooruit building in Ghent as his erstwhile comrade, Oswald Van Ooteghem. Dispa, only sixteen, passed selection, but Van Gyseghem failed due to his poor eyesight – he wore glasses. Hugely disappointed he sought other ways to become involved in the war, and the following year he joined the SS-Vlaanderen where his glasses didn't exclude him from membership. As a member of the Flemish SS he volunteered to go to the Mecklenburg Pomerania region in northern Germany where he received both sports and military-themed training.

HVG: At the beginning of the war the fact that I wore glasses was a stumbling block for the Waffen-SS. After all they were the élite. Christiaan Dispa and I both lived in Ledeberg at the time, and we reported to the Vooruit in Ghent. He was accepted and I wasn't. In fact I was turned down not once but twice. Those standards came from the Leibstandarte SS-Adolf Hitler – they were his bodyguard and only a few volunteers were accepted. Christiaan was an early volunteer, but not the first – the very first volunteers from Flanders left for training in the summer of 1940. As for me, in the end I had to wait until April 1943, things were easier then. In the meantime I went to Mecklenburg with the SS-Vlaanderen. We were trained, we did exercises, but we weren't given any weapons at that time. There were lots of us who went.

Whilst there, he heard his best friend Dispa had been killed in action in the trenches at Kokkolewo near Leningrad at the end of December 1942.[10] Extremely upset at the news, Van Gyseghem returned to Flanders and once again tried to volunteer for the Waffen-SS in early 1943. By this time the manpower shortage was dire, and his less-than-perfect eyesight was no longer such a problem. His application was accepted. He was not alone. Recruitment was even inadvertently spurred on by the USAAF air raid on Mortsel, which happened at the same time and almost claimed the life of his future wife-to-be. On 18th April Herman Van Gyseghem, along with another 283 volunteers, left Flanders for the Waffen-SS training base at Sennheim.

HVG: I was born in Ghent on May 6th 1923. My mother was an activist during the Great War, and then she joined DeVlag. She was a teacher and it was completely normal that I identified so closely with Germany. After all, her maiden name was 'Hermann' as her father, my grandfather, was German. If one wants to understand how it can come to be that someone would volunteer to fight for a foreign country, one should understand the history of that man's country. The Belgian state is an artificial state where the Flemings are the majority but have never been able to exercise this fact against the Francophiles. I will add one more thing to that; it was only in 1930, that is, a hundred years after the Belgian state was established, that a Flemish university was finally founded. Before then it was impossible to become an engineer or a doctor in any language other than French. That is one reason why some freely chose Germany.

A second reason; the cold wind of communism that came from the East, and the influence of the 1936 Olympic Games in Berlin – the pictures and stories of the handsome and happy workers and people, the chance to have one's own house and finally the possibility for a real vacation. I, as a student of the German language, was completely open to these possibilities.

And then the third reason; Moscow or Rome. In the Catholic schools much was said about the 'Red danger'. All of this makes it understandable why I enlisted in the Waffen-SS and why my sister became a German Red Cross Nurse."[11]

I joined in April 1943, and was put on a train to Sennheim in Alsace. We started our training there, it was tough. In Sennheim there were two groups of Flemish recruits; one group were fanatics who wanted to fight, and couldn't wait to fight, and then there were the others who were lukewarm, and who were hedging their bets to see what would happen in the war. I was one of the former. My whole Flemish SS company volunteered at the same time basically. Many of them were members of DeVlag, and we were much more willing to volunteer – to get involved – at that time than the VNV was. At that time the Germans weren't very popular with the VNV. After a few months training at Sennheim we were divided into different divisions: the Frundsberg, the Wiking and so on. The Langemarck Division was established later, at the end of 1944. Most of us Flemish were going in our Sturmbrigade, the Langemarck.

Sennheim was an old French Army barracks deep in the heavily wooded Franco-German border region a stone's throw from the city of Mulhouse. Upon arrival, Van Gyseghem was selected to be trained as an *SS-Funker*, a radio operator. Posted to the 3/2. Replacement SS-Regiment 'Deutschland' on 23rd May 1943, he was then sent on to Debica to join the fledgling the SS-Sturmbrigade Langemarck just days after its establishment. Once there he was assigned to the 14th Company *SS-Nachrichten Ausbildung* (Signals Education) and Replacement Regiment 'Nurnberg'.

Settling into the barracks at Sennheim he was a witness to the open discontent amongst the surviving legionnaires who were told the Legion was henceforth disbanded and that they would be transferred over to the new assault brigade. Some of the volunteers – mostly VNV men – simply refused and were branded as 'rebels'.

HVG: There was always a difference between the Waffen-SS and the Legion Flandern. The legions were formed in each country when the war started with Russia. But the Waffen-SS had started recruiting volunteers much earlier across Flanders, Holland, Norway and so on, about June or July 1940 I think. That was for the Wiking Division, and then later for other divisions. Then in spring 1943 that was around the time the war began to turn against Germany. So the time of the legions was over. The Germans began to form other divisions for the volunteers; for the Flemish, it was the Langemarck, for the Waals it was the Wallonien and so on. Some of the VNV men didn't like that.

Morale was suffering, but received a welcome boost with the arrival of new weapons and equipment straight from the factories – there's nothing like new kit to warm the hearts of soldiers! Van Gyseghem was no different, and put his hand up to join the latest addition to the Flemish arsenal – armour. So impressed were the Germans at the Flemings' performance at the front that they made the highly visible decision to allocate them self-propelled guns, *sturmgeschütze*. These were turretless panzers, cheaper[12] and easier to build than normal tanks, the Germans turned out increasing numbers of them as the war went on, but even so they were still only issued to units the Wehrmacht thought were good enough to make the best use of what was still a very scarce resource. Van Gyseghem's company was number 7, with an establishment of two officers, five NCOs and seventy-six men manning ten self-propelled guns, of which the company had received eight by the end of the year.

HVG: I was sent to Beneschau, in Czechoslovakia as it was then, for my training.[13] *There was a new company of self-propelled guns; Sturmgeschütze and Hetzers.*[14] *I joined them and was trained to be a member of a four-man crew; first in Panzer IIIs, and then in Hetzers. Everybody had a different job. I was a funker, a radio operator, and it wasn't like today with mobile phones and all that, no, this was with wires, so when we went from point A to point B we had to lay out telephone wires, but they were always getting cut by vehicles and shell-fire, so we had then to follow them along, find the break, and fix them, even when shells were landing all around your ears. Now I have to do this with my wife's wool at home when she's knitting a sweater!*

Our senior commander was Conrad Schellong, and my platoon commander was a Flemish officer, August Heyerick[15] *– he was my friend. He was one of the first Flemish officers, before that it was just Germans. He became our company commander later on, but in the beginning we had the German SS-Untersturmführer Gläser. The sturmgeschütze were lower and faster than normal panzers, and were almost invisible. They had no turret. A normal panzer like a Tiger could turn its turret, and it had a crew of five, whereas we had to do our job with just the four of us. I was the radio operator, and I sat on the right side in the Hetzer, and I also had to use the machine-gun on top of it, on the outside. I also had to load the main gun. During the fighting the cabin interior was overloaded with 7.5cm shells for the main gun. The most dangerous place was reserved for the driver. He sat down below ... over there [Van Gyseghem pointed with his right hand to a space below and to his left as if he was back sitting in the self-propelled gun]. He had nothing more than a narrow slit to see through. I was lucky, I was never wounded, 'Gus' Heyerick was injured when a panzer drove over his foot. Serving in panzers like we did, meant you didn't easily get wounded like the infantry guys would. In the infantry, you have man-to-man fighting. In our assault guns things were quite* different. You are driving around, and firing at other tanks and vehicles, not at men. It's all technology, mechanical, and you know; it's either them or us. In the panzers it was all or nothing – dead or alive.

At the same time that Van Gyseghem was beginning his training to become a panzer crewman, Jan Munk was going home for some welcome leave.

JM: It was August 1943 when I was given my first leave. From Apolinovka, I went via Berlin, where I had to register as I had left my unit, and then on again to Holland. I had two big gallon cans of sunflower oil given me by a Dutch doctor in Russia, Dr Hettema, one was for his family and the other was for mine. On reaching my hometown station in Leiden, I said goodbye to another Dutch volunteer I had been travelling with back from the front. His destination was Alkmaar, about forty miles north of Leiden. It was many months later that I heard that he had gone to a barber shop for a haircut before he went home so he looked decent for his parents. Anyway, as he was sitting there in the barbers our 'brave' underground movement emptied a Sten-gun [cheap WW2 British submachine-gun supplied to Resistance movements across occupied Europe] into his back! After hearing of that I never travelled on a bus or a train in Holland without standing with my back to a wall so I could see everyone and no-one could burn holes in my uniform with cigarettes or cut it with razors ... On that home leave I went to visit the parents of a Dutch boy who had been killed in action in Russia, so I went on my bicycle. I cycled quite a way until I came to an old tramway bridge that had been sabotaged, but by walking with my bike over my shoulder I could still cross. I balanced my way from sleeper to sleeper, until I was halfway across when suddenly I was shot at. I put my bike down and pulled out my Luger PO8 pistol that I had 'organised' from the stores. A second shot was fired at me, it sounded like a rifle but it missed – poor marksmanship! I lifted my arm and waved the pistol around. I didn't want to fire it as I didn't know where I was being shot at from, and I didn't want to clean the pistol either. It did the trick and I was able to carry on a few minutes later.

At Maastricht station on the way back to Russia I met another Dutch volunteer, Hans van der Laar, who was serving with the Wiking as a panzer crewman. His panzer had been shot up and he had suffered pretty severe burns to his head. He had been issued with a cheap wig that everyone could see was a wig, but it did hide the burn scars on the top of his head, which were not pleasant. We travelled back to Russia together and then on the 3rd of October I said goodbye to Hans. I never saw or heard from him again.

Even Heinrich Himmler, the Reichsführer-SS himself, was aware of the problem with the growth of the Resistance in hitherto fairly peaceful occupied countries such as Holland, as he acknowledged in a letter he wrote on 19th May 1943 when he sanctioned a three-week leave period for the entire Dutch Legion Niederlande, but banned them from all going home en bloc, 'for political and military reasons, it is impossible to send the entire group on leave to the homeland at the same time.' Munk wasn't the only volunteer to feel the chill winds of hostility at home either. Herman Van Gyseghem noticed the change too.

HVG: I wasn't worried about the Resistance in 1940-41, in those early days there was no resentment towards us, and everything was really quiet. The Germans who arrived in May 1940 were entirely correct and their discipline was excellent, and that helped as people couldn't get angry with them, or with us. Later on, things changed. One of our leaders in the Flemish SS, August Schollen, was killed by the Resistance – he was shot in Antwerp. After that I began to be afraid of reprisals, particularly when I was in my black uniform, the uniform of the Flemish SS.

After their victory at Kursk, the Red Army was pushing the Ostheer in the south back from the Donetz River all the way to the Dnieper. The German Seventeenth Army was in danger of being cut off in the Crimea as the Soviets tried to liberate the city of Kherson on the shores of the Black Sea, and Munk was involved in fierce fighting as the Wiking tried to stem the enemy advance. He was barely back with his regiment a month before being hit by shrapnel in the top of his head in a fire-fight. At first, he was sent to a field hospital near Korsun to be treated, before being evacuated onwards to a hospital in Cracow in Poland.

JM: The field hospital was in the Korsun area and consisted of low wooden buildings and very large tents. I waited an hour and a half and was then taken into a room where a Ukrainian nurse gave me a local anaesthetic, helped me sit up on my stretcher, put my head between her breasts to steady it and started to shave my head. I enjoyed that! When I was operated on the doctor took a piece of shrapnel the size of a pea out of the top of my skull – it had stuck in the bone and no further, thank God. I was taken to a ward and given daily injections of morphine, but they were stopped after a few days to avoid me becoming addicted. In a bed close to mine was a Second Lieutenant who had suffered a very bad head wound and was no longer sane. He would openly masturbate during the day, and a few days after I arrived he died.

In Cracow we had a Flemish lad on our ward who had been very badly wounded in both of his arms and had a special frame fitted around his bed. He had to be washed, fed and helped to the toilet. We used to tease each other of course, and we used to work on our Flemish friend, always before the nurse came around and took our temperatures. He didn't stand a chance! We would tell him dirty jokes, as men do, and told him not to get excited, but the result was always the same! The nurse knew what to expect so when she approached his bed she'd cry out 'Oh my God, Hans has rod-fever again!' and she would tap it with her pencil – we would all laugh our socks off.

Not long after Munk had been shipped northwest to Poland, the German front in the southern Soviet Union was shattered by a powerful new Red Army offensive, with not even the fabled Erich von Manstein able to hold it together.[16] As the Germans retreated west to try and establish a new front-line, almost 60,000 of them were trapped in what became known as the Cherkassy/Korsun Pocket. Munk's Wiking Division and its Sturmbrigade Wallonien running mate were two of the encircled units. The Soviet commander, General Ivan Koniev, wired the Kremlin: 'There is no need to worry, Comrade Stalin. The encircled enemy will not escape.'

The fighting was ferocious as the embattled Germans and their Walloon allies tried desperately to break out of the trap. Casualties were very high, and in his hospital bed Munk heard rumours of horrible atrocities committed by the Red Army.

JM: I was told that the Wiking and my own Westland Regiment had sustained very heavy losses, with many soldiers missing and killed in action … I also heard that the Russians had overrun the field hospital in Korsun where I had been treated. They had behaved true to their nature, which was bestial. The female nurses had had their breasts cut off, and the penises of the male nurses had been found in their mouths, and as for the wounded men – they had all been shot.

For the Flemish Langemarck, the fighting in the Ukraine that winter would leave its mark on them too. Sent to partner the

Das Reich Division, the Flemings were committed to the brutal battles around the town of Jampol in February and March.

Sitting with the Sneyssens in Van Ooteghem's comfortable, *mitteleuropäische* living room, all eyes turned to Herman Van Gyseghem when I asked about Jampol and the Langemarck's time there. It seemed from their facial expressions that he was the only one of that group who was there during that fighting, and they all deferred to him; and yet Van Gyseghem, normally full of memories and anecdotes, so strident in his views and keen to tell his story in his own passionate way, was reticent about Jampol.

HVG: I was at Jampol in Russia during the winter, and it was ice-cold. It wasn't like winter here, a bit of snow, this was something different and we weren't used to cold like that. In Flanders the winter is never that bad, but in Russia it was awful. Jampol was a kessel, we were surrounded. Just like Degrelle in Cherkassy. The Russians used that tactic a lot, to get behind us and use their tanks to encircle us. The fighting was tough. Within a few days our company had shrunk to two officers, four NCOs and just forty-three men.

That was it. A few sentences and then he lapsed into silence, his eyes staring at the table. He raised his right hand, stabbed at the air and then barked out, '*Herr Trigg, it's Jampol, not Yampol or Yampil. You must get the name right.*' (In *Hitler's Flemish Lions* I had referred to the multiple spellings in use for the same place, a common occurrence for place names in Russia, Belarus and Ukraine – this clearly displeased Van Gyseghem).

Then silence once more. Even on that warm summer's evening you could feel the sudden chill in the air. As usual it was down to Van Ooteghem to fill the void, and fill it he did, asking me with a smile how long it would be before this book would be published.

Several months later when I interviewed Theo D'Oosterlinck again – all alone this time except for his wife – I discovered that Van Gyseghem wasn't the only Sneyssen who had fought at Jampol.

TD: I missed Krasny Bor – I was on leave at the time – and then I was sent to Debica for my Unterscharführer course for a few months. After that it was Milowitz, and that's when they formed the Langemarck. The rest of the Legion joined us there, but there were so few of them. We noticed there were hardly any trucks – maybe only two or three I think – with the Legion on board coming back from Leningrad, but there were lots of wounded, lots of them. We trained, did a lot of exercises, and then when they were finished we had a parade through Prague. Around Christmas/New Year 1944 we went back to the front: Jampol and Zhitomir in Ukraine. I was still in 2nd Company, and Martenson was our commander now. Our senior commander was Conrad Schellong. Jampol was the hardest fighting I ever saw. So unpleasant. I lost many comrades. You see your comrades die and you can't help them, there's nothing you can do, that's the worst. I was lucky, you had to be lucky to survive. The fighting was terrible, all my best friends died, all of them, my company lost so many men. We did what we were told. You had no time to think. It was forward or retreat … you were in constant motion. It was survival. Pay attention or you die, and lie as flat as possible, the training had taught us that …Then on the 28th of February 1944 I was wounded, in the left buttock. I ended up in a convalescence company in Breslau. From Breslau they sent me to the leadership school at Bad Tölz, the officer school. I didn't see any more fighting after that, no more war.

You know I lost so many friends at Jampol that I realised I had none left. Ever since then I have never met anyone at any of the reunions who was from my company, not one.

The same day that I interviewed D'Oosterlinck again, I also went to see Herman Van Gyseghem at his house in Ghent. He and his wife met me at their front door, and took me through to their kitchen at the back of the house where I could see out to their large, well-tended garden, and the light streamed in from the big, glass patio doors. Hospitable as usual, the kitchen table was set with small cakes and biscuits, and I could smell the fresh coffee brewing. We exchanged greetings, and I passed on best wishes from Dries Coolens (another Oostfronter whose interviews appear later in this book) in particular, who was a favourite in the Van Gyseghem house. Herman's wife Els, then excused herself and went and sat in the living room, reading the newspaper.

Van Gyseghem sat attentive, awaiting the first question. He was not dressed as formally as our last interview – a grey top and slacks – but still smart. I wanted to know more about Jampol, and the Sturmbrigade's baptism of fire down in the Ukraine, and I wanted to know more about Van Gyseghem himself. His service was very different from the other Oostfronters I had met and interviewed. He wasn't ex-VNV, had never been in the Legion, but had been a crewman in the only Flemish armoured sub-unit ever created – this was rare stuff – but I was concerned that just as in Van Ooteghem's house he would retreat into himself, that it would all be too much, and I had no right to go into his own house and upset him. I needn't have worried.

HVG: The Ukrainians were good friends to the Germans, and to us. They were anti-communist. They wanted independence. We slept in their homes; we slept on their ovens actually. It was so cold and it was the only way to stay warm. In the winter everything was concentrated in one room; cooking, eating, sleeping, everything, and they all had a huge oven which stretched across much of the room and at night everyone would just lie on top of it. The occupation forces were treated well, and the partisans kept away from the villages whilst we were there, but they were still there! When you stood on guard you were sometimes shot at by them, and you could hear the whistling of the bullets over your head. Death was common, and we got used to it. You would hear about a fellow soldier getting killed and you'd barely react; 'Michiels died ah ... that's unfortunate.' Life goes on. You became tough and hard. You washed yourself much less, your clothes looked like rags. All the barracks discipline was gone. You had to be lucky too, or you'd end up dead.

I was a crewman in a panzer then, a Panzer III. We were only issued Hetzers later, at that time it was Panzer IIIs, with turrets – proper panzers. It was heavier than the Hetzer, with more armour. The fighting at Jampol was very hard. The Russians were everywhere, and they were dispersed, all over the steppe. Their aim was always the same, to go around us, get behind us and encircle us – put us in a kessel, whole divisions if they could, why not eh? There was so much space out there, there were never enough troops to fill it all. Then we'd be destroyed, or captured. We had fourteen panzers in the company, and they were all broken or shot to pieces in the fighting. Those men who weren't killed were sent back to be put in other vehicles as crew. Once the panzers were all gone that's when what I call the 'funker period' started. Connecting wires. We all had to have jobs, and I was given the one where I had to connect the field telephone lines between the front line and the different command posts; battalion, brigade, division and so on. I was called the strippensieher. It was a very dangerous job, all out in the open, always under fire. Later, when we were re-equipped, we were given Hetzers, each with a crew of four. Gustaaf Segers was the driver of mine. Every Hetzer needed a funker, so that was my job. But I was also responsible for loading the gun – the cannon loader. The commander had to sometimes *sit on top of the Hetzer with his head outside as there was so little room inside. We had to sit on the ammunition. We were very vulnerable. As for the infantry, they just had to follow us on the outside as we drove forward firing shells.*

NOTES

1. Dank, Milton, *The French against the French*, p129, Cassell.
2. Beutels went on to become a Deputy Chair of Sint-Maartensfonds for the town of Bree in Limburg province in Flanders.
3. Evans, Richard J., *The Third Reich at War*, p22, Allen Lane.
4. Ibid, p363.
5. Ibid, p370.
6. Ibid. p704.
7. Literally the *SS-Flanders*, this was the Flemish branch of Himmler's German Allgemeine-SS and was also called the *Algemeene-SS Vlaanderen* (General SS Flanders), and then later the *Germaansche SS in Vlaanderen* (Germanic SS in Flanders), and also the *Vlaamsche SS* (Flemish SS) – set up in the autumn of 1940 with an initial eighty volunteers from Antwerp and fifty from Ghent by René Lagrou and Ward Hermans – both ex-VNV men. Hermans had also been Dinaso before quarrelling with its founder and leader, Joris Van Severen. The SS-Vlaanderen would eventually peak at around 3,500 members in 1944, with the vast majority serving in the Waffen-SS at some point as Oostfronters.
8. Evans, Richard J., *The Third Reich at War*, p490, Allen Lane.

9. Frieda Van Gyseghem was fluent in German, French and English as well as her native Flemish, and whilst at Koberzyn she met and fell in love with a wounded German patient, Iron Cross 1st Class holder, SS-Hauptscharführer Marten Brandau from the 2nd SS Panzergrenadier Division 'Das Reich'. The couple got engaged in early September 1944 in Ghent in the presence of their families. The wedding – also to be held in Ghent – was planned for the end of October. In the meantime, once the engagement celebrations were over, Frieda went to work in a hospital in Vienna and Marten went back to the Eastern front. On the night of 13/14 September 1944 at 10pm, Frieda was working the night shift when Vienna was bombed and badly damaged. The hospital she was in was hit several times and a large air-raid shelter filled with doctors, nurses and patients was flattened. Casualties were high and included fourteen nurses killed, of whom five were Flemish: Luretia Van Laecke, Yvonne Dieltiens, Katharina Smeets, Inge De Coninck and Margareth Borms. Frieda survived. A few weeks later, on October 21st, just as he was preparing to go back to Ghent on leave for his wedding, Marten Brandau was killed in action in the Ukraine. Frieda was devastated, but continued to work at the hospital in Vienna until the end of the war. When peace eventually came, she stayed for a further year under the occupying American forces, and was then repatriated back to Belgium and arrested and tried for collaboration – regardless of the fact that the Red Cross was meant to be politically neutral. Convicted, she was sentenced to one year's imprisonment. On her release, she settled back in Flanders, but never married. She died in a car accident in Sint Denijs Westrem (Ghent) on 23rd September 1967, aged just 46.

10. Dispa's remains were eventually found in 2009 and were reinterred at the German military cemetery at Sologubowka near St Petersburg.

11. Brandt, Allen, *The Last Knight of Flanders*, p38, excerpt from a letter from Herman Van Gyseghem to the author.

12. At 82,500 Reichsmarks each, a StuG III cost a lot less than even the Panzer III which, although obsolete and small by the standards of the latter half of the war, still came in at 103,163 Reichsmarks.

13. Modern-day Benesov in the Czech Republic, during the war it was the location of the SS-*Truppenübungsplatz Böhmen* – SS-Troop Training Area Bohemia.

14. Sturmgeschütze, StuG IIIs based on an old Panzer III chassis and armed with a powerful 75mm main gun (some 11,300 had been built by the end of the war) and the Jagdpanzer 38, also known as Hetzer ('pursuer/trouble-maker'), was based on a modified Czech Panzer 38(t) chassis with a 75mm L/48 PAK 39 gun. Disliked by many crewmen who found the interior extremely cramped, and often found themselves sitting directly on top of the forty-one rounds of main gun ammunition it carried, it was mechanically reliable, small and therefore easily concealed. It too was cheap to make and some 2,584 were built by the end of the war.

15. The Flemish Waffen-SS officer, August Norbert Heyerick, took over command of the SS-Panzerjäger Battalion 27's 4th StuG Company from the German SS-Obersturmführer Willi Sprenger who was killed in action on 19th April 1945. Heyerick himself passed away on 12th February 1996 aged 74.

16. Mitcham Jr, Samuel W., *Hitler's Field Marshals*, p241, Guild. Hitler said of von Manstein. 'Manstein is perhaps the best brain that the General Staff Corps has produced.'

8

1944: LIBERATION
AND FLIGHT

On the 6th of June 1944, the Allies landed on the beaches
of Normandy and began their assault on Hitler's 'Fortress
Europe'. Two weeks later, on the third anniversary to the day

Oswald Van Ooteghem (centre) talks to the VNV leader, Dr Hendrik Elias.
(Courtesy Oswald Van Ooteghem)

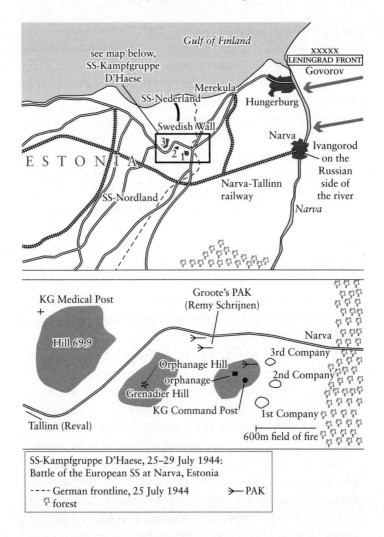

Gulf of Finland

XXXXX
LENINGRAD FRONT
Govorov

see map below,
SS-Kampfgruppe
D'Haese

Merekula
Hungerburg

SS-Nederland

Swedish Wall

Narva

ESTONIA

3
2 1

Ivangorod
on the
Russian
side of
the river

Narva

SS-Nordland

Narva-Tallinn
railway

KG Medical Post
+

Groote's PAK
(Remy Schrijnen)

Narva

Hill 69.9

3rd Company

Orphanage Hill

2nd Company

orphanage

Grenadier Hill

KG Command Post

1st Company

Tallinn (Reval)

600m field of fire

SS-Kampfgruppe D'Haese, 25–29 July 1944:
Battle of the European SS at Narva, Estonia

---- German frontline, 25 July 1944   ➤— PAK
🌿 forest

of the Nazis' invasion of the Soviet Union, the Red Army's
Bagration offensive hit Ernst Busch's Army Group Centre in
Belarus. Bagration was a phenomenal success, annihilating
no fewer than thirty-five Ostheer divisions, and taking the

Soviets to the outskirts of Warsaw itself. In the West, D-Day too was an astonishing triumph – the largest seaborne invasion in history – but it wasn't until the German defeat at Falaise in late August that the Wehrmacht's entire front in France collapsed.

By then, resistance in Belgium had become far more open and deadly. Oostfronters back home on leave were sometimes attacked and a few were killed. Any Fleming wearing a uniform of any of the paramilitary collaborationist organisations was liable to be abused in the streets. Over the border to the north in Holland, it was much the same.

JM: My second home leave was in September 1944, and the welcome from my mother was a little cool this time. I rang the bell, she opened the door, and said nothing. On my first leave she had hugged me and pulled me into the house – not this time. She just stood there and looked uncomfortable. I picked her up, put her to one side and walked in. Our kitchen was at the end of a long corridor, and I could see the tablecloth on the table was moving. I marched into the kitchen and lifted up the cloth to find two men under the table, looking up at me, scared stiff! I found out that they were Belgian Walloons who had deserted from the German Army and who were now being hidden by my parents. Perhaps I should have reported them, but I didn't join the Waffen-SS to betray my parents!

At the end of my leave, to my great surprise, my brother Gerrit – who was very anti-Nazi – asked if he could come with me for a distance. Of course I didn't object. He and I walked for about twenty minutes to a bridge where German guards were posted. I told the guards there to stop the first SS vehicle they saw so it could give me a lift eastwards towards Germany. After the war Gerrit told me he had come with me because he was well-known as a member of the Resistance and so being with him meant I didn't get a knife in the back.

Hitching a ride, Munk made his way back to Germany and down south to the Waffen-SS's famed officer academy at Bad Tölz, to which he had been recommended to receive a commission.

Who would not want the chance to go to Bad Tölz to become an officer? We regarded our Waffen-SS officers without exception as men that you could trust and respect. They were always in the frontline, and when we had a hard time so did they, and they always encouraged us to use our initiative. There was nothing strange in the officer who would help one of his men by carrying a machine-gun or a heavy ammunition box if he was tiring. They were always in the thick of the action and not in the rear where it was safe.

Oswald Van Ooteghem and Theo D'Oosterlinck felt the same about the Waffen-SS officer academy when they were selected as officer candidates at the beginning of 1944.

OVO: It was an honour to go there. After the preparatory course of three months – January, February, March 1944 – in Graz, I went to the officer school in Bad Tölz for six months. Then it was another three months specialist training at Beneschau in the former Czechoslovakia. There we learnt different heavy weapons: artillery, infantry cannons, heavy mortars etc. Finally, in December 1944 I was promoted to Untersturmführer.

TD: I did a course in Graz, then I went to Matzelsdorf, there were so many Flemish it was called the 'Belgian Barrack', it should have been called the 'Flemish Barrack' of course. I started my course at Bad Tölz in July 1944, we were taught in German, and all the commands were given in German, nothing in Flemish.

As Van Ooteghem and D'Oosterlinck were undergoing the extensive training that was one of the hallmarks of the

German military system, back over in the East, the Flemish were about to fight perhaps their most well-known battle – and this despite the fact that there were only around five hundred of them actually there, given the majority were still reforming and refitting after the fighting in the Ukraine. This battle – which would become known as 'the Battle of the European SS' – was Narva.

To call Narva a battle per se, is inaccurate. It was, like the fighting at Lake Ladoga two years earlier, a series of battles fought over many months, with lulls that were then blown apart by bouts of ferocious conflict. The two major periods of combat – from February to the end of March (the Narva Bridgehead Battle), and the July-August Battle of the Tannenberg Line – can be described, albeit simplistically, as a clash between a Red Army that was trying to advance deep into Estonia and the other Baltic States, and an Ostheer force equally desperate to stop them and hold the line in the north, even as the rest of the Russian Front inexorably moved west.

As it was, the Germans held the Soviets in Estonia during the spring battles, and now the STAVKA decreed that Leonid Govorov's Leningrad Front would crush the Ostheer's Army Detachment Narwa and restart the advance southwards down the Baltic coastline. Govorov, a moustached 47-year-old veteran of the Civil War and the invasion of Finland, was an artilleryman by trade, and the Soviet high command considered him an expert at the penetration and defeat of fortified positions. He seemed the natural choice to finally crack the stubborn northern nut.

Under a blazing summer sun that only went down for a few hours a night, Govorov amassed a formidable force approaching 140,000 men supported by several thousand artillery guns and an impressive tank force. By contrast the depleted Ostheer could only muster some 22,250 men and a handful of panzers and self-propelled guns. So far so commonplace at that stage of the war, but what made Narva stand out from so many other bitterly fought battles in the East was the make-up of that 22,250-strong force. More by chance than anything else, the core of the defence was built on non-German units; Dutch, Norwegians, Danes, Estonians, Swiss, Swedes and Walloons; and yes, the Flemish too. The German high command, desperate to try and reinforce the front before the expected Soviet assault hit, ordered the battered Sturmbrigade Langemarck to form a kampfgruppe and sent it northeast to the defensive positions they had called the Tannenberg Line.

It is not my intention to write a comprehensive account of the battle – for that see *Hitler's Flemish Lions* – suffice to say that the kampfgruppe was initially commanded by a German officer, Wilhelm Rehmann, and was composed of several infantry companies and a small anti-tank element of three 75mm PAK cannon. The fulcrum of the whole defensive line was a series of three hills; Orphanage, Grenadier and Love's (this latter also confusingly called 69.9 and Tower Hill as well), that sat astride the main road west to Tallinn. None of the three hills was strikingly high, only rising some 20-50m from the valley floor, with woods crowning the tops, even on Orphanage Hill, named after the orphanage on its summit. Orphanage was also the furthest hill east and hence would be the first that would be attacked, and it was here that Felix Steiner, as the Corps commander, placed his meagre Flemish reinforcements. The company officers, by now almost all of whom were Flemish rather than German, assigned the men their positions and they set to digging in. It was late July and hot. Sweat streamed off their backs and faces as they swung their shovels and picks into the soft Estonian earth, although none of them minded the effort as they were all veterans and knew the value of a deep, safe hole once the Soviet artillery targeted them. The battle they would fight over the next four days would leave the majority of them dead in those holes – over three-quarters of the kampfgruppe were listed as killed, wounded or missing by the end. It would also see Rehmann relieved of his command and his place taken by Georg D'Haese, the very first Fleming to lead an independent Flemish unit at the front – and it would be the only occasion where a Flemish volunteer would win the coveted Knight's Cross of the Iron Cross bravery award. The diminutive Remi Schrijnen, originally turned down for Waffen-SS service due to his lack of the required height, stood at his PAK cannon, loading, firing, loading, firing and firing again until he had covered the valley floor in burning Soviet tanks, and he himself lay badly wounded and close to death.

The 22-year-old Fleming was far from the only casualty over those few terrible days. By the time Leonid Govorov admitted defeat and called off the offensive on the 10th of August, some 2,500 Germans and foreign Waffen-SS volunteers had been killed or were missing presumed dead. Four times that number had been wounded and filled the hospital beds alongside Schrijnen. The Red Army paid a far higher blood price; official casualty figures weren't released during the Soviet era, but since then Russian historians have estimated that some 35,000 Soviet soldiers died in the fighting, and over 150 tanks were destroyed.

Schrijnen himself was extremely lucky. In the middle of all the confusion and bedlam of the battlefield he was found by the crew of a counter-attacking German panzer and evacuated back to a field hospital. Recovering pretty quickly from his wounds, he fought on until the end of the war, but then with the peace he, like many other veterans, found home was no longer to his liking and decamped to West Germany, where he eventually passed away in 2006, almost to the day of the anniversary of his epic fight in Estonia.

With so few survivors, trying to track down an Oostfronter who was at Narva is akin to finding a unicorn, and I thought it would be a giant step beyond what I could accomplish as I drove southeast from Flanders down to southern Germany to my next interview. My destination was Metzingen, a Swabian town in Baden-Württemberg, home to the global headquarters of Hugo Boss and renowned throughout Germany as 'Outlet City', with over eighty top fashion and clothing brands selling their wares at reduced prices in huge stores clustered in the town. Metzingen is a prosperous place, with rich farmland giving way to well-kept houses, shops and streets. Everything is tidy and looked after, the cars are mostly BMWs, Mercedes and Volkswagen – all washed and shiny, the residents likewise – in essence what we think of as very German. Pulling up outside an apartment block high on a hill near the town centre, I gathered my notes and headed to the entrance. The name I was looking for was neatly written in large, black capital letters next to a bell – 'Coolens'. I rang and it was answered immediately by a voice that was clearly expecting me. I was buzzed in and walked up the stairs rather than taking the lift. I noticed that outside the front doors of many of the apartments were walking frames – 'rollators' I think they're called – this was obviously a popular place for the elderly, and since the man I was meeting was in his nineties my mind conjured up an image of a frail gentleman, living in his retirement flat, his mind prone to wandering, his step a trifle unsteady. I didn't need to knock, the man I had to come to see was standing there waiting for me, almost at attention, and in a heart-beat the lazy picture I had built in my imagination was swept away. This was Dries Coolens.

It is a cliché that people look like their dogs – it would perhaps be more accurate to say that people unconsciously choose a dog that looks like them – and the same can usually be said for someone's home. Coolens's apartment was a direct reflection of its occupant; neat, compact, functional – welcoming too. The furniture was mainly wood, dark and heavy. Rugs covered the floor, not scattered haphazardly but deliberately placed and aligned with the walls and doors. Family photos abounded. There was no attempt to hide his past. A photo frame of him and his wife had him in his Waffen-SS uniform, there were etched glass Flemish lions and *berkenkruis* on almost every wall, and the two occasional tables below the lounge window had more framed photos from his wartime service. The large bookcase standing against the far wall was packed with volumes on the Legion Flandern, all of them straight as sentries, with even my own modest work in amongst them.

Pride of place in the lounge though was given to a wooden framed presentation case, around fourteen by twelve inches. It contained a treasure trove of his service; the medals, ribbons, insignia and awards that mean so much to soldiers the world over. Langemarck and Legion Flandern cuff titles were set alongside an Iron Cross, a Close Combat clasp, an Infantry Assault Badge and Wound Medal, and a silver Tank Destruction Badge, proclaiming that Coolens was one of only 18,500 men who received an award created for those infantrymen who by some act of courage had succeeded in destroying an enemy tank with handheld weapons such as a *panzerfaust* (a hand-held, single-shot, disposable anti-tank weapon), an anti-tank mine or just grenades.

Clearly Coolens was extremely proud of his past and didn't care who knew it. We sat around his small dining table, very good coffee and confectionary carefully laid out for us, and then we began.

DC: I get a lot of visitors from Flanders, lots of students, mainly from the Universities of Ghent or Limburg. In fact ever since I was interviewed for that Chris Michel documentary [http://www. chrismichel.nl/tv-reportages/de-laatste-oostfronters originally shown in 2015 on Belgian TV: VRT 'Koppen', and national Dutch TV: NTR 'Eén Vandaag'] I have been drowning in correspondence, I've literally had sackfulls of letters from people asking me all sorts of questions about the war and about us Oostfronters. I also get lots of letters from the relatives of Oostfronters. Once, a man came to see me with his son and grandson – his father, his son's grandfather, and the little one's great-grandfather served with me – the same man of course. I remembered him and I could give them information about him and what he did during the war.

I'm sorry if I have trouble hearing you, my hearing isn't so good now, and neither is my eyesight – that's from being snow-blind a few times from Russia. The hearing problem is from the war too. The artillery bursts and especially from mortars. I was a mortarman and our trick was to load and fire the mortar as fast as possible before the first round hit the ground, dead on your target. We used to get thirteen rounds to hang in the air before the first one exploded, and there was no time to duck, that's why my hearing is bad. Narva was the worst for that…

I stopped scribbling down notes … Narva … had I really heard Coolens say he had been at Narva. I blurted out the question and he looked at me very calmly.

DC: Yes, I was at Narva, that was the most terrible battle. What we experienced was indescribable. Some 1,200 of us went there and only thirty-seven came back, the rest were killed, wounded or missing – some were captured by the Russians [this does not tally with official records, but that is no surprise and no different from the vast majority of first-hand accounts of battles]. We arrived and met the Walloons,

Degrelle's men, and we started to shout insults at each other, and then in no time we were having a huge fist fight, it was just like when I was a teenager and we young Flemish used to meet local Walloons down in the underpass and beat the hell out of each other. I got sent to youth detention for all that sort of stuff. Back then I was raised at home in a Flemish nationalist family, my whole family were politically active; my father Jan-Baptist, my mother Maria, my two brothers Gaston and Victor, everyone was VNV. Our teachers, our clergy – they were all VNV. You can see in our names; so many were French names when we were Flemish – they called me 'André', but I'm not André I'm 'Andries', 'Dries', Flemish and proud of it. I joined the Dietser Youth in 1936. My father had a farm and a construction business, and my brother was an architect and worked with Herman Van Ooteghem [Oswald's father] in the same company, and when I joined the Black Brigade in September 1940 I got to know Oswald. That's also where I met Reimond Tollenaere, in the Black Brigade. I knew his brother too, he lived in Oostakker, both he and Reimond were great guys. After a few months, in January 1941, I joined the Vrijwillige Arbeidsdienst voor Vlaanderen [the VAvV, the Volunteer Labour Service for Flanders, a sort of Flemish version of the Nazis' own Reich Labour Service] and was with them until I enlisted in the Legion Flandern in August. After the invasion in 1940 I had a lot of respect for the Germans because they were so disciplined. Who thought in 1941 that Germany would not win the war? Three-quarters of people were convinced of a German victory, and I remember that after volunteering when we boarded the train to leave Flanders for training we were waved off as heroes by huge crowds. The station was packed. In training though the Germans treated us like livestock, like pieces of meat. We didn't like our German instructors at all, and we always said to each other: 'When we get to the front the first one who will get a bullet in the head will be our company commander.' But after our first experiences at the front our eyes were opened and we realised that we only survived because of the training, because it was so hard.

During training we were visited by quite a few important people; Staf De Clercq, and JefVan De Wiele I remember. De Clercq was the leader of the VNV, a very good guy, I knew him through my father. He died in October 1942 and was succeeded by Elias. I didn't think as much of him as I did of De Clercq. He was a good mayor, but not a good leader of the VNV. As for Van De Wiele, he was a Nazi. That was not my thing. Me and my family were never Nazis, we were 'Dietsers' ['Dietsers' is a term used to describe those who believed in the concept of a Dietsland *– the unification of the Dutch-speaking peoples of the Low Countries, including the Netherlands and Flanders]. I am not a Belgian, I am a Fleming.*

I wanted to steer Coolens back to Narva, but realised there was no rush, he clearly had an excellent memory and was keen to talk.

DC: After our training was finished we were sent to the front near Leningrad. When we arrived there we set off marching looking for our lines, and then suddenly we realised we had passed straight through them and were amongst the Russians; the front there was like that, the distances were so great and there was so much space, so we immediately turned back and got out of there as quickly as we could. We settled into our trenches and they were good, so enemy artillery didn't cause much damage to us, most of the casualties we had were from snipers, the Russians had lots of them and they were excellent shots. I felt sorry for the Russians on the whole, but not for their female soldiers, we used to call them the 'killer divisions'. If they ever caught one of us they would cut off his genitals and hang him up, it was terrible. Like most of us I always kept a last bullet in my gun for me – just in case. I wasn't going to go out like that, I was never going to get captured. Those women were present only at Leningrad. We could see the trams in Leningrad you know, we were that close ... so we used to watch them, what else could you do when it was so cold? Sometimes the temperature was as low as -52C°!

I was wounded seven times at the front. The first time was on 7th January 1942, a head injury at a tiny place called Sapolje. I was hit by a piece of shrapnel on the top of my steel helmet. It hit my helmet so hard that it crushed the steel of it down into my skull, and I got frostbite, very bad frostbite. They took me to Riga for an operation. They cut the helmet off my head and took the steel edge out of my skull, luckily it hadn't pierced my brain or I'd have been dead. Look, you can see the mark on the top of my head and feel the cut.

Coolens bent forward showing the top of his head, covered with a light film of blond stubble. The indentation was there, but was pretty faint after all these years.

DC: The doctors were fantastic, you can barely see it or feel it can you. The German medical services were excellent. After the operation at the hospital in Riga I was taken to another hospital in Königsberg, and then on to Göttingen, for convalescence, before going to the Adolf Hitler barracks in Graz, and from there I was sent back to the front in May 1942.

Coolens then went on to talk of the Volkhov fighting, then Krasny Bor and Jampol in the Ukraine as part of the Sturmbrigade. It was becoming clear that this ardent Flemish nationalist had a service record second to none, and had fought in just about every major engagement the Flemish had during the entire war, getting repeatedly wounded along the way.

DC: I got frostbite in early 1942 as I said, and I was still recovering in May. It was so severe that it looked like they were going to discharge me. My mother wanted me to come home, but all I wanted was to return to the front. By mid-July I was fighting in the swamps, and then I was wounded again in early August, on the 9th – I was shot in the left elbow. Then it was back to hospital: Krasnowardeisk-Riga-Königsberg-Elbingen, and finally Graz again to a convalescence company in October. I went home on leave twice during the war, that was the first time, that October up to November the 6th or 8th, I can't remember exactly which. When I was home I went out, just with comrades, and always in uniform. I wasn't afraid. Did I see things changing over time? Yes I did. I noticed that if we sat in a bar there was whispering among some of the other people in there, and they were looking at us all the time, but they never did anything. I'd like to have seen them try!

The fighting on the Volkhov was hell. It was all a swamp, a morass. If a comrade was hit and fell into the swamp in just a few minutes all you could see was a black heap – they were covered by mosquitoes, thousands and thousands of them, and we used to lose men in the mud, they would get hit and then simply disappear down into the water. It's hard to describe if you haven't experienced it.

Krasny Bor was tough too, very bloody battles. I was there from February 14th until the fighting stopped on March 28th. I was injured again, this time on the right forearm, stab wounds. We were with the Spaniards of the Blue Division. They were good friends, good comrades those Spaniards. You could count on them. I remember when one of our guys had been hit and was wounded lying out in no-man's land. We wanted to go and get him of course, but the Russians had it all covered with machine-guns. We asked the Spaniards anyway and they didn't hesitate, they jumped up and ran in a group to go and get him and bring him back. They shared their oranges with us as well, their brandy too, even their equipment. It was unbelievable.

At this point Coolens was chuckling to himself and shaking his head from side to side. 'They didn't have many heavy weapons the Spanish; mortars, anti-tank guns and so on, and they sold some of what they had.'

Sold? Did the Spanish *sell* their weapons, and if so to whom?

DC: To us of course. We never had enough heavy weapons, and we were always trying to get more, so we bought some off the Spaniards for money, for food, whatever we could bargain with. They were good lads, it was a pleasure to fight alongside them.

After Krasny Bor I was recommended for officer training at Bad Tölz – I'd already done the NCO Course at Lauenburg in Pomerania – but before I was due to go I went sick with jaundice, a remnant from my time in the swamps. Later on in '43 the Legion was disbanded and we went to the Sturmbrigade Langemarck, and as usual I was put in the 4th Company – the heavy weapons company – as I was mortars. My commander was also my best friend, SS-Oberscharführer Karel Goeman. I was wounded again in Ukraine, in late January 1944. A Russian soldier hit my jaw, here on the left-hand side, with his rifle butt. The blow broke my jaw and knocked out some of my teeth. He then tried to stab me in the stomach with his bayonet to finish me off. I grabbed his rifle by the bayonet to stop it, the Russian bayonets were always razor sharp, and you can see here how it cut my fingers down to the bone, you can still see the scars.

Just as with his head wound, Coolens showed us his gnarled fingers, a clear, straight, savage scar ran diagonally across them, it was a wonder he hadn't lost at least two or three fingers.

DC: Anyway, I managed somehow to pull the rifle out of his hands, turn it around, then I stabbed him in the belly with his own bayonet. It was me or him. I still remember his death cry, it was so loud.

After the fight they put some bandages around my wounds and sent me back to the front. They needed every soldier they could get hold of. I was actually wounded twice in Ukraine. I was lucky though, I was still alive. My friend Karel Goeman was not so lucky and was killed in action.[1] All those men … they were constantly falling; then new soldiers would arrive and they'd fall too. We tried to hold the Russians but we were always going backwards. We were fighting with panzerfausts at a place called Bjelgowdka. We were in a kessel, totally surrounded, and we received the order 'save yourselves'. We were 60km behind Russian lines, so we just headed off and we made it – well, not all of us did. By mid-March they were collecting us all at Kamenets-Podolsk, and then back again to the Dniester, to Romania. We had lost so many men, so much equipment, the whole Sturmbrigade only had about four hundred men left out of the original 2,600. After Ukraine some of us were sent to Narva, not all my Company, only some.

Here it was then, an eye-witness account from a veteran of the battle of Narva – an Easten Front historian's Holy Grail.

DC: I always respected the German officers on the front lines, they underwent their baptism of fire with us when we first went to the front, but there was one at Narva who was a coward. He said he was ill and avoided the fighting, I had no respect for him [this was the kampfgruppe's original commander, Wilhelm Rehmann]. Georg D'Haese took over, he was a Flemish nationalist. A great guy. At Narva the élite of the Germanic volunteers were present. They were more non-German Waffen-SS than there were Germans, there were even Swedes, and Sweden was neutral, but they stood with us. The Walloons were there as well of course. I already told you that we fought as soon as we saw each other, then we were fine as we were all there to fight the Russians. Luckily we weren't side by side at the front though, that wouldn't have been good, the Germans knew that and so we were next to the Danes and the Dutch. Outsiders don't understand this because they do not know our history. I hadn't met Remi Schrijnen before Narva. He was in a different company and a different battalion. Our battalions were brought together during the battle.

Narva was harder than Krasny Bor in my opinion, well it was for me in any case. If Remi Schrijnen had not fired his PAK cannon like he did, there would have been nothing left of us. At Narva we sat on Grenadier Hill for eleven days. We were in éénmansgaten [one-man foxholes], all alone. We did that to try and protect ourselves from the shelling. We were fired at from the sea, from the air and from the ground – airplanes, tanks, infantry – everything. When soldiers fight today they need psychologists, for us, that simply was not possible. We fought and endured. We couldn't run away because we would have been shot.

I remember we were ordered to counter-attack to try and recapture Orphanage Hill, but despite all our courage and dedication we couldn't do it, the Russian fire was too heavy. Our only way forward was to crawl, to try and stay underneath all the fire. It was pitch dark. Suddenly I was lying there with my elbow in the corpse of one of our guys. He was half-rotten. The smell was unforgettable, the kind of stench you just don't get rid of. I ended up getting a new uniform, but the smell was still in my nose. We lost so many from our group. Some died in my arms. I lost so many friends.

After Narva we were sent back to Pomerania in Germany. We were put on a ship in Reval [modern-day Tallinn] on the Baltic. The boat went to the north, towards Swedish waters. The Swedish Navy or coast-guard shot at us, so we shot back and then they left. We put in at Swinemünde [modern-day Polish Šwinoujšcie] and disembarked, and then got three weeks' leave in Poland. That's where the accident to Georg D'Haese happened.[2] After the end of the war I saw Remi Schrijnen quite a few times, he lived here in Germany. I don't know of any other survivors of Narva who are still alive.

I joined the Langemarck Division after that, after Narva, and went back to the 4th Company. Then we had to fight on the Oder River, that was bestial. I was an Oberscharführer by then, Steiner promoted me. We would have had more soldiers as well if Van de Wiele hadn't been around. The VNV and Van de Wiele were like fire and water. Van De Wiele tried to get us to fight with boys aged fourteen, fifteen or sixteen years old, that we could not and would not accept. But that was Van de Wiele. Cyriel Verschaeve had no influence on this issue … A lot went wrong over there.

At that point, when we were on the Oder, we were only fighting in order to let civilians from the east escape to the west away from the communists. We were constantly moving around in those last few months. From Stettin, we went to Zadelow and Zachau, we counter-attacked at Reichenbach, and then towards Arnswalde in February, and then ended up in Stargard in March trying to hold the Berlin to Stettin highway. We were split up then, I was put into Kampfgruppe Schellong and fought at Altdamm. We held it for a while but then on March 18th we saw about two hundred Russian armoured vehicles come towards us and that night we were given the order to retreat to a new defensive line between Tantow-Staffelde-Schönfeld. Then another retreat, this time to Damme Prenzlau-Neustrelitz, where we were told to leave all our remaining heavy weapons, not that we had many left by then. I destroyed a Russian tank there, a T-34, with a mine, that's why I got my tank destruction badge. We knew that the war was lost by then of course … the first time I thought the war was lost was back in 1943 after the defeat at Stalingrad. Stalingrad fell because the Rumanians withdrew and the Russians got behind our lines – it was a disaster. I didn't carry on fighting for the Germans – no. I carried on against the communists! For Dietsland! I don't have any regrets. I'm proud of what I've done. Many times since the end of the war I've been asked if I would do it all again and I always reply; 'Yes, but under different circumstances. Only against the communists.' They were the greatest danger to Europe. Then it all finished, the war was over. We burned all our documents at the end of the war, thank goodness, otherwise the Russians would have gone crazy at us if they'd got hold of us with documents saying we were Waffen-SS. That's what I think.

Yes, I was lucky. I was wounded seven times: stab wounds, gunshot wounds, frostbite twice with my feet and hands frozen - in '42 and '43 and I'm still alive, yes, very lucky.

Back in Belgium I came back from Liège and Brussels and stepped off the train in the station in Ghent. I was recognised straightaway and a mob attacked me and almost beat me to death. The next thing I knew I woke up in the hospital in Sint-Gillis in Brussels. I was convicted of taking up arms against Belgium, which is rubbish of course, and I was also accused of betraying someone on a tram to the Germans – a Resistance member – that wasn't true either. Later on it was proven that it had been the police who identified that person to the Germans and not me. I was sentenced to death, not once but twice, and then had my sentence commuted to fifteen years in prison with all my property seized and all my civil rights taken away. I remember in court at my trial they asked me if I knew Oswald Van Ooteghem, and I said of course I knew him, there were photos with the two of us together in them so I could hardly deny it, and anyway, why would I? I was held in the prison at Beverloo for a long time – from 1945 to 1949. My father was in prison with me. He was never convicted of anything, he was in there just because he was a member of the VNV. Then I was sent to Ruislede. I was finally set free in January 1950. My brother paid for my release, he was an important man during the war, in the government, but they didn't arrest him afterwards because he knew too much. When I came out I had no civil rights as I said, and finding work wasn't easy, but I managed to get a job selling animal feed to farmers. I couldn't make a living out of it though, and I had a wife and two children to look after. We were living in Antwerp at the time, in Ekeren, with the Huysmans family. My wife, who was *originally Dutch, was corresponding with her brother who was a senior guy in a power company down here in Metzingen, and he agreed to employ me, so we moved and I got a better job here that paid more, that was in 1954.*

After the war, I had no contact with other Oostfronters for a long time. Then I began to speak to some old comrades and go to some reunions, in Austria, in Aalst sometimes. In Hungary in Bicske, we laid a commemorative stone in memory of the fallen soldiers of the Wiking.

I also did a lot of speeches and talks here in Germany, mainly to students, talking about the Flemish Legion. All the students had great respect for what we did. In Dortmund, after my speech there, I answered questions for three hours – three hours! It was a long time I can tell you. The students knew that Flemings had been on the Eastern Front, but nothing else, no details, so I told them. They always asked me why we went to the Eastern Front, and I always say the same thing; we were not Nazis, we were Dietsers. Some of them asked me about Degrelle, but I don't want to know anything about him. He was a favourite of the Führer of course. Under normal circumstances, you could never be promoted as fast as he was as an officer, especially if you were from Wallonia, but he was.

I still miss Flanders. Back there I believe that there are mixed feelings about us Oostfronters. During the war the majority stood on our side. They still do I think. If I did not have any children or grandchildren I would have returned to Flanders a long time ago. My two sons feel Flemish ... but my grandkids, they feel German. Life goes on.

Now I watch television and see the Americans and their wars. I never fought against the Americans, never, only against the Russians, but from what I have heard of them as soldiers I don't have a good word to say about them. They were poor soldiers, undisciplined, and all they did was shoot and shoot until there wasn't a single living soul left, that's not fighting, and I should know.

Coolens rank was no surprise to me; he was a senior NCO, a colour sergeant in British Army terms, one look at him would tell you that. He reminded me of so many senior NCOs I had known in my own service; ramrod straight, a certain almost elaborate correctness and formality in their manner that only partially hides the essence of who they really are, and who they really are is men who have an intimate relationship with violence. To men like that, violence is as natural as breathing, and such a man would indeed be the type to be wounded multiple times and still carry on fighting, even long after he knew his side couldn't win. I looked again at Coolens over the table, a long, appraising look at this fairly short man, with his blue eyes, glasses and hearing aid discreetly tucked away, his open-necked blue shirt and white cricket jumper, and his dark trousers and polished black shoes. Even now, in his nineties, I had no trouble at all in believing that he would take up a gun and fight for Flanders again given half a chance. That violence can become brutality, and even worse, if not controlled, so I had to ask him – as I always asked – about the Holocaust, the camps, and the horrendous atrocities committed in the East.

DC: I knew nothing of the Holocaust or of the extermination camps. The concentration camps already existed before the war of course, and we knew about them as places where political prisoners and enemies of the state were sent. We knew they were tough places and you didn't want to be locked up there, but as for the rest, all that murder, no, we knew nothing. We just fought for Flanders against Bolshevism. We took Russian prisoners during the fighting at the front and we delivered them to the rear. What happened with them afterwards … we did not know. I did once cut a button off a Russian's uniform jacket, but he was dead already, I've still got the button, it's made of wood you know. We were attacked by partisans a lot, especially when we were near Leningrad. They were dreadful. They didn't wear a uniform or fight like proper soldiers, and they weren't covered by the Geneva Convention. Someone who shoots a weapon while wearing civilian clothes, they have no rights and get what they deserve.

Later on, as it grew dark, we went into town for dinner in a favourite local restaurant where he used to take his wife every Sunday before she passed away a decade earlier. Coolens put on a smart jacket and an old-fashioned German alpine hat adorned with a small feather and several clasps and miniature badges, one of which was a Flemish lion, another a berkenkruis. He greeted his neighbours as we passed and stopped to say hello, they all knew him and clearly held him in some regard. In the restaurant he enjoyed his food, particularly an apple and cinnamon dessert, and drank only sparingly, savouring a glass of local red wine. He chatted about Metzingen, about how the outlet stores drew people from as far away as Russia to stock up on cut-price brands, and he also talked more about the war. He was sad that so many of his friends had died, but overall it wasn't painful for him to recall it all. He was quite matter of fact. I dropped him off back at his apartment building, thanked him for the interview, and watched as he walked to the entrance. He was carrying a walking stick and in the dark of the evening I thought how easily it could be a rifle for Colour Sergeant Coolens.

Back in the war, in the autumn of 1944, hundreds of miles to the northwest of Metzingen, advancing towards the German border, was Charles Foulkes's 2nd Canadian Division, which became the first Allied formation to enter Belgium on 2nd September and begin the liberation. Brussels was freed on the 4th and the Belgian government-in-exile was reinstalled four days later, but bloody fighting in the Scheldt estuary would mean the whole country wouldn't be finally free until February the following year.

In front of the Allied vanguard, some 15,000 Belgian collaborators and fellow-travellers fled east into the Third Reich, where they set up camp around the town of Soltau in northern Germany. Deprived of their Belgian citizenship by order of the new Brussels government, they were bombarded with exhortations to volunteer for the Waffen-SS as a last throw of the dice. Hendrik Elias was among the refugees, but he was still not minded to support these renewed calls. Cyril Verschaeve – whose 70th birthday celebrations Elias had boycotted back in May in protest at the cleric's support for DeVlag and SS recruiting efforts – wrote personally to Himmler to complain about Elias's anti-SS influence:

> Dr Elias is playing his games again. He forbids his men from co-operating in any way. Worse, he is sabotaging one of our main tasks; the expansion of the Volks Grenadier Division Langemarck [the new 27th SS-Freiwilligen Grenadier Division Langemarck (Flämische Nr.1) to give it its proper name]. He is encouraging VNV members to boycott it.

Despite this, DeVlag was now firmly in the driving seat, pretty much eclipsing the VNV, and under Jef Van De Wiele's leadership set up a quasi-government-in-exile – the *Flemish Land Line* – and led from the front in recruiting volunteers for the Waffen-SS, moving around from Soltau, to Waldeck Pyrmont, to Cologne and so on to drum up support amongst the expatriate Flemings. Bruno De Wever estimates that some six thousand volunteers had come forward up to that September, and they were now joined by another four thousand after Belgium's semi-liberation, although he considered it scant return for the effort expended.

> If we consider that a large proportion of volunteers to the Waffen-SS joined under the pressure of circumstances after September 1944, then we can see that recruitment for the Flemish Legion and the Waffen-SS in Flanders was only partially successful despite the heavy work carried out.[3]

Nevertheless, DeVlag had a large pool in which to fish. Uniformed paramilitary formations had proliferated in Flanders under the occupation; there was the *Vlaamsche Wacht* (the Flemish Guard), established to aid the gendarmes in keeping order, the *Vlaamsche Fabriek Wacht* (Flemish Factory Guard, which protected German installations in Flanders), *De Boerenwacht* (Rural Guard, the countryside version of the Flemish Guard), the *VAvV*, as well as VNV DM formations such as the *Militie-Wacht Brigade*, the *Motor Brigade* and even the middle-aged meeting stewards of the *DM-Hulp Brigade*.

While clearly not a tsunami of volunteers, the numbers that came forward were not insignificant, and several thousand new recruits were packed off for some perfunctory training before being committed to the front in the east.

Many didn't heed the call to join the Waffen-SS though, and one such was the SS-Vlaanderen volunteer, Toon Koreman. A good friend of the assassinated Flemish SS leader, August 'Gust' Schollen, Koreman fled Belgium for Germany as the Allies advanced, but instead of enlisting in the Langemarck he went north.

> In September 1944 when the Allied troops came to Antwerp I was already in Germany and my family rightly

thought it was better to destroy all evidence concerning my collaboration with the Germans. Until the end of the war I worked for the Deutsche Arbeitsfront [DAF – German Workers Front] as a Regional Contact for the Flemish workers in Schleswig-Holstein.

It was around this time that the German High Command mooted the possible use of Belgian Waffen-SS men – both Flemings and Walloons – in re-establishing Nazi rule in the country on the back of Hitler's last gamble in the West: the Ardennes offensive of December 1944, the famed Battle of the Bulge. Oswald Van Ooteghem found himself caught up in this half-baked scheme.

OVO: I was sent to the Lüneburgerheide to be part of the creation of the new Langemarck Division. First, I spent two weeks in Wahn, near Cologne. There were lots of Flemish; auxiliaries, Flemish Guards, all sorts, all of them fleeing the Allies in Belgium. We had to recruit these people and train them for the Waffen-SS. I was given command of a company of Flemish Waffen-SS. The Germans told us they wanted to send us west to the Rundstedt offensive [German name for the Battle of the Bulge]. We refused this because we just wanted to fight Bolshevism, not the Allies. But there was one exile group, DeVlag people, who agreed to return to Belgium to take power back once the Rundstedt offensive had succeeded. But on arrival, they had to put on a German uniform, they received a German passport and so on. When the offensive failed, they were told they had to keep the uniform. Everyone could spot who they were, they had beards and wore helmets and stood out a mile away. We called them derisively 'the Minister Company'. They didn't get back into Belgium in the end. After the failure of the offensive all Flemish volunteers, even from other divisions, were gathered on the Lüneburgerheide, and the Division Langemarck was officially founded. Some of the men didn't want to be there, but felt obliged to, and many weren't trained for war. We had three months to train them: January, February and March of 1945, and then at Easter 1945 we went to the front.

NOTES

1. Coolens's best friend, Karen Goeman, was killed in action on 2nd March 1944.
2. D'Haese was injured in a motorbike accident that effectively ended his war and left him with permanent nerve damage. Coolens thought he died in the accident, but in fact he survived the war and went into hiding with his German girlfriend. Years later he became a successful publisher and painter and passed away in the early 1990s.
3. De Wever, Bruno, *Vlaamingen in het Vlaams Legion en de Waffen-SS*, Tielten Wesp: Lannoo, 1984.

9

1945: THE END IS NIGH

As the war drew to a close in 1945, an entire battalion of the SS Langemarck Division was recruited from Flemish youngsters. From left to right; Evrard, Van Doorselaer, Everaert. Casualties were horrendous, only Everaert would survive the fighting. (Courtesy Oswald Van Ooteghem)

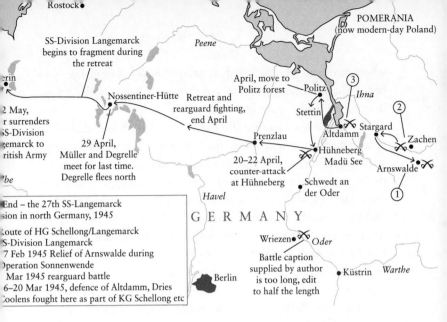

SS-Division Langemarck begins to fragment during the retreat

Peene

Rostock •

POMERANIA
(now modern-day Poland)

erin

Nossentiner-Hütte

Retreat and rearguard fighting, end April

April, move to Politz forest

Politz

Ihna

③

Stettin

② May, r surrenders SS-Division gemarck to ritish Army

29 April, Müller and Degrelle meet for last time. Degrelle flees north

Prenzlau

Altdamm

Stargard

②

Zachen

be

20–22 April, counter-attack at Hühneberg

Hühneberg
Madü See

Arnswalde

Schwedt an der Oder

①

Havel

G E R M A N Y

Wriezen ✗ *Oder*

End – the 27th SS-Langemarck sion in north Germany, 1945

oute of HG Schellong/Langemarck
S-Division Langemarck
7 Feb 1945 Relief of Arnswalde during
Operation Sonnenwende
Mar 1945 rearguard battle
6–20 Mar 1945, defence of Altdamm, Dries
oolens fought here as part of KG Schellong etc

Battle caption supplied by author is too long, edit to half the length

Berlin

Küstrin

Warthe

As New Years' Day 1945 dawned, it was clear to the whole world that the Third Reich was in its death throes. The Luftwaffe had been blown out of the sky, most of the Kriegsmarine lay at the bottom of the ocean, all of Nazi Germany's allies in Europe had been overrun or had switched sides, and with fuel in desperately short supply the remnants of the Army were reduced to relying on horses or on their own feet for transport. Surrounded on three sides by the full might of the Red Army and the Anglo-Americans, Nazi casualties sky-rocketed. In January the Wehrmacht lost 450,000 killed, and would lose just under 300,000 a month from then on until it was all over. Fully a third of all German troops killed in the war would fall in its last four-and-a-half months as under-trained, under-equipped men were slaughtered.[1]

To try and fill the yawning gaps in the ranks, the Nazi Party turned to Germany's old men and created the *Volkssturm*, Germany's Home Guard. Children weren't forgotten either, boys as young as eight were called up by Party authorities in what can only be described as state-sponsored murder. No fewer than 58,000 of these youthful sacrificial lambs were dispatched to the front in March 1945 alone.

DeVlag weren't as morally bankrupt as that, but they did reduce the recruitment age for the Langemarck down to sixteen, with youngsters at the ripe old age of sixteen-and-a-half able to enlist without their parents' permission. Separated from their families and sent to so-called *Wehrertüchtigungslager* (military toughening-up camps), the boys were subjected to enormous pressure to join up, and so many did that the Reich's Hitler Youth supremo, Artur Axmann, announced in early March 1945 that an entire battalion for the Langemarck Division would be formed from them on the Lüneburg Heath training area. Released from his role as a war reporter, newly promoted SS-Untersturmführer Oswald Van Ooteghem was selected to be one of the boys' new officers.

OVO: I was posted into the 1st Battalion of SS-Freiwillige Grenadier Regiment 68, known as the 'Hitler Youth' Battalion because it was composed almost entirely – around seventy-five per cent – of young volunteers from the Flemish youth organisation, the NSJV, that I'd been a member of before the war. I was given a platoon of forty young volunteers, they were all youngsters of 16-17 years – most had been working in the Junkers aircraft factories – and they were convinced they would win the war. My battalion commander was Oluf von Krabbe, a Danish officer and former Danish Army man, as well as Freikorps Danmark. He was the last commander we had when we were fighting on the Oder. Our regimental commander was Hans Stange from Hamburg, an excellent officer. We also had Unterscharführer Dries Callens and Untersturmführer Georges Bruyninckx with us – experienced Flemish volunteers, Callens in particular was a good soldier, he'd been at Narva.[2] Goebbels's propaganda still spoke of the secret weapons that were being developed that would settle the war in our favour, but we knew the war was lost. Nevertheless, they sent us anyway to fight the Red Army on the Oder River. The 'political soldier' Jef Van de Wiele joined us there. He came from Berlin and told us that the war was lost, but that the soldiers were not allowed to know this, they had to stand and fight so civilians could flee from the east to the west away from the Red Army. We saw thousands of refugees from East Prussia pass through our lines at that time. I was ordered to guard a supply depot, containing weapons and ammunition. It was also a communications site. I only took twenty-one of my youngsters, those aged 16-17 years, some were only fifteen and we left them behind in the barracks, and we didn't have enough weapons for all of them anyway. We had been promised that no more Flemish blood would be wasted, and Felix Steiner [by now Steiner was an SS-Obergruppenführer and the commander of the 11th SS Panzer Army] told Hans Stange, our regimental commander: 'Make sure the young soldiers won't be sacrificed anymore. Ensure that they are withdrawn in time.' But we were overtaken by the Russians and our losses were huge. We didn't blame Hitler though. At that time there was no thought of political considerations. The survival instinct was all we had. We had to turn around and fight near Prenzlau, but we had no panzers, no food, not enough ammunition ... it was impossible. Many youngsters were killed there. By chance I was instructed to stay with a group of twenty-one men in a village on the Oder delta. We had to guard the trucks so that our remaining troops could use them to withdraw. After a while we were all alone and were surrounded by the Russians. We escaped into a nearby wood, but were soon surrounded again. That night I managed to lead a break-out with a few of the young lads, and we headed west as fast as we could. We went west on a compass bearing passing lakes, forests .... trying to hide from Russian tanks and troops. We only moved at night to avoid the Russians and Allied aircraft, and on the journey many other soldiers joined my group. I had almost a whole company, and because they could not pronounce my name, we called ourselves 'Kampfgruppe Oswald' [Kampfgruppen were usually called after their commande, hence 'Oswald']. We still had to engage in some short firefights but we made it. Once in the West, I took off my uniform and put on civilian clothes and went into hiding in West Germany.

To the south, down in Bavaria, Jan Munk and Theo D'Oosterlinck were still on their officer training course when Bad Tölz received the order to halt all instruction and form the instructors and cadets into a new Waffen-SS division – the last one that would ever be established – the 38th Nibelungen. Ordered to assemble in the Black Forest area, Munk, D'Oosterlinck and their comrades set off.

JM: We started the journey in trucks, but myself and Kees Gerritsen – another Dutch friend of mine from Bad Tölz – realised we were sitting on boxes of mortar rounds, so we got off and walked the rest of the way as Allied aircraft were shooting at everything on the roads, and didn't we both have two good feet?

TD: At the end of the course a few of us were promoted to Untersturmführer, but not me, I was an Oberjunker, but I'd received the rank insignia, and a month later I would have been appointed as an officer. We were then sent to the Black Forest to form the Nibelungen Division. We were sent on buses; they were the buses from the local public school in the town. We were given Hitler Youth lads to lead; they were just boys, some were only fourteen or fifteen years old. We were always pulling back and trying to get out unscathed, trying not to lose anybody, you understand? Then we surrendered to the Americans.

JM: I was given a company of Volkssturm, Hitler Youth and RAD [Reich Arbeit Dienst – Labour Service] boys and old men. We had no equipment, morale was poor and the desertion rate from these new companies was very high. We were employed as guards on the roads, and we saw quite a few troops who were just trying to escape south to Italy to surrender to the Americans or the British. After a few days we sent everyone home ... We all went back to Bad Tölz and stayed there for a few days in the almost-deserted barracks, and were then issued with orders to find our way back to our old divisions. Mine was still the Wiking of course, which I was told was in Hungary, so that's where I decided I would go.

Munk packed his kit, slung it over his shoulder and headed off east in the general direction of Hungary. He was soon scooped up, along with three other Dutch volunteers, by an SS-Standartenführer, but not before an encounter with some former Italian allies.

JM: I have no idea how long I was marching for and I really wanted to find some transport, and then one day I met two high ranking Italian officers who had a very new looking lady's bike with them. I really wanted that bike. My opinion of the Italians as soldiers was not very high as we had fought next to an Italian unit back in Slavyansk [in the eastern Ukraine in 1943 before Italy switched sides] and they were more trouble than they were worth. I told these officers I wanted the bike and they just handed it over without a protest.

The last few months of the war found Herman Van Gyseghem in eastern Germany right in the path of the advancing Red Army. Transferred to SS-Jagdpanzer Abteilung 560 Z.b.v. 'Kampfgruppe 1001 Nacht' codename 'Suleika', Van Gyseghem's company became the battalion's 3rd, alongside two companies of Hetzer-equipped Latvian SS men. The fourth company, equipped with Sturmgeschutz IIIs, was made up of German staff and students from the Janowitz training school (home of the Waffen-SS anti-tank training school), and accordingly called *Company Lehr* (Training Company).

HVG: Those last few months were typical of what we faced with the Russians. It was chaos. The Russians were everywhere, and all heading in the direction of Berlin. On a map you could see it very clearly. All the roads fanned out from Berlin and out to the east, and from February 1945 onwards they were all loaded with Russian tanks. For us this was an advantage. We didn't have to hunt them out – they were all there – and there were so many of them that you just couldn't miss. We drove on the narrow roads in eastern Germany, about sixty to seventy kilometres from Berlin, and laid up in a small village to wait for the Russians.

Sent to the tiny village of Alt Wriezen, about 60km east of Berlin near the Oder River, Van Gyseghem was the radio operator in Hetzer number 322, alongside two other Flemings; Gustaaf Segers the driver, and Michel Parmentier the gunner, and their Austrian commander, SS-Oberscharführer Wiesener. It was mid-April 1945, Wednesday the 18th to be exact, and spring was finally arriving. It wasn't warm as yet, but neither was it cold as winter faded into memory, its vestiges being the light frost on the ground in the still mornings. The Flemish of 3rd Company had moved into blocking positions and camouflaged their tank destroyers, their main guns pointing east towards Alt Wriezen's namesake village, Wriezen, over a kilometre away on the Old Oder. Over the preceding few days 3rd Company had been involved in bitter fighting, constantly having to retreat in front of overwhelming Soviet attacks. Now, they sensed an advantage, their low and hard-to-spot Hetzers lying hull-down and half-hidden by the narrow lanes and tightly packed houses that were typical of this ancient rural landscape. The Flemish crews were extremely experienced by this time, and they could all see how good their new positions were to face the oncoming Soviet advance. They didn't have to wait long. Tank engines could be heard, and minutes later a convoy of seven Red Army T-34s, carrying groups of infantrymen on their hulls, turrets and engine decks, came driving into the village.

HVG: Wiesener gave his commands through his throat microphone to all of us crew. Parmentier knew exactly what to do and sighted the cannon on the approaching targets. It was all routine, but even so in the close confines of the hull we found ourselves bathed in sweat, our faces streaked with lines of black powder. The adrenaline was pumping, all was silence, we all held our breath, and then Wiesener shouts: 'Fire!' In an instant Parmentier fires and a fraction of a second later a 7.5cm tank shell flies out of the long barrel with an enormous bang. We shot the first Russian T-34 tank in the convoy – direct hit! It came to an immediate stop and caught fire. A few Russian infantrymen were burning too and there were cries of pain as a few of the Russian crew members from the T-34 tried to climb out of the tank just as the turret exploded. The narrow street was now blocked and the Russian convoy was at a standstill. All the Russians could do was reverse back the way they had come, but we didn't let that happen.

Just as they had done so many times before, the crew all knew what they had to do and their actions were automatic. Van Gyseghem quickly reloaded the cannon with a fresh armour-piercing round, and Parmentier fired again. The Russians didn't get any time to react. 'We shot the last Russian tank next. That blocked them all in.' The enemy couldn't move, either forward or backward. The crew took full advantage, it was like shooting fish in a barrel.

HVG: *Then we shot the ones in between. The Russians thought the roads were completely open to Berlin and that we had all run away, and the next thing they knew we were hitting them and they were trapped. We were so euphoric as we destroyed all seven in a matter of minutes and we watched all these tanks burning. At one point it was so easy, and even almost funny, that we forgot our own safety and ignored all the rules we had learned, and the next thing we knew the tables had turned, the Russians started to bring their guns to bear on us and it was our turn to take punishment.*

The Hetzer hull was filled with smoke and gunpowder which stuck on their sweaty faces and matched the black of their panzer uniforms. Wiesener was elated at his crew's success, and in the heat of the moment he made a fatal mistake – one you wouldn't expect from an experienced veteran. He jumped out of the cupola, shouting to the other crews about their success, and began to run towards his comrades in the nearby Hetzers. A previously unseen Soviet tank emerged from another street and pointed its gun directly at Hetzer 322. The Soviet cannon barked, and Wiesener took the full force of the round in his chest, which blew him apart as it exited from his back and sped on towards his Hetzer. That round missed. But having seen what happened, Van Gyseghem jumped out and ran towards his stricken commander. Reaching the tattered remains of the body, all he could do was break Wiesener's identification tag in two, take half with him, and leave the shattered corpse lying in the street. Under hostile fire Herman ran back to his Hetzer and climbed back in. Without a commander the remaining crew hesitated for a moment as to what to do next. That hesitation proved disastrous for them.

The Soviet tank fired again and this time hit Hetzer 322 full on. The blast rocked the assault gun and in seconds it was on fire and burning. Gustaaf Segers was severely wounded, but somehow managed to climb out of the vehicle. Parmentier and Van Gyseghem were pulled out by some paratroopers from SS-Fallschirmjäger Battalion 600 (the Waffen-SS's only airborne unit). The impact of the Soviet tank round had left Van Gyseghem unconscious, but otherwise unwounded. Parmentier was not so lucky. Badly wounded by shrapnel and with severe burns, he was taken to the neighbouring village of Bliesdorf, a couple of kilometres to the southwest, where a field hospital had been set up. Segers was sent there too. For Parmentier, one shoulder and part of his back were stripped of flesh, and you could see the bones showing through. Medic and fellow Fleming, Stan Scheltjes, helped to treat the wounded gunner and tried to comfort him: 'It's not so bad Michel my friend, you'll be alright.'

It wouldn't be. Scheltjes said that Parmentier was crying, partly from the pain, but also because he knew his death would leave his younger brother – who had joined the Waffen-SS a few weeks earlier despite Michel's objections – all alone at the front. As darkness began to fall the field station had to be abandoned for fear of being overrun by the Soviets. The staff and wounded had no option but to find cover in the woods to the west. In the chaos Scheltjes lost contact with Parmentier. Another wounded Fleming from 3rd Company, Alexander 'Alex' Colen, was the last man to see the young gunner alive. Officially listed as 'Missing in Action', neither his body, nor that of his commander, Wiesener, was ever found. Van Gyseghem soon recovered and fought on, while Gustaaf Segers's injuries were so severe that even though he survived the war he was disabled for life.[3]

All in all the 3rd Flemish 'Langemarck' Company destroyed sixteen Soviet T-34 tanks that day, with seven claimed by

Hetzer 322. For this action all the crew members from Hetzer 322 were awarded the Iron Cross 2nd Class.

HVG: We fought hard, but our losses were so large. Near to Berlin we were running out of everything; panzers, guns, no Luftwaffe, no ammunition, and always more and more Russians. Many of us were killed or wounded. After the Oder we lost control of the battle and were just fighting to try and stay alive. Everyone was fleeing west. But we were Waffen-SS, we had committed ourselves, and even though we knew the war was lost, we still fought on, we just had to.

As the war came to an end, Jan Munk was drawn into preparations for last ditch Nazi resistance, before having his one and only skirmish with the Americans.

JM: We were with this Standartenführer from the 14th to the 29th April and it was a marvellous time. He told us he wanted to collect as many pistols, machine-guns, mortars and panzerfausts as we could get hold of, and so we stopped military convoys, took what we wanted, loaded it into a truck and took it to a hiding place on a farm. I believe it was all connected to the 'Werewolf' organisation who were meant to be SS men who had vowed to undertake guerrilla fighting and never surrender. In reality nothing like that happened ... We were then split up and I was once again given command of a company of Hitler Youth and Labour Service boys. Most of them were seventeen but some were just sixteen years old. We were in Eggenfeld about 200km north-east of Munich. It was the 1st of May and my orders were to take up a defensive position where a road entered a wood, and stop any enemy tanks getting through. I put my boys to digging foxholes and told them to keep under cover at all costs. They were all extremely keen and determined to do their bit for the war. A few hours later ten or twelve American tanks appeared with no infantry. The road was very narrow and built high above the surrounding fields, which meant the tanks were forced to drive in convoy, one after the other, making our job easier. I fired first and crippled the lead tank and then the Americans fired all their ammunition blasting the wood until I think they ran out of shells. I watched as the crew of the stricken tank were taken on board another one, and then they all reversed back the way they had come. None of my boys had been injured, which was all well and good, but the situation was hopeless. I told my boys we had to move out before the nearest enemy aircraft came and bombed us. Back in the safety of a nearby village I told the boys that was it and they had to go back to their homes. Some of them were bitterly disappointed and cried. This was my only encounter with the Americans. I returned to the farm and to the news that Hitler had committed suicide – the war was over.

For Herman Van Gyseghem, news of the defeat of the Third Reich and the end of the war came from his Flemish company commander, Remi Bertels, on the edge of a pine grove near Parchim in Mecklenburg-West Pomerania, some 170 kilometres northwest of Berlin.

HVG: I was in the East facing the Russians still when the war ended. Bertels stood in front of us – the few who were left – and said; 'Comrades, it's over! The war is done, and we lost.' It was dark and I remember it was so quiet, no guns, no sounds of shooting, no bombers roaring overhead, nothing. Then he went on and said that he had received word that Germany had surrendered and that we should try and get to the West, to the Americans. Arguments broke out, with some men saying they didn't trust the Americans, but most said anything had to be better than the Russians – no-one wanted to go to Siberia, it was too cold! We all knew we couldn't surrender to them, it would have been a death sentence. Bertels said we should find civilian clothes to change into, and someone asked him if he knew somewhere we could get some clothes, and he said; 'How you play it is not my concern, but you all have been soldiers long enough to be able to sort yourselves out.' That was it. We said goodbye to each other, and we all promised to meet up on the exact same day in May the following year in Brussels' Market Square. I was speechless I can tell you. I couldn't believe that it was over and that we had lost. Then I felt a tap on my shoulder, turned around and it was my three best friends; Godfried Cardoen, Jupp Timmermans and Cyriel Roels. They persuaded me that the four of us should stick together and try and make it home, so we headed down the road to the village to find shelter. Masses of people —Germans mostly of course — were fleeing west away from the Russians to try and find safety, and so we planned to join them. The whole place was filled with refugees and soldiers like us, and it took us until around midnight to find a large farm where we found some other men from our company who were busy changing into some clothes the farmer had given them; old jackets, trousers and the like. There wasn't enough for us though, so we just tried to make ourselves as comfortable as we could in a barn, but we couldn't really sleep, and Jupp talked all night to try and keep our spirits up. The next morning a crowd of ex-prisoners-of-war burst in, all of them shouting away in all sorts of languages; French, English and German. There was a bit of an argument, they wanted guns, and it all looked a bit dangerous, and then Godfried stepped toward the ringleader and punched him right under the chin. He fell backwards into the door but jumped straight back up again so I hit him over the head with my pistol, and he went down like a wet sack. The pistol went off as well, but no-one was hurt and the four of us ran outside to try and get away, but suddenly there were Americans there all shouting at us; 'Hands up!' That was it, we were prisoners-of-war, and we were marched to a truck full of German soldiers.

The roads were packed, thousands and thousands of people with all their possessions packed into suitcases and onto carts, and all moving west to the River Elbe, that's where safety was, away from the Russians, you had to get over to the other side of the river, to the western side, to be safe, and it wasn't easy. There were guards everywhere and the Russians were stopping people all the time. After a while they took us south to Wittenberge where we crossed over the Elbe to the west and were put in a large prison camp surrounded by barbed wire. They handed us over to the French. They put me and some others in an old bunker where we were guarded by some French-speaking Senegalese soldiers. They kept us there for some time and we talked to the French about joining the Foreign Legion and carrying on the fight against the communists, but it didn't work out. We realised that the blood group tattoos we all had on our arms singled us out as SS, so we tried to cut them out, well most of us tried anyway. That's when it really hit me that the war was over and we had lost. They then sent us to Belgium later on that year.

The fighting might have been over, but not the suffering, particularly for Germany's womenfolk, who now became the target of a deliberate Soviet policy of rape and sexual violence on an industrial scale. The true figures will never be known, but estimates place the number of women raped across East Prussia, Pomerania and Silesia at 1.4 million, with a further 100,000 assaulted in Berlin itself. Gang rapes were the norm, and no account was taken of age.[4] Bestial though this undoubtedly was, it was perhaps predictable from the soldiers of an army which had lost over 11 million men killed during nearly four years of total war.[5]

That does not lessen the horror of what was visited on the hapless victims, as Lucie Lefever knows to her cost. The Red

Army advance found her trapped in Breslau, as the city was put under siege.

LL: I felt it was my duty to stay. We felt protected. Afterwards we found out that this was not the case when we had to surrender. The Russians came closer and closer to the Oder. On 21st January 1945 we left the train station and went to a castle about a kilometre behind the Oder. There we prepared a dressing station for the wounded. The Russians came later. The wounded kept on being brought to us from the fighting on the Oder. It went on day and night. We had no proper ambulances. Our wounded soldiers were brought in on trucks, on wagons pulled by horses, on anything and all of them were being transported to us in the military hospital in Breslau. And at the very end, when it was really critical, an officer asked if I wanted to leave with the last flight out from the airfield at Gandau.

As so often in our interview, Van Ooteghem complimented his Sneyssens comrade: 'Yes, during the siege of Breslau, Lucie stayed. She was given the opportunity to leave Breslau on the last Luftwaffe flight out. She refused. She wanted to stay with the wounded soldiers.' Lefever nodded slightly, her head bobbing forward.

LL: In Breslau itself in Frankfurterstrasse, near the Gandau aerodrome we all crawled into the cellars and set up a dressing station. The Russians bombed us for two whole days. Then later we were obliged to flee into the Jahrhunderthalle[6] in Breslau – a large modern building for exhibitions.

Van Ooteghem interrupted again, jabbing his finger at me to make his point:

OVO: But before the end, the fortress commander Besslein of Breslau[7] honoured her with the award of the Iron Cross 2nd class.

There were only two non-German women who have received this: a Danish nurse and Lucie.

Another nod and a bob of the head from Lefever.

LL: After the surrender we had to flee to the west. We were lucky, we went in some cars and the Russians shot over our heads. We had to keep on going west. During the day we hid, then at night we ran on. Once there was a Russian commissar who stopped us. I had my Red Cross pass, I showed it to him and he took it from me and just ripped it up. When I got back to Flanders I hid the papers I had left in the top of our curtains. They were my salvation as at my hearing I told them I had to spend my time being forced to work in Germany.

Lefever did not escape the Red Army as easily as she let on. It became clear during the interview that she had been assaulted herself, and whilst she had obviously come to terms with it after so many years, it was still an immensely traumatic subject. It doesn't come easily to any man to ask a woman in her nineties (any woman) about a rape she had been subjected to. At that moment I remembered the words of the American Civil War general, William Tecumseh Sherman, 'War is cruelty, and you cannot refine it.'

Horror and cruelty aside, the war was now over, and it was time to go home – for some, but not all.

OVO: When the war ended I thought of committing suicide, but instead I got rid of my uniform, changed into some civilian clothes and decided to stay in Germany rather than risk going back to Belgium. I knew I had to hide and deny I had served in the Waffen-SS, that's when I had those photos taken of me in German Army uniform, so I could show them to anyone who asked. The shoulder boards and collar tabs were all made of paper and stuck onto the uniform, but they looked real enough to fool anyone. I had to do it, they were looking for SS men, and there were signs everywhere saying that if someone offered shelter to an SS soldier they would get twenty years in prison. So I made my way to the French sector of Germany and called myself Hans Richter, pretended I was a German, and married a German woman because I just didn't trust the Belgian authorities. I became an architectural draughtsman down in the Black Forest.

After hearing of Hitler's death, Jan Munk knew there was no point in trying to reach the remains of the Wiking in Hungary, or wherever it was, so he decided to try and make it back home to Holland. He knew he would need help to get there; food, shelter, clothes etc. There was no money. Nazi Reichsmarks were basically worthless and there was no way he could get hold of American dollars or British sterling, so he helped himself to the best currency he could find among the stores intended for the Werewolf – cigarettes. Cigarettes had become the new cash. He could buy a meal for two cigarettes, and a woman cost five. Stuffing a rucksack with as many cartons as it would hold, he and another Dutch ex-volunteer began to walk.

JM: We passed by an old wooden hut, and heard a woman crying. When we investigated we found three Hiwis and a young German girl stripped naked. She was about to be raped. We didn't rape women and the Hiwis weren't going to rape this young girl either. We shot them … A few days later we came to a big farm where we told the family that if they gave us civilian clothing – shoes, socks, trousers, shirts, jackets – then we would tell them where we had hidden a truck full of supplies for the Werewolf. That sealed the deal and we got all we wanted. I kept those trousers for over two years before they were worn out.

NOTES

1. Evans, Richard J., *The Third Reich at War*, p682, Allen Lane. The Wehrmacht lost 450,000 men killed in the month of January 1945, 295,000 in February, 284,000 in March and a further 281,000 in April.

2. Oluf von Krabbe was an ex-captain in the Danish Royal Army who commanded the 3rd Company of Freikorps Danmark from August 1941 onwards. After the war, he conducted a study into his fellow Danish Waffen-SS volunteers which was published as *Danske Soldaten i Kamp pa Ostfronten 1941–45* in 1976. Dries Callens was a twenty-year-old veteran of the fighting at Narva, having fought on Orphanage and Grenadier Hills, while Bruyninckx was actually born in Hull on 27th March 1917 after his family fled Belgium during the previous war. He went back to Belgium, joined Degrelle's Rex and then the Legion Flandern. He fought on the Leningrad front, was wounded and went to Bad Tölz before joining the SS-Sturmbrigade Langemarck. He was wounded for a second time in the Ukraine, and then became a company commander in SS-Grenadier Regiment 68. After the war, he settled in France and passed away in 2002.

3. Hetzer 322 was not the only Flemish assault gun to be knocked out that day. Alex Colens's Hetzer also took a direct hit and had to be abandoned. With every member of the crew injured, Colens, the 25-year old vehicle commander from Antwerp, was extremely lucky, with only a slight wound to his knee. His radio operator-cum-machine-gunner Jan Hayet got a shrapnel splinter in his buttock which left him with a large scar, while the gunner, Jozef Pintens, was more severely wounded and had to be evacuated on a Red Cross train. The train

was hit during an Allied air attack and Pintens was killed. Colens survived the war and ended up in Ireland, raising a family before returning to Flanders many years later. He passed away in Ghent on 30th December 2008. Colens wasn't the only ex-Flemish SS veteran to end up in Ireland, her Catholic heritage and neutral stance during the war also drew several other veterans after the conflict including Albert Folens who was invalided out of the Waffen-SS and served in the SD before becoming an educational publisher in Ireland. An ex-Skorzeny commando, Staf Van Velthoven, lived in Kinvarra, Co. Galway until his death a few years after Colens. Most famously, Albert Luykx from Limburg went there. He ended up being accused of complicity in the Arms Crisis of 1970 alongside the then-Minister of Finance, Charles Haughey. Luykx had been a member of the VNV's Black Brigade but never joined the Waffen-SS. The latter three were the subject of an Irish TV programme for RTE One, *Ireland's Nazis*, broadcast in 2007.

4. Evans, Richard J., *The Third Reich at War*, p711, Allen Lane.

5. Ibid, p707.

6. Breslau's Hundred Years Hall was the largest exhibition space in Germany and could accommodate crowds of up to 10,000 people.

7. SS-Obersturmbannführer Georg-Robert Besslein was the commander of SS-Regiment Besslein which was a major part of the defence of the besieged city. After surrendering along with the rest of the garrison on 6th May 1945, he was held in captivity by the Soviets until October 1955, after which he settled in West Germany. He died in Heidelberg in April 1993.

IO

PAYING THE PIPER

With the war over, Oswald Van Ootegehm went into hiding in southern
Germany. He had photos taken of himself dressed in German Army uniform to
hide his membership of the Waffen-SS. His collar tabs and shoulder boards are
made out of cardboard. (Courtesy Oswald Van Ooteghem)

With liberation and peace came justice or retribution; whether you saw it as the former or the latter depended on your view point. For members of the Resistance in the formerly occupied nations – men and women who had lived in fear day and night, who had fought bravely against the odds, and seen so many of their friends tortured and executed – it was only right to see collaborators hunted down and punished. For returning Oostfronters and the likes of Jan Munk, Lucie Lefever and the other Sneyssens, it was victor's justice; revenge by any other name.

The aftermath of the liberation of almost every country in Western Europe – and especially France – was marked by an orgy of killing as scores were settled and summary justice was meted out to known collaborators, often with a bullet to the head. Thousands died and many more just 'disappeared', no doubt ending up in unmarked graves in Europe's dark and silent forests and woods.

For the Oostfronters, if they survived the initial bloodletting, they were hauled before military courts in Belgium and put on trial. Once convicted, many were given long prison sentences ranging anywhere from ten years to life, and a few were executed. However, tempers soon calmed and the desire for national healing overcame the urge for revenge. In the end most of those convicted were quietly released within five years of the end of the war. Bitterness at their treatment though, still remains among the veterans:

LL: After the war I was naturally obliged to get rid of my Iron Cross. after all, I had told the authorities that I had been a conscripted worker. In the detention camp we were treated very badly. We had to wash naked in public, and we were also medically examined and interrogated.

OVO: The nurses were meant to be under the protection of the Red Cross in Geneva. After her Russian captivity Lucie was then imprisoned and punished in Belgium.

LL: I looked for my Pro Justitia to show you [official document given to her by the Belgian government on her conviction for collaboration detailing the charges on which she had been tried and convicted] but I haven't been able to find it. It said that I had 'taken up arms against Belgium' and was sentenced to nine months in prison. I ended up serving three months. I received no recognition for my work for the Red Cross, no recognition or understanding that I was a nurse helping the wounded and sick, just nine months' imprisonment and years of being treated by the authorities as a criminal – Belgian justice, it's a joke!

Jan Munk remembered his experiences of the detention and displacement camps as he headed back to Holland posing as a liberated foreign worker:

JM: In one of the many camps I went through I saw two men walking in step with one another. The Russian guards immediately grabbed them and checked under their left upper arm for the blood group tattoo all Waffen-SS men had. They found it on these two men and shot them on the spot in front of all the other men, women and children in the camp.

On arriving back in Holland, Munk was recognised by someone who had known him as a student before the war, and thrown into a cell.

JM: I cried my eyes out that night. The next day I was taken to Roermond with four others and we were put in cells in a row along a corridor. At one end was the guardroom and at the other was an enclosed quadrangle. At about 10 o'clock that night I heard one of the cells being opened and the occupant taken out into the quadrangle. After the guards had their fun with him they returned him to his cell and took the next one, and then it was my turn. Three guards sat on a bench and I was ordered to do the goose-step. They tripped me as I went by them and that was it – I had disobeyed their order to do the goose-step! I was beaten up with fists and sticks. This went on for three nights. Waiting for your turn was the worst part.

Shuttled from camp to camp, Munk wasn't subject to any official judicial process until more than two years after his ordeal in Roermond.

JM: On 17th September 1947 I was taken by truck, along with seven other men, to Alkmaar to spend the night in a cell there before being taken to Leiden the next morning where our cases were to be heard by a tribunal. My case was heard at 11 in the morning and then we were all taken back to our prison at Erfprins. The whole process was repeated on the 30th of September, when the verdicts were read out. I received five years' imprisonment and the loss of my civil rights, so I couldn't vote. This was what happened to all of us who were aged over twenty-one. I was finally released on 9th November 1948. I then went home and finally made peace with my father.

Toon Koreman, an SS-Vlaanderen man, but not a Waffen-SS soldier of course, was still in Schleswig-Holstein near the Danish border when the war ended.

I was arrested in Kiel by British soldiers and locked up in a local jail at first. During the next ten days I was thoroughly maltreated and tortured by soldiers from a Scottish unit, especially one sergeant in particular. Afterwards I was sent more dead than alive to a camp in Neuengamme ... I was held in the same jail in Antwerp as my old

DeVlag chief – Jef Van De Wiele – and finally after six years I was a free man; but Van De Wiele was held for nearly fifteen years![1]

D'Oosterlinck and Van Gyseghem weren't physically abused like Koreman but had similar experiences of judicial punishment and the imprisonment that followed.

TD: We surrendered to the Americans at Ludwigsburg and were put in a camp there. We kept our uniforms but had to remove our shoulder boards and rank slides. The Americans saw how young we all were and treated us well. They used to ask us to help them round the camp, fixing things and keeping it clean and in order. Then that November some officials and policemen came from Belgium, they came to search the various camps looking for Flemish soldiers. I was arrested, along with some others, and put on a truck to the jail in Liège. Then from there I was sent to Brussels, and then on to Antwerp. Finally, I ended up in the detention camp in Lokeren. We were treated badly there. There were fifteen barracks, and the eighth barrack block was the chapel where the priest held Mass every Sunday. The barrack blocks were too small for so many people, it was very crowded, and some inmates died there.

Every year there is a reunion mass to remember those who died in Lokeren, and every year I get an invitation to go. I was there until my conviction in 1946. I was sentenced to five years in prison. My father was convicted alongside me, he was sentenced for being in the VNV. We were taken to a small prison in Leuven, and while there we had to work in Charleroi for 2.10 francs an hour on the railway tracks. Afterwards, we were transferred to Merksplas and we had to work in Brasschaat. There was an airfield nearby that the Germans had made unusable by blowing holes in the landing strips. We had to fill them up again. It was hard but it wasn't forced labour. There were only two guards and they were pretty slack. I served three years in the end. My father was released and then I did another five months, and then one day in May one of the guards just said to me; 'D'Oosterlinck off you go, you're free.' That was it. It was crazy – Belgian justice eh? Some people were sentenced to death, some to twenty years and more, and then for me it was three years and then 'you're free', crazy. I just went home.

I found out later that some old Oostfronters who were at Lokeren went and fought in Korea against communism. They were the new heroes. History repeats itself.

D'Oosterlinck's spouse burst into the conversation at that point, wagging her finger excitedly to make her point:

Yes, Belgian justice! It was no justice at all! We knew lots of people who had really done nothing at all – they were just members of the VNV or something like that – and they were all punished, it wasn't fair, not fair at all.

My family wasn't wealthy, when the Germans entered Belgium my father was unemployed, and there were four of us children to feed, life was hard. My father went to the barracks, and spoke to the Germans and asked if they had work for him, they did, and he worked there for eight or nine months. And then they suggested to him that he should go and work in Germany. The pay was good and he could send it home so we could eat and live. He worked in Germany for four years in all, and for that the Belgian authorities locked him up in St Peter's after the war, he was just honest and told them he volunteered to go to Germany and wasn't a forced worker. Neither of my parents had a party card –they weren't in any political party, they weren't interested in politics. I'm a Flemish nationalist and so I joined the DMS [the Dietsche Meisjes Scharen – the Dietsers Maidens Platoons – the girls branch of the VNV's youth wing the NSJV] and became a leader for East Flanders. But after the war times were hard. I was the daughter of a collaborator and had been in the DMS. It was bad.

Up to that point she had been quiet in both our interviews with Theo, content to sit and listen as her husband talked about his service, so I was taken aback at the way she reacted when we started to discuss the aftermath of the war; this was not a woman who could let it go, she was genuinely angry at the way she and her family had been treated by a system that she felt was capricious and had no legitimacy.

HVG: We arrived in Strasbourg, where the gendarmerie took us by train – two gendarmes per prisoner – to Brussels to a small castle there. I was held there for some time and was then sent to court and convicted of bearing arms against Belgium and of helping the enemy. They also convicted my sister of the same charge, the bearing of arms, when she had been a Red Cross nurse in Vienna! She got one year in prison, and I got four. They put us in Sint-Kruis prison. From there, every day we went on the tram and then the train to the coast between Den Haan and Knokke where our job was to help clean up the Atlantic Wall, all the defences the Germans had built to stop an invasion. The sand dunes were full of bunkers, barbed wire and mines – thousands of mines – and we had to move them all. Accidents happened. The trenches between the bunkers we had to fill in as well. Some of the bunkers had walls half a metrer thick, and while some we blew up, some couldn't be destroyed like that because they were too close to houses and other buildings. To clear those ones we had hammers, big hammers, sledgehammers about five kilos in weight. We used to stand round the bunker in a circle, and then one after another hit it with our hammers – bang, bang, bang – until it was demolished.

As for my parents, they escaped to Germany at the end of the war. Lots of people left Flanders to protect themselves. They left our house empty and just went. The Resistance was looking for collaborators, God knows what would have happened if they had been taken.

I spent time working in the villages of Wenduine and Blankenberge, and I also had to stay in Merksplas for a while. There, they told us that we were all 'saboteurs', I don't know why. We grew potatoes there, and our job was to keep all the bugs and insects off them. We used to walk between the rows of potato plants and pick the beetles off them. The one good thing there was the food; we got herrings every day, very good nutrition. I was finally released in 1949.

Unlike his compatriots, Oswald Van Ooteghem made the decision to stay away from Flanders and let things play out. His married life down in southern Germany was a good one, he worked hard and lived well enough in comparison to so many of mainland Europe's war-ravaged, half-starved people. However, he knew his time in Germany was only a stopgap, at some point he would need to make a choice as to his future. Like so many former SS men he contemplated emigrating to South America, and he made a successful application to go and live in Argentina. Whilst still deciding whether or not to go and make a new life on a new continent, his mother went to see him in the Black Forest and made up his mind for him.

OVO: It was 1949, I had a German passport and was all ready to leave, and then my mother came to Germany and asked me to come back to Flanders. My wife also wanted to regularise my situation – she didn't want to live in the shadows any more. So I submitted an application to the Belgian Embassy to be allowed to return to Belgium. They didn't send me any papers, but they did send the French gendarmes. I was arrested and taken back to Belgium, first to Brussels, where I spent a few days, and then later to a prison in Ghent.

Van Ooteghem was tried, convicted and sentenced to three years' imprisonment. As so often in his life, luck was on his side. The war had been over for four years by now, and the authorities in Belgium had little appetite for yet more lengthy trials and harsh punishments, so Van Ooteghem's three-year term was far more lenient than the sentences passed down earlier to other Oostfronters. Dispatched to Ghent's *Nieuwewandeling* ('New Walk' in English) gaol, he was put in a cell with his father and Hendrik Elias.

OVO: Yes, I was lucky not to get a harsher sentence, but at my trial I told the court that I had saved someone's life – it was back in 1940 just after the German invasion. My father and I were hiding out in the woods from the Belgian government when the Germans arrived. Remember the Belgian police were arresting lots of prominent Flemish nationalists and taking them away, and many were shot. As it was the Germans put up posters everywhere saying that anyone who was found with a weapon would be shot on the spot. The mayor of our town informed everyone that all weapons had to be collected and delivered to the town hall so no-one would be found to have a weapon at home. These were two contradictory orders. A farmer's son who was walking with a bag full of weapons to hand them in at the town hall, was arrested and executed on the spot. A second young man was arrested for the same 'offence' and would have been shot. Nobody wanted to intervene, they were all scared, but I wasn't afraid, and even though I was only sixteen years old I got on my bicycle and rode to where the boy was going to be shot. I told the officer in charge of the firing squad about the mayor's order on guns, and the officer accepted this and let the boy go, just like that. At my trial, the father of the boy testified for me. This went hugely in my favour. Also, another act of kindness went in my favour. The father of a childhood friend of mine had died. His mother had then remarried a Russian Jew who smoked like a chimney. I knew him and used to send him the cigarettes I was given in my rations – I was a non-smoker. He ended up being sent to a concentration camp and didn't return, but his wife also testified for me at my trial that I – an SS soldier – used to send cigarettes back to a Jew. That was helpful for me.

At this point Van Ooteghem gave one of his trademark smiles, the ones that stretched across his whole face and went all the way to his eyes:

OVO: My lawyer also knew one of the officers of the court – very well indeed if you know what I mean – so the case was settled in bed by the two of them!

Times were different too, communism was on the march everywhere; in Prague, in Berlin, and Korea of course, and suddenly what the Oostfronters had done didn't seem such a bad idea, they needed us really, so I was lucky once more. I was reunited with my father in jail. Elias was there too, the last president of the VNV. In the prison there were seventeen other architects alongside my father, and we set up an office inside the prison, working on designs for all the new buildings being constructed across Flanders. We designed numerous buildings in Ghent: tax offices, a police station, schools … all the official government buildings were designed and drawn in prison, except for the National Bank in Ghent, which my father was offered, but only on the proviso he denounced his nationalist politics. He said he wouldn't and was still a supporter of the VNV, so he didn't get the job. I spent fourteen months there and used my time to get more qualifications. I was then released and settled back in Ghent.

On release from prison, most Oostfronters started life anew. Some managed to shed their past as they shed their uniforms, although many found their problems had in some ways only just started.

TD: After I was released it was time to work! I went to evening school for four years and studied to become a draftsman. I worked hard and did well, and I got a job with OIP. They worked for the army and I was worried they would find out about my past, but one of my teachers recommended me and they never asked me anything about the war.

I kept silent. So I didn't tell my children, just in case. They didn't need to know, I'd moved on anyway. The first contract I worked on was for the F104, the Starfighter. Together with a company from Hamburg, IA, we made the optical sights for them. We had to make optics for 1,100 aircraft. The Germans bought 800, Belgium bought 110, and the Netherlands and Italy bought them too. The company sent me to Germany, to Hamburg, because I could speak German. I told them I had learned German at school, that wasn't true of course, I learnt it in the Legion. There were terrible problems with the Starfighter – more than 130 of the German ones crashed, but that was because they were left on the ground too long – up to ten years some of them! In other countries they didn't have those problems.

As for Oswald Van Ooteghem, he was the heir of a well-known name in Flemish nationalist politics, and he was always going to pick up that mantle again at some point.

OVO: It wasn't long before I joined the Volksunie[2] and soon after that I was asked to stand for election on their behalf to the provincial council. I was always open and honest about my past, I found this never gave me any problems as everyone respected it, so at my first speech in a theatre I stood up and told everyone there about my past – about my volunteering for the Legion, my service at the front, and my time in prison. People could either vote for me then or not. Lots of Oostfronters got involved in the Volksunie, they had no fear. They went around sticking up posters and turning up to meetings; most were militants that the party could always rely on. Once again we were fighting for Flanders and also for amnesty for all those who had been deprived of their rights after the war. We wanted electoral power to help those affected by repression after the war.

Van Ooteghem was treated remarkably leniently given his family history of involvement in the upper echelons of Flemish nationalism, but then perhaps the Belgian state felt relatively secure, given so few prominent nationalist leaders were left alive after the war; Staf De Clercq, Joris Van Severen, Reimond Tollenaere – all were dead. Having said that, some high profile senior survivors of the hierarchy were punished severely.

OVO: Dr Elias, I think, spent fifteen years in prison and was only released due to illness; he had stomach problems, ulcers I think. He couldn't return to Ghent and lived for a while in the Netherlands. Eventually he returned to Laeken in Brussels. There he wrote a masterful book: 1914–1939 – Twenty-Five Years of the Flemish Movement – the history of our struggle for independence. The idea for the book originated while he was in prison. While he was locked up he wasn't allowed to write, but the chaplain smuggled him in paper and pen and documents he needed. Dr Elias was a historian and also studied law, and he had a chance to become a professor at the University of Leuven, but instead went into politics and chose the VNV.

After his release I visited him several times in the Netherlands and Brussels, where he lived, and after he died I kept in touch with his wife. There's a story there; when Elias was a young lawyer, one of his very first clients was a young woman who wanted to divorce her husband. Elias helped her and the next thing you know, she became his wife! She remained faithful to him throughout the war and his time in prison, and all the time until he died. When he was serving his sentence she used to visit him every week and pick up his laundry – she was very devoted.

In Flanders, many of the Oostfronters organised themselves into old comrades' associations to help look after each other. I asked the Sneyssens about how their group came into being.

OVO: First of all, there is nothing that beats the camaraderie of the front. If someone is hurt out in no-mans' land, you go get him, no matter what. That is obvious. But that feeling has stayed with us after the war. Our invalids had no prosthetics. They had to beg for them. We had to beg for wheelchairs too. So we decided we had to do it all ourselves. We supported the widows, we delivered Christmas trees, money, gifts etc. As a group of friends we established the 'Friends Sneyssens' here in Ghent, it was 1950 or 1951 I think.

We called it Sneyssens after a historical figure, the flag bearer of Ghent who fought against the French hundreds of years ago. His right hand was chopped off but he didn't drop the flag, he just took it up in his left hand and carried on. Symbolism you see – something was taken away from him but he fought on – just like us! We all joined: and then the children and grandchildren of the Sneyssens come together too on a regular basis, all among friends.

TD: After the war I kept myself to myself and didn't join any groups of old comrades. I was angry though as I saw that all the priests, the clerics, those who taught us in school and so on – all the ones who encouraged us to go and fight communism, to go and join the Legion, they just washed their hands of us, they said they knew nothing of it, that they hadn't been involved. I just got on with work, my family, with my life. Then I retired around 1980, and it was different then, I could get involved. In the Sneyssens we don't talk about the misery we've seen, all the horror, we speak about the reasons we did it, why we did it, the fight against communism. We talk about life and friendship. Occasionally we would tell a story, an anecdote, but only occasionally.

OVO: There was a second group like us in Antwerp; the Sint-Maartensfonds. Toon Pauli, another Oostfronter, was president of the Sint-Maartensfonds, and we kept in touch. There were reasons that we had several groups. The Belgian police would raid our meetings, so we had to spread out into small groups all over the place to escape from the Belgian courts and persecution. Earlier this year we'd been in existence for sixty-five years. We dissolved *the Sneyssens group a few months ago as we are all too old now. The Sneyssens wasn't just for Oostfronters though, we had many supporters and friends – Oostfronters' relatives could join as well of course. The association may be gone now but we still look after each other so that comrades from the war never stand alone.*

As we talked about the Sneyssens I turned to Madeleine De Kie, Van Ooteghem's 'guardian angel' sitting quietly to his left, sipping her champagne, attentive to his every need and word. Well-dressed, well-kept, her short, dark brown hair neatly cut. During the interviews with Van Ooteghem and the other Sneyssens I had always been interested about her connection with the group. She definitely wasn't their age so couldn't be a contemporary of Lucie Lefever from the DRK or anything like that, but Van Ooteghem's line about relatives being involved in the Sneyssens gave me the push I needed to ask her outright how she had become involved.

MDK: Yes, my father Marcel De Kie was in the Legion Flandern. He signed up in April 1941 for the German Army, before the war in Russia began, and not for political reasons but because of social injustice and the prevailing poverty that his family and friends suffered before and during the war. His neighbourhood was so poor, that sometimes in winter the whole street had just one bucket of coal to share for heating for a whole week. He was the eldest child in the family and was intelligent, but his parents couldn't afford to send him to be educated, so he became a tailor like my grandfather. He was due to be conscripted into the Belgian Army, but the invasion came before he enlisted. Some of his friends were killed in northern France by French soldiers, and this made him very angry, as it also did that almost all officers in the Belgian Army were French-speaking and not Flemish, so Flemish soldiers didn't understand what they were being ordered to do. After the invasion, during the occupation my grandparents started to make German uniforms. My grandmother used to take my father with her to the barracks to deliver the uniforms when they were finished. When he was at the barracks he used to see all the propaganda posters urging young men to join the German Army or the Waffen-SS, and after a short time he enlisted.

OVO: I first met Marcel when he was in the Nordwest Regiment [SS-Standarte Nordwest] in Hamburg, in Langenhorn. He was a National Socialist, while I was a Flemish nationalist. We served together in Leningrad, and at Krasny Bor. He was wounded several times. He was a Scharführer in the Langemarck - a serious, conscientious man and a disciplined, élite soldier. When I first joined up he was my instructor in the Flemish Legion.

MDK: My father was in the 1st Company of the Legion along with men like Marcel Behaegel. He went out to Russia – to Leningrad – and was wounded by shrapnel in the right shoulder at Weschky on 2nd March 1942. He was awarded the Wound Medal in Black for that. Much later on, as the war was ending in 1945, he served in the Langemarck Division's panzer unit, and then finally in around March or April 1945 he was in the 1st Platoon of Kampfgruppe Schellong's 3rd Company, his commanding officer was a man named Oehms I think [this was probably the German SS-Sturmbannführer Johannes Oehms]. My father was captured by the English at the end of the war. He was then handed over to the Americans and sent to Breendonk[3] before being put in Ghent's Nieuwewandeling prison. He was given the death penalty but that was later commuted to life imprisonment. They released him in 1948. My father and mother (my mother was French) mostly spoke French together. My mother's family was liberal and French-speaking, and my father was more of a social democrat. At home we had to speak Flemish, and in school we learned French.

Father was not happy with the outcome of the war. He was embittered and disillusioned, and kept himself to himself, and he never really spoke to us about the war and what he did. We all knew about his punishment of course, for example the government took away his civil rights as part of his sentence, so he didn't have the right to vote, but what we didn't know until much later was that he was in contact with some of his old Oostfronter comrades. He did it in secret and never told us, he just did it in his own way – all very quietly. We used to see Oswald though, as he used to come to my father to tailor his suits.

My father eventually got his Belgian citizenship back in 1980, but he never voted again. He always used to get a doctor's certificate as an alibi to say he couldn't vote – for him not voting was a matter of principle.

OVO: Justice was not even, not balanced, I can tell you. For example, during the war I had a girlfriend. She was a lovely girl, but we lost touch as you do during war and when you're young, anyway, after the war she was punished because she'd been my girlfriend. I met her in Ghent after I was released from prison, and she told me that she had been tried and convicted and had lost her civil rights for life – I only lost my civil rights for five years! Belgian justice! As for so many other Oostfronters, they suffered very badly. Many were sentenced to ten, twenty or even thirty years' imprisonment, and they lost their citizenship. They still supported me after my release, even though I had gotten only three years, served fourteen months and then got my civil rights back a few years later. They saw me as a 'lampist', someone who carries a lamp on a tram or bus and leads the way for them.

MDK: I was a nurse, for my whole working life, and I was once working in a hospital when another female nurse heard my name and asked me if I was related to Marcel De Kie, I said yes he was my father, and she turned to me and said that if it had been her choice he would have been shot – she was very angry. I was angry too and I said I am a nurse and wouldn't hurt anyone, even her if she was hurt and brought in to hospital and I had to treat her. She was quiet after that.

Across the border to the north the situation for veterans was much the same as it was in Flanders.

JM: In the Netherlands we were denied careers in the civil service, the armed forces, in academia, and employers wouldn't give us jobs. So we had to do it ourselves. Those who could employ a comrade did so, those who could provide a home for a comrade did so. Furniture was donated and cash donations were collected, especially for the disabled. An association was formed in Holland called the 'Foundation of Former Political Delinquents', and outings were organised to reunions in Germany. But after a year or so this was forbidden by the Dutch government, as was another organisation – the Jan Hartman Foundation. Reunions in Holland became impossible due to hostile publicity, so Dutch veterans could only attend those in Germany or Flanders, which were also attacked by protest marches and demonstrations.[4]

Munk, like many other former Waffen-SS men, ended up leaving his native country to begin a new life elsewhere.

JM: My younger sister, Marietje, was employed as a private secretary tor an Englishman, John Thompson, who worked for an organisation that organised exchanges between medical students from different countries. An English group was arriving on 29th July 1952 and was being met by a Dutch student who was going to take them sailing. He developed appendicitis and John asked Marietje to arrange a replacement who could sail a boat – by complete luck that was me. Mauveen was one of the party, and that's how we met. We married in 1956 and moved to England. On 1st January 1957 I secured a job with Perkins Engines in Peterborough. I disclosed my past to them but they accepted me anyway. I was with the company for twenty-six-and-a-half years. I retired in 1983 and after a few years, Mauveen and I moved to Devon, where we lived for nearly twenty years with our two dogs. As for my past? I'd put it away until a young author [not this author] contacted me with a request to supply information on my experiences in the Waffen-SS for a book he was writing. I was reluctant to drag up the past, but Mauveen persuaded me to try. She died in 2008.

State-sponsored repression – understandable though it may have been given both the Belgian and Dutch governments' desire to downplay all talk of collaboration and focus on the activities of the Resistance instead – seems to have backfired to some extent though, especially in Belgium as the issue of Flemish independence resurfaced once again. Flemish Oostfronter groups like Sint-Maartensfonds and the Sneyssens were all slap bang in the heart of Flemish nationalist politics and that hasn't changed. The prevailing popular image of the Oostfronters in Flanders is still of young men who were strongly pro-Catholic, pro-Flemish and anti-communist. It may be a simplification to view the Oostfronters as idealists who went far away to fight for 'hearth and home' on the Russian Front, and once there were deceived by the Nazis only to return and be punished mercilessly by a harsh Belgian government – but it's a very powerful simplification and one that still holds sway today among both the Oostfronters themselves and their natural supporters amongst the Flemish populace. Among the interviewees Oswald Van Ooteghem was the most forthright and thoughtful on the subject.

OVO:The Flemish movement was eroded by the repression, no doubt about that. But I think that the state of Belgium made a big mistake by tackling the collaborators so hard. She created a sort of class of underdogs that have become a symbol for the Flemish, and that the

Flemish Movement has been only too happy to put back in play. In Germany, the leaders were condemned but the followers were left alone, not so here where there were no fewer than 600,000 people with a record of collaboration.[5] That means it is the masses, whilst in Germany it was just the headline, and what's been the result? In Germany the process destroyed Nazism, and here it has created a reaction. The same happened in the Netherlands.

Now you ask me, will there ever be an independent Flanders? I tell you, yes. It will take a while. One of the leaders of the Volksunie was Hugo Schiltz, an MP from Antwerp. An intelligent man. He told me: 'In all federal states there are hierarchies. In Germany they have federal legislation and then below it Landes law [regional law]. Due to the absence of that same hierarchy, Belgium will break.' We here in Belgium cannot bring in any law without the agreement of the Walloons. There is always a grendelgrondwet[6] that blocks everything, even though the Flemish are in the majority, the Walloons can block a bill at any time. The Flemings are conservative, the Walloons are semi-communist. These are two total opposites. Sooner or later it will all fall apart.

I wanted to find out more of these people's views on some of the most famous Belgian – both Flemish and Walloon – individuals from the war; Léon Degrelle and Remi Schrijnen among them.

HVG: We had one Knight's Cross winner from Flanders in the Langemarck: Remi Schrijnen. We thought that if he could drive the Russians off with his anti-tank gun, then we can too. But the Walloons had more Knight's Cross winners. Degrelle took care of that. He had an audience with Hitler himself, and Hitler said 'If I had a son I would want him to be like you' – that's the legend anyway. But Degrelle was a good Waal [a Flemish name for the Walloons]. A good Belgian. He did not have the same ideals as we Flemings.

It could well be that he would have had a lot of power in Belgium after the war if Germany had been victorious.

OVO: After the war I met Schrijnen, and Degrelle. Degrelle was an idealist for the Waal, and we had nothing against the SS Walloons of course. I remember he had an elegant castle in the Bois de la Cambre in Brussels. I was received there as a war reporter. He was a master propagandist. Suddenly there was a little girl next to me and he says, 'Voilà, ma petite Godelieve a l'intention de la Flandre. The point: he had a daughter, a girl ... Godelieve is a Flemish name, so he was suggesting that Flanders was his daughter.

Van Ooteghem seemed fairly positive about the Walloon leader, but Van Gyseghem and Lefever seemed less certain about both him and his followers.

HVG: In southern Spain near Malaga – Alicante I think – Degrelle built a castle like the one he had in Belgium. If he was there, in residence as it were, then the Belgian flag flew above the place. This personified his pretensions – after all that's what the King does when he's at home in his palace.

LL: I never met Degrelle, and never thought much of him, but I will tell you that SS Walloon soldiers regularly bullied and humiliated Flemish nurses. Despite everything though we still helped them when they were wounded.

Toon Koreman was of much the same opinion regarding Degrelle as the two latter Sneyssens.

He didn't understand us or the whole Flemish movement because he always refused to learn our language – the language of the majority of people in Belgium. Plus, he was always a Belgian patriot, very royalist, and that is the exact opposite of the Flemish movement. However, I admit that Degrelle distinguished himself on the Russian Front through his bravery and courage. There is no doubt he wanted to use his personal relationship with Hitler and Himmler to lead Belgium as a whole – even though he didn't speak the language of the majority of the population.

I wanted to know if any of the interviewees had any regrets about their service, even though I felt I knew exactly what their answer would be.

HVG: No regrets. We became men. We are lucky that we are still alive to talk about it, others aren't. You can't give ten out of ten to Bolshevism and to Russia, there was so very much wrong with that system, and yes, Stalin was much worse than Putin, but Putin was the head of the KGB you know. Some things never change.

Before the discussion headed off into present-day Russian geopolitics, Van Ooteghem stepped in, as he usually did when he thought the conversation was veering off topic.

OVO: It was hard. But it has given me many things for the rest of my life. Since then I have had discipline, survival instinct, energy, and I learned perseverance too. When you've done something as a young man full of conviction, and in good conscience, then you should not regret it. The intention was 100% pure and in hindsight of course we can look back, and we have been attacked for what we did, but there was a journalist who said that 'if the million volunteers hadn't been there, then the Russians would have flooded across all of western Europe.' Because the intention of the Soviet Union was nothing less than world revolution. Stalin's intent, his plan, was to make all of Europe communist. And that journalist also wrote that in all probability the Germans and western European volunteers weakened Russia so badly that they weren't able to carry out their plan. Our fight was then maybe not so useless after all. You cannot forget that the Waffen-SS consisted of about a million men, but more than half were non-Germans – they were other Europeans and even Muslims who fought for Europe against communism.

Van Ooteghem took a breath, his eyes seeming to cloud over, his voice getting a little rawer.

OVO: I say again, I don't regret it, but I'm not terribly proud of some things that happened either. I don't need to apologise, I was idealistic and I didn't know what was going to happen. We weren't aware of the crimes of the Third Reich. What we did we did out of our Flemish nationalist convictions, our anti-Bolshevik beliefs and also a bit of adventurism, a bit of romanticism, with youthful enthusiasm even.

D'Oosterlinck was adamant, clenching his right fist to emphasise the point.

TD: No regrets at all. It has helped me in life. All that hard training made us into men, and it has shaped me to where I am now.

Lucie was the same.

LL: No regrets. Not at all. I'm glad I can handle what I've been through... I know the misery that I have experienced, I can put it in its place. It's just my life, I have lived it. And also thanks to the Sneyssens, they have helped me a lot. It is good that we could do something for each other.

One last time Oswald leapt her defence.

OVO: She continued the work of a nurse you know. She visited sick people, did home visits, delivered packages and gifts to widows, etc. She was our social worker as well was our Lucie, we all owe her a lot.

The treatment the interviewees received when they returned home after the war (except Olbrechts who didn't return home of course) was the one subject they all felt the strongest about. Both Belgium and Holland had been invaded, defeated and occupied, and none of them had played a part in that – except Olbrechts again, who had fought the Germans as a member of the Belgian artillery. Their governments had gone into exile, as had the Dutch queen, whilst the Belgian king had 'retired' from public life to his palace, and as countries they were essentially leaderless. None had taken up arms against their own country or people, but had fought and bled hundreds of miles to the east, combating an enemy that they were told was the epitome of evil and was intent on the destruction of European civilisation. This message was most vociferously preached to them by a Roman Catholic church that almost all of them fervently believed in. As far as they were concerned they had served with courage and honour, only to be maliciously punished once the war was over, when their only real offence was to have lost. Lucie Lefever was the epitome of this viewpoint; a Red Cross nurse who had done nothing except treat the wounded and sick, who was sexually assaulted by the Red Army and then abused once more back in Belgium with a trumped-up conviction and subsequent imprisonment. Most of the Oostfronters suspected that what really sat behind the state's judicial retribution was really another attempt to smother the Flemish independence movement; but as in so many other instances across history, the very harshness of the reaction had the exact opposite effect to what was intended.

Undoubtedly brutal as much of the treatment was, there can also be no denying that the Flemish and Dutch volunteers wore the uniform of their occupiers and fought alongside an army that had invaded their homelands, terror-bombed Rotterdam and killed well over twenty thousand of their countrymen and women. Obviously there was going to be a judicial process and punishments when warranted, but the inconsistencies seem not only harsh, but also random and driven more by a desire to even the score rather than achieve justice. The fact that over seven decades later the Oostfronters and their sympathisers still rankle at the inequity of it is testament to the Belgian government's failure to lay the chapter to rest.

NOTES

1. Toon Koreman passed away in hospital in October 1996 following an unsuccessful operation.
2. The Volksunie – the People's Union – was a moderate Flemish nationalist political party in Belgium, formed in 1954 as a successor to the Christian Flemish People's Union.
3. Fort Breendonk (Dutch: Fort van Breendonk, French: Fort de Breendonk) is a military fortification situated at Breendonk, near Mechelen in Belgium, which is best known for its role as a Nazi prison camp during the German occupation. Originally built for the Belgian Army 1906-13, during the Second World War the fort was requisitioned by the Germans as a prison camp for the detention of Belgian political dissidents, captured Resistance members and Jews. Although technically a prison rather than a concentration camp, the Fort was infamous for its prisoners' poor living conditions and for the use of torture. Most prisoners who were detained at the camp were later transferred to larger concentration camps in Eastern Europe. Of the 3,590 prisoners known to have been imprisoned at Breendonk, 303 died or were executed within the Fort itself but as many as 1,741 died subsequently in other camps before

Paying the Piper

the end of the war. Fort Breendonk was then briefly reused after the war as an internment camp for Belgian collaborators. This period of the Fort's existence is known as 'Breendonk II'. Trials of the Fort's Flemish SS guards were held during 1946 in Mechelen, with fourteen sentenced to be executed by firing squad; two appealed their case and had their sentences commuted to life imprisonment. Four others were sentenced to life, one to twenty years in prison, and one other was acquitted. Two guards were sentenced to life but were never caught. The Nazi camp commandant, Philipp Schmitt, was tried in Antwerp in 1949 and sentenced to death. He was shot on 9th August 1950. He never showed any remorse and denied all of the atrocities that occurred at Breendonk, claiming he was merely re-educating the inmates as he had been ordered. Today, the site is a national memorial and museum, which is open to the public.

4. Jan Hartman (1887–1969) was a Dutch fascist and collaborator. After the war, he was active in far-right politics, and was one of the two founders of the *Stichting Oud Politieke Delinquenten* – SOPD (Foundation of Former Political Delinquents), a right-wing organisation founded by and for formerly jailed and convicted war criminals and collaborators. Hartman was born in Beilen and as a young man spent time in Germany. In the 1930s he joined the NSB and worked in propaganda before he volunteered for the Waffen-SS in 1941 and saw action on the Eastern Front. After the war he was sentenced to ten years in prison but was released early, in 1950, on probation. He founded the SOPD together with Jan Wolthuis in 1951. Hartman became the organisation's

secretary. The SOPD was the first and the largest of the former collaborationist organizations in the country. In 1952 he and Wolthuis played a never fully explained part in the escape of seven convicted war criminals from the *Koepelgevangenis* in Breda, including Klaas Carel Faber. From the mid-1950s on Hartman was particularly active in attempts to rehabilitate veterans of the Eastern Front. After his death in 1969, a Jan Hartman Foundation (*Jan Hartman Stichting*) was established; it claimed to be a charitable institution offering various kinds of assistance including legal aid.

5. After the war, a total of 400,000 Belgians – both Flemish and Walloons – were investigated for possible collaboration. Of these around 56,000 were prosecuted. The majority received prison sentences and loss of civil rights, although several hundred were executed. Waterfield, Bruno (17th May 2011). 'Nazi hunters call on Belgium's justice minister to be sacked.' (*The Telegraph*, UK.)

6. The *grendelgrondwet* or 'latch constitution' was introduced in 1970 and enshrines the fact that a number of issues come under special laws, which can only be amended by a two-thirds majority in the parliament, plus a majority in each language group. The purpose of this lock is that constitutional changes can then only be enacted if endorsed by both Flemings and Walloons. This means that neither the majority Flemish community, nor the minority Walloons can unilaterally change the constitution.

SEVENTY YEARS ON

It is now more than seventy years since the end of the war, an ocean of time to reflect on what was really a very brief episode in the Oostfronters' lives. The veterans have spent far more

Members of the Sneyssens veterans group, standing from left to right; Oswald Van Ooteghem, Lucie Lefever, Theo D'Oosterlinck. Sitting, from left to right; Herman Van Gyseghem, Karel Linseele, Oswald Cromme Lynck. (Courtesy Theo D'Oosterlinck)

time in civilian jobs, getting married, raising their children and grandchildren and even spent a lot more time being retired than they ever did in the uniform of the Waffen-SS. Yet the few short years that they did spend in the Legion Flandern, the Wiking, the Red Cross or the Langemarck, has been the defining time of their lives for most – though not all – of the men and women I met. They carry it with them; for some it is a badge of honour, for others it's the burden of Atlas. For almost all of them the cause they fought for was the most important thing in their young lives, and many of them still believe in it – whatever '*it*' is or was. Sitting there, in a sunny room in peaceful, prosperous Flanders or Germany, staring into a glass or a coffee cup, what do their minds conjure from the past? Horror, remorse, pride?

One Oostfronter who epitomises this dilemma is Albert Olbrechts. Though in comparison with the veterans interviewed for this work, Olbrechts stands out in many ways. Firstly, having volunteered in 1941 at the age of twenty-six, he was one of the oldest recruits in the original Legion, as well as being the oldest veteran interviewed for this book; he was actually 101 years old when I saw him. Secondly, his wartime service at the front was by far the shortest. Olbrechts went with the Legion to Leningrad, and after a few weeks became seriously ill. Sent home to convalesce, he served in the SS-Fürsorgeamt in Antwerp for the next three years looking after the welfare of the families of serving volunteers, his repeated requests to return to the frontline continually being turned down until he was assigned to the Nibelungen Division in the dying days of the war. Thirdly, he was not a Flemish nationalist in any way – Olbrechts was a pre-war member of Léon Degrelle's Rex Party, and considered himself a proud Belgian – albeit one who has now lived in Germany for the majority of his life.

Last but not least, he was also the only Oostfronter I met who was born in the UK; in Croydon, in south London. His old house is gone now, replaced by new apartment buildings advertising one bed flats for over a third of a million pounds – 'spacious one bedroom apartment ... modern high specification interior and exterior. Allocated parking included.' Back then he and his entire family – mother, father, nine children and grandparents lived in a large house, refugees from the First World War raging on the other side of the Channel. Now he, and his second wife Hildegard, live comfortably in a first floor flat of a house in Ettlingen near Karlsruhe. Their home is light and airy, large windows looking out to the road and their neighbours (maybe Sydenham Road is not all that different after all), the furniture by contrast is heavy and dark and too big for a flat, presumably left over from their previous house. Unlike Coolens's home you would never guess at Olbrechts' service in the Waffen-SS by looking at the possessions and nick-knacks with which we all fill our lives. The pieces that do stand out are a couple of stuffed birds of prey, high on shelves and incongruous; and everywhere, carved elephants of all shapes and sizes, their significance becoming clear only later during the interview. Then suddenly you could see it, a clue to his past, hidden behind a whole family of wooden pachyderms – two, three, four books in all; Léon Degrelle, Jan Vinckx – Rex and the Legion.

We conducted the whole interview in English (again another first for a Flemish Oostfronter) with me sitting next to him on the sofa so he could hear my questions, and Hildegard, a lovely woman, keeping us topped up with coffee and very tasty cake, although Olbrechts only drank water and weak tea himself, his breakfast bowl empty on the table by the window.

AO: I was born in Croydon in England, and my name is 'Albert George' after the king you see, I even have a letter from the king congratulating me on my name you see. I was born there because my family left Belgium when the Germans attacked at the beginning of the First World War. My mother was pregnant with me at the time and so I was born on the 4th of February 1915, one of nine children. I will speak to you in English because my English is better than my Flemish. I left Flanders a long time ago and the language has changed since I was there. My grandfather was the President of the Belgian Refugee Society in London, he died in Croydon before we returned to Belgium. Apart from my father, who died in his sixties, my family has always been long-lived, of the nine children eight passed ninety years of age, and my sister and mother were both 101, like me. Most people say I've lived so long because of sport, I was world champion seventeen times for long distance running – marathons and so on – in the senior's category, even though sometimes I was the only one running! When I was the only one running in my category it was great because I didn't have to run fast! I ran everywhere, all over Europe, even in England, in Gateshead. The last race I ran was when I was ninety-five. I ran the Great Wall of China once, well, some of it. I was due to run a marathon on it, but the night before I ate some of the local food, God knows what it was, cat, dog or something, I don't know, anyway I was sick all night long and the next day I could only run ten kilometres before I had to stop. I was eighty-six then. I only drink water now, from the tap, and I don't eat much, cornflakes for breakfast, maybe an egg, I can't taste food now, not really you see, and my teeth aren't so good anymore.

A dun-coloured blanket covered his legs, the skin of his hands and face seemed almost translucent, the veins standing out, only the length of his bony fingers giving a hint at how tall he still is. An image of Dries Coolens sprung to mind, unbidden.

How different these two men are now in physical terms. Olbrechts looked and sounded his age, whereas Coolens still moved like a boxer.

AO: I spent three weeks at the front during the war, and then I came back. Our food was frozen over there and my stomach got frozen too and so they sent me to hospital. When I was discharged I wasn't allowed to go back to the front, I don't know why, it was a mystery. I protested and even qualified for the Sports Medal to show I was OK, but they didn't believe me. I was sent to Graz to a convalescence company, and then back to Antwerp to the Fürsorgeamt for both the Flemish and the Walloons, and I spent the rest of the war there.

I looked up from my pad – just three weeks? Olbrechts' war was three weeks? I felt deflated. Had I come all this way to hear about three weeks of service? I shouldn't have worried. His story was fascinating and revealing.

AO: I didn't volunteer to sit in an office, I volunteered to fight, and towards the end of the war I was sent to Prague and I saw my official file with all the letters in it that I had sent to the SS-Hauptamt requesting a posting to the front. All the letters had notes on them from my boss in Antwerp who said that it was OK for me to go back to the front as long as they sent him – that is the SS authorities sent him – someone just as good, who was a good worker and someone he could trust to do the job. So it was him who stopped me from going back to the front in fact. I suppose I should be grateful to him as I survived the war and I am still alive now.

His blue eyes clouded over – another sip of water.

AO: I went back to Belgium when I was fifteen, in 1930. I went to university to study Biology, and that's where I first met Léon

Degrelle. He was already well-known for his political views, and I was sympathetic to those views and found his speeches very inspiring, that's why I joined the Rex Party. I was very pro-Catholic and pro-Belgian, a Belgian nationalist, that was what I was. My father was very traditional and devoutly Catholic, and he wasn't a Rexist. I remember once when one of Degrelle's speeches was being broadcast across the road from our house in a cinema, my father became very angry, he didn't want to hear it, or have a lot of Rexists hanging round near our house. So yes, I was a Rexist, and that was a big difference between the likes of Dries [Coolens] and me, they were all pro-Flemish and against Belgium, but I was for Belgium. So when I volunteered I wanted to go to the Walloon Legion, that's where Degrelle was and where all the other Rexists were going – well almost all of them. There were other Flemings in the Walloon Legion you know, there always were, I wouldn't have been the only one, but Degrelle said to me; 'Albert, no, you must go to the Flemish Legion and be my best propagandist there. Tell them all about Rex.'

As it turned out I didn't talk politics with the other Flemish volunteers, not really, yes we were all anti-communists, it was Rome or Moscow we were always told. I always remember that back in Flanders every Sunday the Catholic Youth would march through the streets singing anti-communist songs. My father was anti-communist but not a Rexist, and he always said I shouldn't join the party, but I did of course, and I had a black Rexist uniform and a cap, but I never wore them in Mechelen where we lived just in case my father saw me. Anyway, one day we had a meeting in Mechelen and I went in my uniform as I was sure my father wouldn't be there, but a friend of my father did go and he saw me, and he then spoke to my father later, and said 'oh I didn't know your son was in Rex' and my father said no he isn't, and his friend said 'yes he is, I saw him in his uniform.' So my father then said to me that I had twenty-four hours in which to bring my uniform home and burn it in the garden, or he would throw me out. He was like that my father, a very strict man, a dictator – for example, he used to insist that all we children had to go to church three times every Sunday, and he only went once, in the afternoon, but we couldn't question him or say anything to him about that or he would have hit us round the head.

Anyway, I didn't burn my uniform, instead I left home and went to live with an uncle. I rarely saw my father after that. I saw him once much later in Brussels at the train station after I had volunteered and I was wearing my *Waffen-SS* uniform. We were both waiting for the same train – the same carriage actually – and he looked at me and just walked away and got into another carriage. I heard later that he told my mother, 'Oh I saw our German son today, he was wearing a very smart German uniform.'

I was in the Belgian Army when war broke out, doing my military service. I was a Wachtmeister [sergeant] in the artillery, and I fought the Germans in 1940. My whole unit ran away to the coast and I became a prisoner. I was only a prisoner for three weeks though as the Germans sent all the Flemish home. I just had to answer a few simple questions; who I was, where I lived and so on, and that was it, they waved me way and I was allowed to go free. I went home and saw how the Germans behaved – always so polite and correct. We had some billeted with us in our house and they were very respectful and brought German black bread back to the house each day for my mother. She liked it but my father refused to eat it.

I joined the Legion in 1941 with the first batch of volunteers. That was when I met Oswald Van Ooteghem for the first time. I was one of the tallest men in the Legion then so they made me a flag bearer when we marched through the streets of Brussels.

We were sent to Debica to train and when we got there we were all in different uniforms; VNV, Verdinaso, Rex and so on, and we were ordered to stand in a field and a German officer came along on a horse – his name was Reich [SS-Standartenführer Otto Reich] and he said to us, 'Look at these gypsies. You have come here to eat and to shit. You should be proud that we allow you to fight alongside us.' He then went to our Flemish flags and just grabbed them and moved them around with no respect. I will never forget his words or what he did, we were idealists and he looked down on us. That night in the barracks you could hear people crying. Lots of the volunteers wanted to go home. I spoke to a good friend of mine who was also from Antwerp and a Rexist like me, and he said; 'Albert, what will they think of us back home if we leave now, they'd think we were cowards.' So we decided to stay. We had no Flemish officers to look after us, and the Germans just saw us as foreigners and didn't respect us – later Tollenaere came and so did Suys [Paul Suys, the leader of Rex Vlaanderen) and then things started to get better.

As the war drew to a close, Olbrechts joined the cadets and instructors of Bad Tölz – Jan Munk amongst them – in the ranks of the Nibelungen Division.

AO: We called it the 'Niegelungen' Division – that means 'out of luck'! We didn't even have enough weapons, so one day all the companies were called together and we were told to hand all the weapons we had to just one company so at least they could fight. I just kept my Belgian Army pistol that I had right from the beginning of the war. We were in a wood and American tanks were passing by to the left and right. The officers told us it was over, and they said we should go and hide in the nearby farms. I was a squad leader and I went off with two or three seventeen-year-old lads to a farm where we took off our uniforms and put on some civilian clothes we had stolen. We decided to hide in a barn that night and surrender the next morning. That night there was shooting in the next-door village, and when I woke up under the straw the next morning the Americans had arrived at the farm. A black American

sergeant was shouting at us to get out of the hay and put our
hands up. He took me to an officer, and I showed him my Belgian
passport. I told him I had been taken from Belgium to come and
work in Germany, and he said OK and directed me to a refugee
centre.

Olbrechts' war was over, but not his wanderings. As it
turned out he would never leave Germany and never return
to Flanders. Like so many survivors of the conflict without
documentation, his journey became an odyssey.

*AO: I knew two women who lived in Fulda [in the region of Hesse
on the river of the same name] and so I walked there – it took
me about four or five days. They took me in and I made myself
useful by begging for food off local farmers during the day and
then bringing it home each night. But one day we heard that the
Americans were searching all the houses for SS men or people
without papers, so the local priest sent me to the bishop, who in
turn sent me to a nunnery to help out with the farm animals. They
looked after me very well until one of the sisters – Sister Francia –
said to the local policeman who used to come for a free meal that
I was very responsible and hard-working but wasn't a German. He
wanted to see my papers then of course. The Mother Superior was
very angry and sent Sister Francia to east Germany, and told the
policeman that I was German, and that if he caused any trouble
his free meals would stop. Three days later I was called to the local
administration office and given a new passport. I was now Albert
Olbrechts from Königsberg [now Kaliningrad in Russia).*

From then onwards, Olbrechts' life was anything but
straightforward. He worked for an American Army rabbi –
Major Pfeiffer – for a while, until Pfeiffer began to suspect
Olbrechts was not what he pretended to be.

AO: I said I had something to tell him so we went into his office and in front of his menorah I told him my story and threw myself on his mercy. He could have called the MPs and had me arrested, but he didn't. He looked after me and even told my parents back in Belgium that I was alive and well. I had been condemned to death in Belgium, because I had joined the Waffen-SS and I was a member of Rex, but not for any act as I hadn't done anything. I knew about the camps like Dachau and Sachsenhausen, but I didn't know about the death camps. If I'd have known I would never have volunteered. Those things were horrible, truly horrible.

By now Olbrechts was working full-time for the American armed forces, including a stint helping to break the Soviet blockade of Berlin in the famous air-lift. He was injured in a road accident, and after his recovery he spent time on various construction projects, eventually building up his own company and settling in Ettlingen. Not content with having started one successful business, Olbrechts founded another – *Jumbo Reise* – a bus and coach company with an elephant logo, hence the name and the elephants dotted throughout his apartment. He ran Jumbo Reise until his retirement, whereupon he decided his adopted home town needed a sports stadium, so he gave it one, a 30,000-seat outdoor stadium, all of it built by him. It took him ten years to finish and was finally opened in 1980.

He kept himself to himself for many years after the war, not contacting any of his old comrades, not joining any Oostfronter organisations or going to any reunions, but keeping discreet tabs on it all nonetheless.

AO: I subscribed to Berkenkruis and always read the magazine. I didn't get in contact with anyone though, I was always worried that I'd get arrested and sent back to Belgium. I miss Flanders but I'm happy here in Germany.

It seemed to me that Olbrechts was doing all he could to live down his time in the Waffen-SS and to make amends, although amends for what exactly I don't know as his service seemed to be utterly blameless, but he is haunted by it nonetheless. However, he told me one story that seemed to be the spur for so much of his life since.

AO: I was never afraid of being attacked when I walked around Antwerp in my Waffen-SS uniform, but sometimes it was not easy to wear it. My best friend was called Paul and he was going to volunteer like I did, but first he had to sort out some family business, so he told me that he would join with the next batch. I saw him several weeks later and we went for a drink, and while we were in this bar he told me that he had found two English pilots who had been shot down and were trying to get home. We didn't have any quarrel with the English so he decided to help them escape. Two weeks later I got some home leave and I heard that he had been arrested by the Germans for trying to help the pilots. I thought I had to help him so I wrote a letter to Goering [Hermann Goering, Head of the Luftwaffe] but my father insisted I not send it as I could get into trouble and it could backfire. Then later I saw my friend's father at the station in a black suit – they'd shot Paul. I tried to avoid him by going out a different exit from the station, but we passed each other anyway and he just looked at me in my uniform. I was so ashamed, standing there in my Waffen-SS uniform, with his son, my best friend, shot. Paul had written me a letter from prison and I went to his house to get it – making sure I didn't go in my uniform of course. His mother opened the door and started to shout at me, saying I was just like them, the people who had murdered her son. I didn't know what to do, it was awful, truly awful. I got his letter, took it home, sat and read it and it said that by the time I was reading it he would be dead.

His voice trailed off into silence. This was guilt. This was remorse. After seventy years it is still there. Olbrechts didn't shoot Paul, neither did he betray him to the Gestapo for trying to help two shot-down English pilots, indeed he even tried to help him, and yet he clearly felt responsible in some way, that by wearing the uniform of the Waffen-SS he was guilty by association and somehow responsible for his friend's death.

AO: I don't regret joining the Legion. I know that what I did is something the rest of the world sees as bad, and I do regret that they only see the bad. Most of the volunteers thought that they would get an independent Flanders, they were fooled for sure. As for me, I was just anti-communist and I wanted Belgium to stay together as one country, that was a big part of being a Rexist, and I didn't want Flanders to be independent, to leave Belgium and split the country apart. Now I see things differently. Belgium is not a normal state, I am Flemish but at school everything was in French, and then at university it was all in Flemish, I found that very confusing. French is like Latin or Greek, whereas Flemish is Germanic, and I see now why so many Flemish want independence, I didn't back then, but now I see that the Flemish were treated like second-class citizens.

Olbrechts subsided into silence, his breathing a little laboured; it was time for me to go. I shook his hand to say my goodbyes and thank yous and was struck again at just how big it was – the hands of a strong, powerful man, now more bone than flesh; brittle and dry like autumn leaves.

Remorse, regret; these were emotions the Oostfronters and other veterans understood, but for them it was nuanced; they expressed utter horror at the Holocaust, other crimes perpetrated by the Nazis, and the individual acts of brutality that impinged on their own lives, but they did not feel blanket regret.

OVO: I feel no remorse for what I did at the front. It was me or them. For years I comforted myself with the thought that if I hadn't pulled the trigger and shot them, then they would have shot me instead. I still think about it every night, when I lie awake. I'm a convinced pacifist now, I hate war. You can think of it as a kid who burned his fingers while playing with fire, and now never wants to play with fire again. That's me and war. But I don't feel sorry for what I've done. I was convinced that I was fighting for the right cause. But I wouldn't call what I feel remorse, no, not that. Yes, we lost. And back then we didn't want to admit that. Not yet. It's like in football. You're behind on the scoreboard and you know that the battle is lost, but you continue to cheer for your team. Because it's your team. You do it out of solidarity. Now I can put it into perspective and it makes no sense to speculate about what would have happened if we would have won. But then it really was us or them, and I stood on the side of 'us'.

Oswald Van Ooteghem is now in his nineties. A survivor, both of war and the always-dangerous arena of politics, with a flourish he clenches his left fist, holds it in the air and tells me that his personal motto is '*Nie pleuje!*' – 'Never give up!' Underneath the bravado and knowing smile, there is something else, doubt perhaps.

OVO: I realize that I'm in my final years, and that makes me humble as I think back, and think of all the young men I killed, or saw killed. I've had a good life, they haven't. Now, my last wish is to pay my respects to those that died. But there is no nostalgia, none. Of course we were naive back then, and we were used and abused. I am glad that we live in an open, democratic society, but the message of Reimond Tollenaere is still very topical for me: 'We strive for an equal place for Flanders in a new Europe.' I tell you now that from the cradle to the grave, I am now, and always have been, a Flemish nationalist.

Not all the Sneyssens felt the same.

TD: I do not know if we will ever have an independent Flanders, but I'm now ninety-two years old, I'm not interested any more. In ten years, we will all be gone and nobody will be interested in what we did for Flanders.

JM: There was a time when most Europeans agreed that communism was evil. Everyone knew about the communist camps in Siberia for political prisoners, and the regular purges they had to rid themselves of people who didn't toe the line. I believed then, and still believe now, that my motives in opposing that system were right. You can't measure that with today's yardstick. The terrible thing is that the Waffen-SS have all been labelled as criminals and beasts under the concept of 'blanket guilt'. This was deliberate. The Waffen-SS was composed of European volunteers who were frontline soldiers with a minimum of political affiliations, whereas Himmler's SS were members of the Nazi Party. We in the Waffen-SS were plain, ordinary soldiers, perhaps a bit better than the average, but that was because we were volunteers. I never saw or heard about any poor behaviour at all in my regiment!

Having said that I do regret that I was part of a regime that was able to establish concentration camps, and order mass slaughter, but my comrades and I were not aware of this, and this happens to be true.

HVG: I don't have any regrets, that's for sure. But I didn't want to be involved in politics after the war. I've always been a big fan of the

Flemish cause, and it remains an eternal struggle for the Flemish to get respect, just like it has been for the Germans. For Flanders look at history, look at Belgian history, Flanders has always had history, but Wallonia has none. I took my punishment and then it was done. It's all so long ago now. Let it rest.

JM: I don't regret it – my service in the Wiking that is – but that doesn't mean I am comfortable with everything that I saw, or what we had to do sometimes. Death just became part of our everyday existence. We had a young Russian lad with us at the front who had deserted from the Red Army. He used to help us out, carrying ammunition and supplies and so on, and at night he would sometimes go out across no-mans' land and persuade some other Russians to come back over with him and desert. One morning he didn't come back, and we found him several days later in a village we captured. In the centre of the village was a tree, and there he was. It was sickening. Someone who had knowledge of dissection, a butcher or a surgeon or something, had nailed one end of his intestines to the tree and the whipped them around the tree until there was no more gut left in the body.

Most of the time we regarded Russian soldiers as cannon-fodder, as cattle sent for the slaughter because they just kept on attacking, no matter what, and we just didn't understand that. Very often their soldiers were forced to attack by their political Commissars. They even forced soldiers who didn't have any weapons to keep going. If they faltered or disobeyed they were promptly shot in the back. We sometimes knew when they were going to attack as well as they would start singing, which meant they had been given their 'encouragement ration' of vodka. They did have some very well-trained units as well though who fought very hard and were very successful. But the majority were just herded forward like animals. They just kept on coming regardless of casualties. Once, we were on the edge of a wood with a wide, flat patch of ground and a few bushes between us and another wood. We saw some Russians come out of that wood pulling some sort of anti-tank gun. There were about five Russians and we just watched as they turned the gun around and began to get it ready to fire. At that moment, we shot them all. A second group of Russians then came out of the wood, not running but walking as if out on a Sunday afternoon stroll. The same thing happened again and we shot them all too. Then another group appeared and we did the same to them before they finally abandoned the gun. We just didn't understand why they walked out to be killed.

TD: I have to tell you that my children, none of my family, know what I've done. I had to be silent: my firm worked for the Belgian Army and the air force, and I might have lost my job or lost my firm its contracts. I couldn't risk that. My kids suspect what I did, but they don't know for sure. They'll be fine with it, it's time they knew.

D'Oosterlinck is a man used to secrets. I interviewed him in his home, a comfortable and homely flat in a modern block by the canal in Ghent. He looked as he always did; calm, contented, his cardigan and slippers testament to a man at ease with himself. As for his home, just as with Olbrechts there are no markers, no clues of his past in his furniture, photos or possessions. He is surrounded by photo albums of his travels; a whole cupboard groans with them, all neatly labelled and logged, the memories of decades. The rest of the place though was cluttered, and that surprised me, until I learnt the reason why: he had just married the week before! His new wife, his second, was beaming smiles, and she was midway through moving her stuff in, hence the clutter. Sorting it all out would have to wait though, as the two of them were off on their honeymoon the following day, a river cruise down the Rhine. None of his friends in the

Sneyssens knew yet. 'That was why we were quiet when we met you at Oswald Van Ooteghem's house Herr Trigg. My wife and I knew we were getting married back then but we weren't telling anyone so we just kept quiet.'

The two of them beamed at me and at each other, a couple in their nineties smiling at the thought of another fresh start, looking forward and not backward. They offered to take me to their favourite local spot for lunch, a five-minute walk away, it turned out to be the canteen of the nearby hospital. Seven euros bought the daily special, which on that day happened to be a typically Flemish dish of spinach and greens wrapped in ham and served with masses of mashed potato and gravy. The room was packed with staff from the hospital; paramedics, ambulance teams, doctors and nurses, and quite a few other elderly locals who were clearly regulars like the D'Oosterlincks. Over lunch we talked about the book and what would happen next once the story was out and Theo's secret was a secret no more. They were both sanguine about it, in the run-up to this second interview his daughter had finally found out the truth, and her reaction had been one of understanding – she said she had always suspected it anyway.

D'Oosterlinck seemed relived his daughter now knew the truth, and in that self-same atmosphere of candour at the lunch table as I drank my beer and the D'Oosterlincks drank their white wine, I broached the topic of Nazi atrocities, of the Holocaust, and what, if anything, he knew or had seen.

TD: We knew that there were concentration camps, everybody did. We knew they were where enemies of the state were sent; members of the Resistance, communists and so on, but we didn't know what was happening in them, no-one ever told us about it and we didn't talk about it. Perhaps the people who lived close by knew about it, I don't know.

I was just a soldier. I was fighting Bolshevism and trying to stay alive – nothing more.

Oswald Van Ooteghem has always insisted that while he knew that opponents of the Nazis and Jews were imprisoned in concentration camps during the war, he believed that this was more about internal security and the almost traditional anti-Semitism that was prevalent at the time across most of Europe. He has always said that personally he never had any problems with the Jews, and that, on the contrary, he even had a good relationship with the Jewish stepfather of a childhood friend, the same story of course that helped him at his trial after the war. He says that like so many others, he only found out about the extermination camps after the war, and was completely shocked at the realisation that he fought for such a gruesome regime. 'It took a long time for this to sink in.'

It is like a mantra, a rote response all the Oostfronters came out with. That doesn't make it a lie, not at all, but at the same time it leaves a tiny flicker of doubt. What I can say with absolute certainty is that I believe that none of the veterans I met and interviewed were ever involved directly in the Holocaust. I don't think that any of them participated in the war crimes that have made the SS – and by implication the Waffen-SS – a byword for brutality and inhumanity. The fact remains that the regime they fought for did commit those crimes, it did try and perpetrate genocide, and for that it rightly stands condemned for all time.

For these men who wore the uniform with the double lightning flash runes on their collar tab, it will, rightly or wrongly, forever blacken their reputations.

HVG: We didn't know about the camps – we knew they existed of course, and we knew that the Jews were imprisoned, but as to what was happening in there, we knew nothing. There simply wasn't time to think about those things.

OVO: That's why I'm mad at Himmler. We were soldiers, nothing more. The Waffen-SS has come to represent a whole panoply of people – innocents, but also men who committed war crimes. Therefore he has given us a bad name. We did not deserve it. Of all those crimes we knew nothing. Don't forget as well that war crimes and cruelty weren't limited to just one side, everybody did it. There were horrible things that happened during the liberation; in France alone about 10,000 people were murdered in the street. I cannot approve of or condone any of the crimes that happened. I cannot condone the atomic bomb dropped on Hiroshima, or the terror bombing of Dresden, or the abuse of one million German women by Russian soldiers – no, not at all. What I can tell you is that when I was at Bad Tölz there were concentration camp inmates there who worked in the barracks [the inmates were from Dachau]; cleaning the paths, tending the gardens, working in the kitchens and so on, and we always treated them with respect. They worked hard, but no more than we did. Sometimes we'd give them cigarettes and extra food, and I remember one I saw after the war who said to me: 'You were good to us during the war, now after the war, we will be good for you.'

Theo D'Oosterlinck said exactly the same of his time at Bad Tölz, that there were camp inmates who worked in the grounds and the facilities, and who were not mistreated or abused in any way.

TD: At Bad Tölz there were camp inmates there, in the barracks. They had to clean the hallways, the grounds etc. They never told us what it was like in the camps, or what happened. They were kept separate from us, but at night they slept in the same barracks we did. They were treated fine, I never saw them being abused. It was the same at the front, we never talked to any prisoners or saw them being abused.

The Dutchman, Jan Munk, echoed this view but with one important admission:

JM: **During my last leave my father told me that he believed that Jews were being killed in concentration camps** *[author's emphasis]. I told him that in the officer school at Bad Tölz we had many inmates from Dachau working there. Dressed in their blue and white stripped trousers and jackets they kept the roads clean or worked in the gardens. They stood to one side and took their caps off to us as we passed, no more and no less, and if we laid a finger on them they complained to their Kapo [their overseer, usually another inmate] and we were reprimanded, and whilst we were issued with two cigarettes a day, they were issued three, and that is the absolute truth. Was I to believe my own eyes or my father?*

Personally, I have never met a former Dachau inmate who was at Bad Tölz during the war, and so have never been able to ask the question myself, but I hope that in the midst of a camp system that would have provided Danté with a new vision of Hell, that against all the odds the Waffen-SS officer academy in the quiet Bavarian countryside was an oasis of relative humanity.

My long series of interviews ended as they had begun, with the former Belgian Senator and teenage Waffen-SS volunteer, Oswald Van Ooteghem. This extremely polite, hospitable, mischievous old man in whose house I had sat for hours and hours, talking about the war and his life since; eating his food, drinking his champagne, his whisky, his coffee, all the time being treated as an honoured guest as he walked me through the halls of his memory, reliving the few, brief years that have forever shaped his life. Did I know him at all? Did I really know everything about his service, about what he knew was going on in Russia, what the Nazis were really doing, or was I just seeing what he was allowing me to see? I don't know the answer to that question.

What I came to believe was that communism was the most important force that drove the interviewees to volunteer. As a political ideology it was detested, and it was also seen as an existential threat to their beloved Roman Catholic faith. Allied to this, for the Oostfronters at least, was the belief that fighting alongside the Germans would lead inevitably to the independence of Flanders in the Europe that would follow the war. The Dutch volunteers clearly believed their own country's place in the new order would also be assured by their service too. That idea of a 'new order' in Europe was important in its own right. There was no sense of the Waffen-SS as a 'European army' – the idea of it being the forerunner of today's NATO alliance was dismissed by the Oostfronters and their compatriots – but there was definitely a feeling among the interviewees that what the Nazis had to offer was something fresh, something powerful, something youthful that spoke to their generation, a generation scarred by the hopelessness of the Great Depression and the apparent exhaustion of multi-party liberalism. What perhaps they didn't see – or didn't want to see – was what came with that self-same new order; oppression, authoritarianism and the unbridled savagery of an ideology based on race hate.

What I can also say is that I *felt* that OVO, and all the other Oostfronters and interviewees, had told me the truth as they saw it, and as for OVO himself he had one last message for me, one last thought as I went to switch off my dictaphone for the last time. He looked at me, his blue eyes focused, and lifting his right arm from the sofa he poked his forefinger at me, stabbing it at me like a bayonet:

I was lucky. My whole life has depended on such good fortune. I survived the war, I became a senator, I have a great family and a wonderful grandson, Alexander. But make no mistake Herr Trigg, war is the worst thing that can happen to everyone and anyone, the worst thing of all.

I thought long and hard on that comment, turning it over in my mind. The world has learned a lot in the last half century and more; the number of authoritarian dictatorships has fallen from over ninety to twenty, and the corresponding number of democracies has risen from less than forty to around one hundred today. Perhaps most encouragingly of all, the number of people dying every year from war has plummeted by a dramatic seventy-five per cent, and this despite a rocketing global population, the collapse of the former Soviet Union and the empires of Britain and France, the so-called Arab Spring and ensuing ethnic conflicts and violence that fill our television screens and newspapers every day.

So, hope springs eternal as the cliché goes, and it was hard not to agree with that sentiment as I sat there in Van Ooteghem's comfortable lounge as the sun began to set, thinking of Theo D'Oosterlinck and his new wife on their honeymoon on the Rhine; imagining them happily chattering away as they unpacked their suitcases in their cabin, before going out on deck to toast their future together as their river cruiser glided effortlessly by the imposing slate massif of the Lorelei.

APPENDICES

Appendix A – Krasny Bor Grave Registration List 2008
In 2008, near Krasny Bor, the remains of thirty-one missing Flemish Waffen-SS soldiers were found, identified and reburied at the military cemeteries of Novgorod and Sologubowka. All of them died in 1943, almost all over a two-week period in the fighting in March (in fact most of them over the space of just three days). They are listed below by the date they were originally reported as 'Missing believed Killed in Action'.

Florimont De Smedt: Born 20.02.1911 in Berlaar–Heikant – killed 03.03.1943

Lodewijk Tielemans: Born 22.11.1914 in Antwerp – killed 13.03.1943

Lode Peters: Born 01.09.1911 in Bornem – killed 19.03.1943

Herman Vinck: Born 17.08.1909 in Beveren – killed 19.03.1943

Oskar Waegemans: Born 14.10.1918 in Berlaere – killed 19.03.1943

Theo Luysmans: Born 16.08.1923 in Maaseik – killed 22.03.1943

Jozef Verhoeven: Born 17.03.1923 in Etterbeek – killed 22.03.1943

Ferdinand Van den Brouck: Born 14.06.1923 in Balen – killed 22.03.1943

Hendrik Commissaris: Born 17.09.1918 in Antwerp – killed 23.03.1943

Pieter Diesmans: Born 29.8.1919 in Waltwider – killed 23.03.1943

José Wilkin: Born 05.03.1912 in Schaarbeek – killed 23.03.1943

Roger De Smet: Born 05.01.1912 in Lokeren – killed 23.03.1943

Jan De Wreze: Born 31.01.1923 in Antwerp – killed 23.03.1943

Oscar Delecluyse: Born 01.04.1923 in Roeselare – killed together with his brother Frank Delecluyse on 24.03.1943

Eugen Deplae: Born 25.01.1922 in Kortrijk – killed 24.03.1943

Walter Molenaers: Born 29.08.1924 in Izegem – killed 24.03.1943

Frans Van Gasse: Born 19.11.1922 in Sint-Niklaas – killed 24.03.1943

Jan Leopold Vranken: Born 10.10.1920 in Stokkem – killed 24.03.1943

Jan Van Roy: Born 26.08.1912 in Mol – killed 24.03.1943

Achiel Nicassie: Born 19.09.1919 in Vorst-Kempen – killed 25.03.1943

Van der Bracht: Born 27.02.1913 in Voorde – killed 25.03.1943

Vital Flament: Born 22.12.1922 in Dampremy – killed 25.03.1943

Jan De Cock: Born 02.09.1922 in Boom – killed 25.03.1943

Gullaume Schamps: Born 31.12.1920 in Antwerp – killed 25.03.1943

Maurits Temmermans: Born 17.11.1922 in Ghent – killed 25.03.1943

Antoine Wene: Born 09.01.1924 in Antwerp – killed 28.03.1943

Jaak Van Reck: Born 22.04.1922 in Krefeld – killed 29.03.1943

Robert Van de Caveye: Born 24.12.1923 in Lebbeke – killed
01.07.1943

Christian Malysek: Born 14.02.1902 in Gryboniwe –
killed March 1943, exact date unknown

Henry Van den Eeden: Born 01.10.1923 in Antwerp – killed
March 1943, exact date unknown

*Appendix B – Flemish Wehrmacht and Waffen-SS Officer
Personnel and Bad Tölz Attendees*
There were five courses held during the war at Bad Tölz specifically
for 'Germanics' i.e. non-German candidates intended to rapidly
increase the pool of trained and available officers amongst the
foreign volunteer formations including the Flemish and Dutch units.

Dates and titles of the first four courses are below. There was a
fifth course held in the second half of 1944 – number 18 – which
was not completed due to the ending of the war. This was the
course attended by Jan Munk.

Lehrgang für germanische Offiziere/SS-Junkerschule
Tölz 01.02.1943 – 30.04.1943

Lehrgang für germanische Offiziere/SS-Junkerschule Tölz
15.06.1943 – 01.10.1943

Lehrgang für germanische Offiziere/SS-Junkerschule Tölz
18.10.1943 – 11.03.1944

Lehrgang für germanische Offiziere/SS-Junkerschule Tölz
01.04.1944 – 31.08.1944

The following is a list of Flemish officers who graduated from Bad
Tölz and their ranks.

Untersturmführer

Bachot Jozef, Barrie P. Albert, Bauwens Theophiel, Beernaert Ferdinand, Bertels Remy, Bogaert Remi, Bollen Alfons, Borghgraef Wilfried, Boterman Gilbert, Bottu Lucien, Bouten Jan, Buntinx Eduard, Buyse Jan, Callebaut August, Ceuleers Ome, Claes Emiel, Claeys Huibrecht, Cornelissens Albert, Coninckx Robert, Cornil Jan, Dams Ludwig, De Brandt Gaston, De Clerck Philipp, De Coster Robert, De Glas Arthur, De Gruyter Bert, De Kesel Frans, De Lepeleire Frans, De Meester Henrik, De Meyer Anton, De Meyer Herman, De Moor Frans, De Munck Achiel, De Pillecijn Remy, De Prijcker Albert, De Rijcker Walter, De Saedeleer Albert, De Vriesere Georges, De Vuyst Aimé, De Wilde Constant, De Backer Julius, De Wilde Kamiel, De Witte Gilbert, Donckers Victor, Deblaer Jack, Debusschere Herman, Decru Andries, Dekesel Frans, Demeyer Henri, Dewit Albert, D'Haese Georg, D'Hulster Michael, Dujardin Marcel, Duynslaeger Arseen, Eggermont Emiel, Elbers Marcel, Ensch Albert, Everaert Henri, Geerkens Frans, Geunes Albert, Gombert Tony, Govaerts Peter, Goyvaerts Frank, Groenvynck Roger, Guldentops John, Gyssens Ferdinand, Grysolle Joris, Heip Rudolf, Heirbaut Marcel, Hellemans Albrecht, Heyerick August, Heyman Heinrich, Hubert Gilbert, Jans Albert, Joyeux Wilhelm, Jacobs Alfons, Jacobs Ferdinand, Kemps Hugo, Kersters jan, Lauwers Hendrik, Leysen Siegfried, Lippens Gustaaf, Luyten Jozef, Lagast Karel, Laperre Marcel, Laporte Ferdinand, Marien Jozef, Mertens Leopold, Moens Roger, Mortier Hugo, Nijland Albert, Nijs Jan, Ooms Ludwig, Oosterveld Dirk, Osselaer Ernst, Pasques Theo, Pouliart Staf, Pouget Albert, Reckers Lodewijk, Ranst Jan, Raskin Hendrik, Raveyse German, Roekens Julien, Schollen August – (Germanische SS Flandern), Swinnen Albert, Stevens Andreas, Thielens Arthur, Tollenaere Reimond, Truyts Joris, Van de Ven Wilfried, Van den Abeele Hendrik, Van den Borght Albert, Van den Bossche Viktor, Van Damme Maurits, Van Dyk Willem, Van Eeckhout Florent, Van Geenhoven Eduard, Van Hamme Gustaaf, Van Hileghem Gustaf, Van Nuffel Leo, Van Offel Horace, Van Ooteghem Oswald, Van Sintjan Filip, Van Bockel Jozef, Van der

Weeën Leo, Van Hilst August, Van Leemputten Walter, Van Mol Henri, Van Nitsen Ferdinand, Vereenooghe Rafaël, Verhaeghen Paul, Vaes Jaak, Velleman Robert, Verbeken August, Verbist Leo, Verfaille Alfons, Verhulst Eduard, Verleye Roger, Verlinden Karel, Vierendeels Frans, Vincx Jan, Wachterlaer Alfons, Wentein Karl, Willems Hugo, Wouters Robert, Wouters Ludwig

Obersturmführer

Delombaerde Karel, D'Helft Godfried, Knockaert Serphin, Petre Viktor, Thijs Idefons, Van der Smissen Rene, Vanackere Jozef, Willaert Gaston, Arckens Eugeen, Beyens Lodewijk, Bruyninckx Georges, Buyse Eugeen, Delbaere Jan, Francois Jef, Geerts Cäser, Geerts Leo, Gillis Gaspard, Inghels Jeroom, Janssens Carolus, Kennes Frans, Meulemans Clement, Peeters Alfons, Suys Paul, Peeters Willem, Uyttersprott Ortair

Hauptsturmführer

Anthonissen Gommaar, Callens Josef (d. R.), Cambie Andreas, De Meulder Jan, Hendrix Hubert, Klimmer Jozef, Michel Daniel Dr., Moulaert Fernand Dr., Uten Jan, Van de Perre Gerard

Sturmbannführer

Urbain Bohez

Obersturmbannführer

Jef Van de Wiele Jef – Leader DeVlag

SS Junker

Renaat Bauweraerts

Standartenoberjunker

Caramin Eugen, De Weber Franciscus, Vermeulen Walter

The following are Flemings who achieved officer rank in the German Army and Luftwaffe rather than the Waffen-SS.

Leutnants Stobbe Ernest (unit not known), Voet Ferdinand (unit not known), Walbers Gerard – Luftwaffe Oberleutnants Bocqué Isidoor and De Bruycker Bert, and Hauptman Jughters Maurits – all from Luftwaffe Fläm. Flak Abt. 590.

Appendix C – Wehrmacht and Waffen-SS Bravery Awards and Classifications

As with all things in the Wehrmacht, when it came to bravery awards there was a thorough system and process in place. Courage, and the citations and medals that went with it, was taken very seriously and based on a pyramid structure, with the Iron Cross being the standard basis of measurement, along with a series of specialist awards such as the Close Combat Badge, the Wound Badge etc. Up the pecking order from the Iron Cross was the German Cross, the Honour Roll Clasp and then finally on to the pinnacle, the Knight's Cross. Most of the awards had at least two grades, with the Knight's Cross having four; the Knight's Cross itself, then awarded with Oak Leaves, then Swords and finally Diamonds.

Close Combat Day – *(Nahkampftag)*

A Close Combat Day was designated as a day of fighting the enemy at hand-to-hand level. These days were acknowledged in a soldier's individual *Soldbuch* by his superior officer and noted as such.

Iron Cross – *(Eisener Kreutz)*

Awarded in two classes:

The Iron Cross 2nd Class was authorised for a single act of bravery in combat beyond normal duty, some 2.3m were awarded during the war.

The Iron Cross 1st Class required you to already have the 2nd Class award and a further three to five additional acts of bravery; some 300,000 were awarded.

Honour Roll Clasp of the German Army – *(Ehrungsblattspange des deutschen Heeres)*

The Honour Roll Clasp required you to have both classes of the Iron Cross as a prerequisite, and was then awarded for an additional act of unusual bravery which fell just short of deserving a Knight's Cross. Some 166 Waffen-SS soldiers won this prestigious award.

German Cross – *(Deutscher Kreutz)*

Awarded in two classes, the lower being Silver, the higher in Gold: This award was instituted by Hitler personally as a median award between the Iron Cross and a full-blown Knight's Cross. It only required the winner to already have the Iron Cross 2nd Class, and was awarded for repeated acts of exceptional bravery in combat that didn't merit a Knight's Cross. One thousand and sixteen Waffen-SS soldiers won this award. There were twenty men in the Waffen-SS who held both the Honour Roll Clasp and the German Cross in Gold.

Knight's Cross – *(Ritterkreuz)*

Highly coveted, this was the highest award for bravery available to members of the Wehrmacht. Worn on a ribbon around the neck it was colloquially known as 'curing your throat ache'. While it could be earned by all ranks for exceptional acts of courage, it was also awarded to officers as recognition of the deeds of the units under their command; hence many were earned by battalion, regimental and divisional commanders.

A holder of the Knight's Cross could then go on to be awarded three higher grades for additional service and acts of bravery. Firstly Oakleaves *(Eichenlauben)* would be awarded, then Swords *(Schwerter)*, and finally Diamonds *(Brillianten)*. The Luftwaffe pilot, Hans-Ulrich Rudel, had a special category created just for him – the Golden Oak Leaves – as the Third Reich had effectively run out of existing awards for him.

Appendix D – Waffen-SS Unit Organisations
Starting at the smallest unit size – the Gruppe – and then upwards to the largest – the Armeegruppe.

SS Section *(Gruppe)*

Commanded by a junior NCO, such as an SS-Rottenführer or an SS-Unterscharführer. Made up of anywhere between 6 and 12 men, depending on casualties, the section was the foundation and the building block of the Waffen-SS fighting formations, as in all armies. When a man passed his Waffen-SS recruit training, he would be posted to a division, which would then send him internally to a regiment and a named battalion. In the battalion, he would be detailed to one of the companies and a specific platoon within that company. He would then finally be allocated to a section in the platoon and that *Gruppe* would become his home and sanctuary until killed, wounded, captured or told otherwise. If Sections in a unit don't function, then nothing else does either. All unit cohesion and performance rested on them within the Waffen-SS.

SS Platoon *(Zug)*

Commanded either by a junior officer such as an SS-Untersturmführer, an officer candidate such as an SS-Oberjunker or a senior NCO such as an SS-Oberscharführer. The platoon had its component sections, usually 3 or 4 again depending on casualties, with a young officer commander and a veteran platoon sergeant who would act as second-in-command. The platoon sergeant would also control the platoon's supplies (ammunition, food, water etc.) and provide a steady hand and voice of experience to his young officer. In SS panzer formations a platoon would usually comprise five tanks. A soldier's closest friends were his section, but his home was his platoon.

SS Company *(Kompanie)*

Commanded by a more senior and experienced, though usually still young, officer such as an SS-Obersturmführer or an SS-Hauptsturmführer. In the British Army, a company is commanded by a Major, around early 30s in age, and no less. Normally consisting of three platoons the company was the lowest tactical unit that external attachments were made to, including forward artillery fire observers and forward air controllers. In panzer formations, the company would usually comprise four tank platoons, and two command and control tanks.

SS Battalion *(Abteilung)*

Commanded by an older and more experienced officer such as an SS-Sturmbannführer. An average battalion would be made up of four companies and could have sections of specialist troops such as assault engineers attached as necessary for a particular operation. A battalion would be numbered with a Roman numeral in front of its parent regiments designation, such as *II/SS-Panzergrenadier Regiment 6 Theodor Eicke*, which denoted the 2nd Battalion of the Theodor Eicke Panzergrenadier Regiment number 6.

SS Regiment *(Standarte)*

Commanded by a senior and very experienced officer such as an SS-Oberführer or SS-Standartenführer. Equivalent to a brigade in British Army parlance, the regiments were a division's major sub-units and as such would have their own integral staff as well as supporting elements including at the very least a heavy gun company, an anti-aircraft defence company, a combat engineer company and its teeth arms of either three foot borne infantry, armoured infantry battalions or two panzer battalions depending on its designation as an infantry, panzer grenadier or panzer regiment respectively. This was a major difference between Army and Waffen-SS regiments with Army formations having the same number of panzer battalions but crucially only two infantry battalions in each panzer grenadier or infantry regiment. This heavily reduced the unit's combat power and meant that Army units tended to burn out far more rapidly in the battles of attrition so prevalent on the Russian Front.

However due to manpower shortages later on in the war many Waffen-SS regiments raised in late 1944 and 1945, including those in the Flemish Langemarck and the French Charlemagne, mirrored Army formations and only consisted of two battalion regiments. This reduction in strength meant the units combat effectiveness could be quickly eroded in periods of intense fighting. The regiment would be described by type, Roman numeral if it had one, and then honour name if given one, so for example in the Das Reich there was *SS-Panzergrenadier Regiment 3 Deutschland*. If composed of Germanic volunteers the term 'Freiwilligen' i.e. 'volunteer', would be added. So, in the Dutch SS-Nederland Division there were two regiments, *SS-Freiwilligen Panzergrenadier Regiment 48 General Seyffardt*, and *SS-Freiwilligen Panzergrenadier Regiment 49 De Ruyter*. Non-Germanic volunteer units were designated as 'Waffen-Grenadier der SS', i.e. 'Armed Grenadier of the SS', such as the Latvian *Waffen-Grenadier Regiment der SS 42 Voldemars Veiss*.

SS Division *(Division)*
Next up the chain came the mainstay of the Waffen-SS formational system, the division. This was entirely different from the British Army system where the much smaller regimental formation was the building block of the field army and a soldier's spiritual home. A British soldier in the Second World War would feel loyalty to the Royal Norfolks, the Cameroonians or the Irish Guards – famous regiments all, but in the Waffen-SS, it was to the Das Reich or Hitlerjugend Divisions. This 'division as home' concept was a great help in maintaining morale and combat effectiveness during the frequent decimations of the Waffen-SS divisions. There were three main types of Waffen-SS division each with its own structure: the Panzer *(tank)* division, the Panzergrenadier *(mixed tanks and infantry)* division and the non-mechanized division *(infantry, cavalry or mountain infantry)*. All three types were commanded by either an SS-Gruppenführer or SS-Brigadeführer. Just as with regiments,

the division would have a structure of support units and these would typically comprise a headquarters staff, military police, transport, medical support, logistics, a signals battalion, an engineer battalion, an artillery regiment and an anti-aircraft battalion (almost all entirely mechanised in panzer and panzer grenadier divisions). The teeth fighting elements of the different types of divisions were as follows:

Panzer division – these were the armoured fists of the Waffen-SS and each had two panzer grenadier regiments of three battalions each and a panzer regiment of two battalions. There were seven full panzer divisions in the Waffen-SS and they comprised the crème de la crème of the Waffen-SS fighting strength, such as the *1st SS-Panzer Division Leibstandarte SS Adolf Hitler*. Of the non-German Waffen-SS formations, only the famous 5th SS Panzer Division Wiking attained this celebrated status.

Panzergrenadier division – comprising two panzer grenadier regiments of three battalions each and a single panzer battalion, these were not full panzer divisions but were still very powerful formations with their own integral armour. In the 'combat pecking order' these formations were still an élite within the Waffen-SS. There were seven panzer grenadier divisions including the only Waffen-SS division to fight exclusively on the Western Front, the ethnic German *17th SS-Panzergrenadier Division Götz von Berlichingen*. Five of the divisions that attained this status were non-Reichsdeutsche formations including the Nordic *11th SS-Freiwilligen-Panzergrenadier Division Nordland* and the Hungarian volksdeutsche *18th SS- Freiwilligen-Panzergrenadier Division Horst Wessel*, the Götz and the Langemarck and Wallonien.

Lastly there were the non-mechanized divisions (either infantry, cavalry or mountain infantry). These formations formed the bulk of the Waffen-SS order of battle during the war, and indeed the vast majority of foreign formations came under this designation. As non-mechanized units, they were the least well-equipped of the Waffen-SS formations and were of widely differing quality, organisation, strength and combat effectiveness. Usually called 'grenadier' divisions, they normally comprised two grenadier regiments of three battalions each with supporting arms, but in practice this was chopped and changed to suit the availability, or not, of both equipment and manpower. In the French *33rd Waffen-Grenadier-Division der SS Charlemagne (französische Nr.1)* for instance there were only two grenadier battalions in each regiment (for more information see Book 1 in the Hitler's Legions series *Hitler's Gauls*). Crucially these formations lacked any integral armour and the necessary transport to give them the mobility on the battlefield that was increasingly essential as the nature of warfare, particularly on the Eastern Front, became one characterised by rapid movement. In total, there were some twenty-six grenadier divisions including two number 23s, two number 29s and two number 33s (the number being re-used when the original formation was disbanded). Thus, the original *29th Waffen-Grenadier Division der SS (russiche Nr.1)* under Bronislav Kaminski, became the *29th Waffen-Grenadier Division der SS (italienische Nr.1)* under Heldmann when Kaminski's men were absorbed into Vlasov's ROA.

There were four SS cavalry (*Kavallerie*) divisions, including the short-lived *33rd Waffen-Kavallerie Division der SS (ungarische Nr.3)* which was overrun before formation and its number reused for the French Charlemagne division. There were also six mountain infantry (*Gebirgs*) divisions including the German *6th SS Mountain Division Nord*, and the Yugoslav ethnic German *7th SS-Freiwilligen-Mountain Division Prinz Eugen*. A few of these formations were excellent combat formations, especially the three Baltic grenadier divisions, the Nord, the Prinz Eugen, the Langemarck and the Wallonien. The majority however, were of questionable quality and many were formed as defeat loomed and were of little value at the front. Some of these latter were the lowest of the low and deserve to be remembered with nothing but horror and contempt for their records, which were brutal beyond belief. Probably the most infamous being the *36th Waffen-Grenadier Division der SS* under Oskar Dirlewanger, whose misdeeds in Belorussia and especially Warsaw will forever stain the reputation of the Waffen-SS order of battle.

SS Corps (Korps)

Commanded by either an SS-Obergruppenführer or SS-Gruppenführer. The Corps was the next level up in organisational terms and consisted of a number of divisions, the minimum of which was two but could rise to three or even four. The Corps was a fully-functional field force in its own right with a full-time staff comprising complements of headquarters staff, transport, logistics, and military police, medical and signalling units of different strengths. Component divisions would then be placed under Corps command but did not 'belong' to that Corps, as it were, for any more than the specific campaign the Corps was involved in, or even for no longer than a single operation. The Wehrmacht's ability to swiftly regroup formations under differing Corps commands during often complex phases of battle was one of the reasons that the German forces held out for so long towards the end of the war. During the latter defensive stages of the Russian campaign, formations would often rapidly switch Corps control to face and close off Russian offensive threats, and its true to say that few armies have ever mastered this incredibly difficult art. During the war a total of eighteen Waffen-SS corps were formed including Felix Steiner's famous *III Germanic SS-Panzer Corps* and the *I SS* and *II SS-Panzer Corps* of Kharkov, Normandy and Ardennes fame.

SS Army Group (Armeegruppe)

Commanded by either an SS-Obergruppenführer or SS-Oberstgruppenführer – only Sepp Dietrich ever achieved this latter rank, see Appendix on Waffen-SS Ranks. Largest formations ever fielded by the Waffen-SS during the war, including Dietrich's *Sixth SS Panzer Army* and Steiner's *Eleventh SS Panzer Army*. This grouping would normally consist of several corps-sized units, but was extremely unwieldy to handle even for the well-trained Wehrmacht General Staff corps. During the early stages of the war the separate Waffen-SS formations were distributed between the different Wehrmacht Army Groups, such as Army Group A, B or C for the invasion of Soviet Russia, and it was only when to all intents and purposes the war was lost that Waffen-SS formations were brought together in this way (in an interesting volte face often with Army formations integral to them).

Appendix E – Waffen-SS Ranks and Equivalences

SS-Schütze	Private (this was the basic private rank; any speciality would be reflected in the title, e.g. *Panzerschütze,* tank trooper)
SS-Oberschütze	Senior Private (attained after six months' service – this may seem strange to have 'grades' of Private but in the modern British Army there are no less than four Private grades and it can take two years or more to move from Class 4 at the bottom to 1, with soldiers gaining greater qualifications in the process as well as increased pay)
SS-Sturmmann	Lance corporal (first NCO rank)
SS-Rottenführer	Corporal
SS-Unterscharführer	Lance Sergeant (this rank, above full Corporal but below Sergeant, is only used in the British Army in the Brigade of Guards – the Household Cavalry use slightly different rankings)
SS-Junker	Officer candidate (acting rank only, substantive rank of SS-Unterscharführer, non-university

	graduates hold this rank in the British Army while training at RMA Sandhurst)
SS-Scharführer	Sergeant
SS-Standartenjunker	Officer candidate (acting rank only, substantive rank of SS-Scharführer, this was a step up from SS-Junker)
SS-Oberscharführer	Colour/staff Sergeant
SS-Hauptscharführer	Warrant Officer Class 2
SS-Standartenoberjunker	Officer candidate (acting rank only, substantive rank of SS-Hauptscharführer, yet another step in the process of becoming a fully-fledged officer in the Waffen-SS)
SS-Sturmscharführer	Warrant Officer Class 1 (could only be achieved after fifteen years' service)
SS-Untersturmführer	Second Lieutenant
SS-Obersturmführer	Lieutenant
SS-Hauptsturmführer	Captain
SS-Sturmbannführer	Major
SS-Obersturmbannführer	Lieutenant-Colonel
SS-Standartenführer	Colonel
SS-Oberführer	Brigadier equivalent
SS-Brigadeführer	Major-General
SS-Gruppenführer	Lieutenant-General
SS-Obergruppenführer	General
SS-Oberstgruppenführer	Colonel-General (only Sepp Dietrich ever attained this rank)

Appendix F – Waffen-SS Training Establishments
As the Waffen-SS grew it established a network of training sites across Germany and Occupied Europe. The vast majority were outside the borders of the original Reich as the Army guarded

its own training bases jealously and therefore there was very little land and few facilities available to the fledgling force. The SS's solution was to either take over existing bases from defeated armies – Deba in Poland and Sennheim in the Alsace were examples of this approach – or to create new bases through eviction and forced resettlement. The most infamous example of this strategy was the establishment in September 1942 of SS Truppenübungsplatz Beneschau (Benesov in the modern-day Czech Republic). The first stage saw the forced resettlement of the inhabitants of 71 villages in the 44,000 hectares around the town of Neweklau. A total of 17,647 people were displaced. In September 1943 the facility was expanded and renamed the SS Truppenübungsplatz Bohemia. Further clearances then took place, with 144 more villages and hamlets emptied and an additional 30,986 people expelled.

Within the training area were several specialist schools:

- the SS Artillery School II Beneschau
- the SS Panzer-Grenadier School Prosetschnitz (this later became the SS Panzer-Grenadier School Kienschlag)
- the SS Tank Destroyer School Janowitz
- the SS Pioneer School Hradischko
- the SS Pioneer Technical Institute
- the SS sanitary school Prague Beneschau, including the SS military hospital Prague Podol.

Other training camps were as below, the list is not intended to be comprehensive and any omissions are the responsibility of the author.

Bad Tölz, Germany – officer training
Berlin, Germany – war reporters, mechanics, medics and interpreters
Braunschweig, Germany – officer training
Breslau, eastern Germany – infantry training

Göttingen, Germany – cavalry training
Grafenwöhr, Germany – former training area for the inter-war
    Reichswehr, multi-disciplinary training was carried out here
Graz, Austria – basic military training (alternative to Klagenfurt)
Klagenfurt, Austria – basic military training & NCO training
Neustift, Austrian Tyrol – Mountain warfare training
Posen-Treskau, eastern Germany – NCO training
Sennheim, Alsace – pre-military basic training for the majority of
    Germanic foreign volunteers
Sterzing-Vipiteno, Austrian South Tyrol – signals training

The Waffen-SS also used several other existing training areas to
form and reform units, such as Wildflecken in Germany.

BIBLIOGRAPHY

Ailsby, Christopher, *Hell on the Eastern Front: The Waffen-SS War in Russia 1941–1945*, Spellmount, 1998

Ailsby, Christopher, *Waffen-SS: The Unpublished Photographs 1923–1945*, Bookmart, 2000

Bauer, Eddy, Lt. Col, *World War II*, Orbis, 1972

Beevor, Antony, *Berlin – The Downfall 1945*, Penguin, 2003

Bellamy, Chris, *Absolute War – Soviet Russia in the Second World War*, Macmillan, 2007

Bishop, Chris, *Hell on the Western Front: The Waffen-SS in Europe 1940–45*, Spellmount, 2003

Bishop, Chris, *The Military Atlas of World War II*, Amber, 2005

Brandt, Allen, *The Last Knight of Flanders: Remy Schrijnen and his SS-Legion "Flandern"/Sturmbrigade "Langemarck" Comrades on the Eastern Front 1941–1945*, Schiffer, 1998

Bruyne, Eddy de and Rikmenspoel, Marc J., *For Rex and for Belgium – Léon Degrelle and Walloon Political and Military Collaboration 1940-45*, Helion, 2004

Butler, Rupert, *SS-Wiking*, Spellmount, 2002

Butler, Rupert, *The Black Angels*, Arrow, 1989

Butler, Rupert, *Legions of Death*, Hamlyn, 1983

Carell, Paul, *Hitler's War on Russia Volume One*, George G. Harrap, 1964 (translated by Ewald Osers)

Carell, Paul, *Hitler's War on Russia Volume Two: Scorched Earth*, George G. Harrap, 1970 (translated by Ewald Osers)

Dank, Milton, *The French Against the French*, Cassell, 1978

Davies, Norman, *Europe at War 1939–1945*, Macmillan, 2006

Estes, Kenneth W., *A European Anabasis – Western European Volunteers in the German Army and SS, 1940-1945*, Columbia University Press, 2003

Evans, Richard J., *The Third Reich at War*, Allen Lane, 2008

Foot, M. R. D., *Resistance – European Resistance to Nazism 1940-45*, Eyre Methuen, 1976,

Glantz, David M., *The Battle for Leningrad 1941–1944*, BCA, 2004

Graber, G. S., *History of the SS*, Diamond, 1994

Hausser, Paul, *Wenn Alle Brüder Schweigen – Grosser Bildband über die Waffen-SS* ('When all our brothers are silent'), Nation Europa, 1973

Hillbald, Thorolf (ed.), *Twilight of the Gods – A Swedish Waffen-SS Volunteer's Experiences with the 11th SS-Panzergrenadier Division 'Nordland', Eastern Front 1944-45*, Helion, 2004

Jones, Michael, *Leningrad: State of Siege*, John Murray, 2008

Jurado, Carlos Caballero, *Resistance Warfare 1940–45*, Osprey Men-at-Arms series, 1985

Landwehr, Richard, 'The European Volunteer Movement of World War II', *Journal of Historical Review*

Larsson, Lars T., *Hitler's Swedes – A History of the Swedish Volunteers in the Waffen-SS*, Helion, 2015

Le Tissier, Tony, *With our backs to Berlin – The German Army in Retreat 1945*, Sutton, 2001

Littlejohn, David, *The Patriotic Traitors: A History of Collaboration in German-Occupied Europe 1940/1945*, William Heinemann, 1972

Littlejohn, David, *Foreign Legions of the Third Reich Volume 2*, R. James Bender, 1981

Michaelis, Rolf, *Panzergrenadier Divisions of the Waffen-SS*, Schiffer, 2010

Mitcham Jr, Samuel W., *Hitler's Field Marshals and their Battles*, Guild, 1988

Munk, Jan, *I was a Dutch Volunteer*, self-published, 2008

Pierik, Perry, *From Leningrad to Berlin – Dutch volunteers in the service of the German Waffen-SS 1941-1945*, Aspeckt, 2001

Quarrie, Bruce, *Hitler's Samurai*, Patrick Stephens, 1983

Reitlinger, Gerald, *The SS: Alibi of a Nation, 1939–1945*, Heinemann, 1956

Rikmanspoel, Marc J., *Soldiers of the Waffen-SS – Many Nations, One Motto*, J. J Fedorowicz, 1999

Rikmanspoel, Marc J., *Waffen-SS Encyclopedia*, Aberjona, 2004

Roberts, Geoffrey, *Stalin's General – The Life of Georgy Zhukov*, Icon, 2012

Sourd, Jean-Pierre, *True Believers: Spanish Volunteers in the Heer and Waffen-SS, 1944–45*, Europa Books Inc, 2004 (translated by Antonio Munoz)

Taylor, Brian, *Barbarossa to Berlin Volume Two: The Defeat of Germany, 19 November 1942 to 15 May 1945*, Spellmount, 2004

Verton, Hendrik C., *In the Fire of the Eastern Front – The Experiences of a Dutch Waffen-SS Volunteer on the Eastern Front 1941–45*, Helion, 2007 (translated by Hazel Toon-Thorn)

Villani, Gerry, *Voices of the Waffen-SS*, self-published, 2015

Weale, Adrian, *The SS – A New History*, Abacus, 2010

Williamson, Gordon, *The Blood Soaked Soil*, Blitz Editions, 1997

Williamson, Gordon, *Loyalty is my Honor*, Brown, 1995

Williamson, Gordon, *The SS: Hitler's Instrument of Terror*, Sidgwick & Jackson, 1994

Williamson, Gordon, *The Waffen-SS – 24. to 38. Divisions, & Volunteer Legions*, Osprey Men-at-Arms series, 2004

INDEX